Maine

Charles C. Calhoun
with revisions by Michaela Colquhoun, Patricia Harris, and David Lyon
updated by Conrad Little Paulus

Photography by Kindra Clineff and Thomas Mark Szelog

COMPASS AMERICAN GUIDES
An imprint of Fodor's Travel Publications

Compass American Guides: Maine

Editor: Diane Mehta
Designer: Tina R. Malaney
Compass Editorial Director: Paul Eisenberg
Compass Creative Director: Fabrizio La Rocca
Editorial Production: Linda Schmidt
Photo Editor and Archival Researcher: Melanie Marin
Map Design: base maps provided by Erik Potter, Matchbook Maps, LLC; cartography by Mark Stroud, Moon Street Cartography

Cover photo: Kindra Clineff

Fourth Edition
ISBN 1–4000–1237–6
ISSN 1542–3468

The details in this book are based on information supplied to us at press time, but changes occur all the time, and the publisher cannot accept responsibility for facts that become outdated or for inadvertent errors or omissions.

Compass American Guides, 1745 Broadway, New York, NY 10019
PRINTED IN CHINA

10 9 8 7 6 5 4 3 2 1

*To the Estys: Don and Mae, Bob and Karen, Kristen and Laura,
and in memory of Donald — C. C.*

*To my wife, Lee Ann Szelog,
the heart and inspiration of these photographs — T. M. S.*

C O N T E N T S

Literary Extracts

Topical Essays

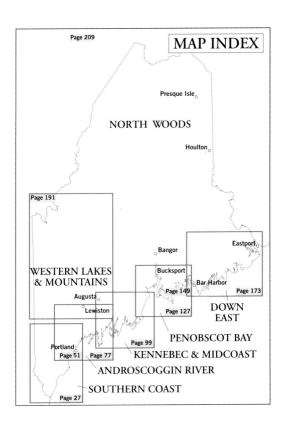

MAP INDEX

Page 209

Presque Isle

NORTH WOODS

Houlton

Page 191

Bangor

Eastport

WESTERN LAKES
& MOUNTAINS

Bucksport

Bar Harbor

Page 149

Page 173

Augusta

Page 127

DOWN
EAST

Lewiston

Page 99

PENOBSCOT BAY

Portland
Page 51

Page 77

KENNEBEC & MIDCOAST

ANDROSCOGGIN RIVER

Page 27

SOUTHERN COAST

Maps

FACTS ABOUT MAINE

The Pine Tree State

CAPITAL: Augusta

ENTERED UNION: March 15, 1820 (23rd state)

STATE MOTTO: *Dirigo* ("I lead")

STATE FLOWER: White Pine Cone and Tassel

STATE BIRD: Chickadee

STATE FISH: Landlocked salmon

STATE CAT: Maine coon cat

STATE TREE: Eastern White Pine

STATE ANIMAL: Moose

POPULATION (2003): 1.3 million

FIVE LARGEST CITIES:

Portland	63,635
Lewiston	35,922
Bangor	31,550
South Portland	23,553
Auburn	23,313

ECONOMY*:

Principal industries (by payroll employment): manufacturing, services, trade, government, finance, insurance, real estate, construction

Principal manufactured goods: paper and wood products, leather products

International airports at: Portland, Bangor

Per capita income (2003): $28,935

Sales Tax: 5%

---

*Tourism, though not coded as a distinct industry, brings in big bucks.

Small boats dock harborside in Portland.

GEOGRAPHY:
Size: 33,215 sq. miles
Highest point: 5,267 feet: Mount Katahdin, Piscataquis County

CLIMATE:
Highest temperature recorded: 107°F (42°C) at North Bridgton on July 10, 1911
Lowest temperature recorded: -48°F (-42°C) at Van Buren on January 19, 1925

FAMOUS MAINERS:
L. L. Bean ▪ George Mitchell ▪ James G. Blaine ▪ David E. Kelley ▪ Stephen King
Hannibal Hamlin ▪ Marsden Hartley ▪ Henry Wadsworth Longfellow
Edna St. Vincent Millay ▪ Margaret Chase Smith

INTRODUCTION

A visitor once remarked to a reporter for the weekly *Maine Times* how disappointed she was on her bus tour to shop-filled Bar Harbor, "I thought we were going to see quaint little villages and fishing boats along the coast." She was, of course, a 15- or 20-minute ride from places where she could have seen all that and more; if she'd only had the opportunity to set out on her own, she might have experienced the Maine she had envisioned.

This book is written for travelers of an independent frame of mind, people who are curious enough to take an occasional risk and traipse to some offbeat, out-of-the-way village or historic sight. If you have limited time, certainly hit the obvious spots. But if you have even one day to spare, let yourself be lured away from the U.S. Route 1 and I-95 corridor and the overcrowded resorts—one almost indistinguishable now from another. You'll see a state whose most remarkable aspects are barely known to the tourist industry.

The basic framework of this book harks back to the WPA guides of the 1930s: a series of itineraries reflecting the shape of the land. In the case of Maine, then and now, the best way to perceive this land is not as a coastal strip edging a huge, unexplored backcountry, but as a series of great river valleys reaching into the heart of the Northland, connecting the interior and the sea. This is the way the early French and British explorers saw the country, and the route the earliest settlers took in search of timber and farmland. The Piscataqua, the Androscoggin, the Kennebec, the Penobscot, and the St. Croix rivers flow through the forests and mountains of western and northern Maine, then meet the Atlantic along the state's legendary rocky shore. These are not simply rivers of great beauty but keys to understanding the land and people of Maine.

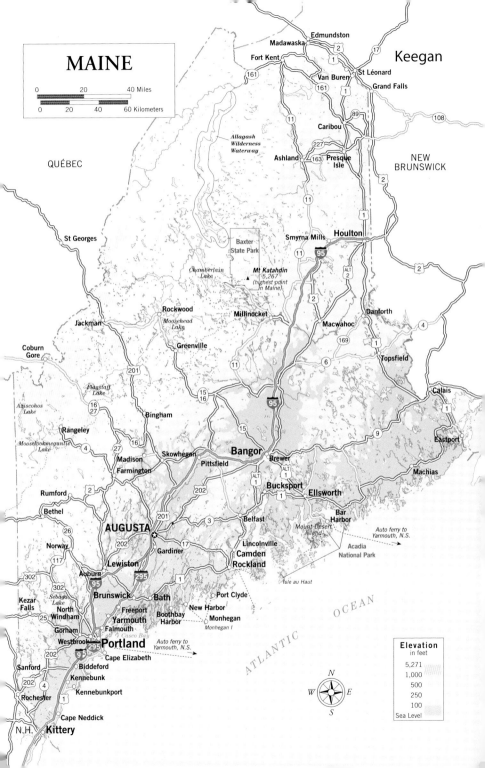

LEARNING MAINE

■ THE FOUR SEASONS

■ WINTER

Maine is the kingdom of the cold. Aside from skiers headed for the resorts in the western mountains, few people visit Maine by choice between the first heavy frosts of November and the leafing out of the trees in May. Yet winter, more than any other season in this far corner of New England, has shaped the look of Maine's townscapes and the character of its people as fundamentally as the last retreating glaciers of the Ice Age sculpted its hills and valleys some 18,000 years ago. So much that seems quintessentially "Mainer"—the low-key personalities, the ability to spend long periods of time alone, the warmth and loyalty demonstrated once a friendship has been established, the willingness to make do with what is at hand— so much of this can be explained by the fact of winter.

And it is a glorious season. Snow comes in dramatic bursts. People who can avoid traveling stay close to home. But once a storm passes, the landscape comes alive: children skate or slide on frozen ponds, older kids play ice hockey, ice fishermen socialize in little huts, and intrepid birdwatchers search for tree sparrows, cedar waxwings, hawk owls. The harbors—full of mallards, harlequin ducks, and eiders amid the lobster boats—never completely freeze. In the distance clouds of sea smoke wrap themselves around the islands. Cross-country skiers, noisy snowmobiles, and daring young men sliding their four-wheel-drive trucks in circles on the ice animate the winter woods.

At night the quiet returns. Dark comes by 4 P.M. Now and then icy slush cascades off the roof. On the very coldest nights, when the countryside seems unearthly quiet, the bare trees make cracking noises in the dark. In the clear air the Milky Way turns out to have so many stars that it really *does* look like spilled milk. On some nights the aurora borealis flickers and progresses leisurely across the sky. Back indoors, locals read seed catalogues around the wood stove and await the next growing season.

■ SPRING

Everything conspires to make you believe it cannot happen. At some point in January a thaw arrives, leaving the ground bare of snow for several weeks—the beginning of mud season. There will be another false start in February, and several more in March. The daylight hours lengthen, but the trees remain stubbornly bare and the turf, soggy by day, freezes crisp after dark. Sand off the roads blows in your eyes. What elsewhere might promise to be a spring shower turns into more snow. By day the only sign that nature is stirring is the excitement of the herring gulls dining at the town landfill.

Then two things happen. Sometime in April you hear the ice crack. The breaking up of river or creek ice is a more certain sign of spring than any daffodil. As the surface crust breaks up and the snow in the distant hills begins to melt, modest streams become torrents. Years ago the spring freshet marked the beginning of the season, when logs crowded the rivers. After a winter of cutting in the forest, the new timber would have been floated downriver, collected in huge booms where the white water had ceased and the rivers widened, then parceled out to the sawmills. The heroic age of logging is past; now it is more highly mechanized and dominated by large corporations. But to all who know Maine's story, the churning waters of springtime evoke the days when a forest economy fed into its rivers.

A quiet sunset during a snowy winter in Waldoboro.

In May, depending how far you are from the moderating touch of the sea, color washes over the drab countryside. The transformation takes several weeks, perhaps more in truculent years. A few warmish days will bring out the maples and birches, then the oaks, as a band of color marches up the brown and gray hillsides in a reverse image of fall. It is still sweater weather—and on the coast may remain so, at least after dark, all summer long—but the natives will slowly emerge from their cocoons of Gore-Tex and wool, exposing pale skin to the thin springtime light.

■ SUMMER

"Where are you are going this summer?" someone will inevitably ask.

"Who wants to go anywhere?" is the triumphant reply. "We're in Maine!" Suddenly the long wait proves to have been worth it. Forgotten are the chilblains, the fuel bills, the cars skidding on black ice. It's time to sit in the sun and smell the balsam sap rise from the woods or the sweet stench of the rockweed the tide has left exposed on the shore. The fiddleheads of June give way to the peas and raspberries of July, and then to the tiny wild blueberries of August. At night, while most of the rest of the country swelters or turns up the air-conditioning, it's time to build a log fire. The cool breeze off the ocean or out of the hills lets you wear wool and go barefoot at the same time. True, summer has its irritations—an exasperating array of flying insects (some too small to see, some almost too large to swat), sudden thunderstorms inland, and days when it seems the fog will never lift along the shore. But the intense sweetness of the very best days is all the more valued by a people who know that winter will return.

For about 150 years now, a good number of outlanders have also come to enjoy Maine's summer climate and scenery. In fact, this seasonal migration of summer visitors can be traced back many thousands of years; at least some of the indigenous peoples of the Maine forests came downriver by canoe each summer and lived for the warmest months on the shore, leaving shellheaps and other reminders. (Their distant descendants, selling sweetgrass baskets and other crafts they had made to supplement a meager income, were still a familiar sight in summer resort towns as late as the 1940s.) Modern tourism, however, began with the arrival of a group of painters—including Thomas Cole, Frederick Church, and above all Fitz Hugh Lane—in the two decades before the Civil War. Their romantic depictions of Maine's harbors and most especially of Mount Desert Island's rocky shores inspired a first wave of "rusticators"—well-to-do families seeking an escape from urban Boston, New York, and Philadelphia in the 1870s. Some built huge summer "cottages," rustic or palatial, in a string of fashionable resort towns along the Maine coast, Bar Harbor the most famous of them. Other waves of summer visitors headed for the woods and lakes, where weary businessmen sought to restore their health and their sense of manliness by close encounters with bear, moose, and trout.

Some of the descendants of these late-19th- and early-20th-century summer people still spend Fourth of July through Labor Day in their great-grandparents' cottages; a few have even settled in the state year round. Some of the patterns of modern Maine tourism reflect the earlier models, though on a vastly different scale. The state today accommodates a mass migration of admirers in July and August, many of whom do not stray very far from the coastal strip threaded by U.S. 1 (also known as Route 1). Given that many year-round residents choose to go off to their "camps" (the local name for any kind of house on a lake) in the same months, the brief tourist high season puts a strain on some of the state's resources,

The Cottage Door, *a summer scene photographed by Emma D. Sewall.*
(following page) The shore walk in Bar Harbor.

not least its sense of calm, slow-moving, rather sparsely settled rusticity. (No wonder some Mainers hate the "VACATIONLAND" label on their license plates!) Mercifully or not, the season is brief, and the roads soon empty.

■ FALL

September is the ideal month to visit Maine. The summer crowds thin dramatically, yet the weather remains near-perfect through early October. Seacoast towns that were uncomfortably crowded at the height of the season are manageable again after Labor Day. Although some attractions close once the public schools are back in session, there is a growing awareness of a fall tourist season, one that has less to do with the foliage—which, incidentally, is as splendid in the hills of Maine as anything to be seen in Vermont or New Hampshire—than with an informed search for the qualities that made Maine desirable to start with: its remoteness and unspoiled scenery, and the rare commodity of solitude.

On the coast, the light performs tricks. In the early morning fog the trunks of the paper birches, normally white or gray, appear a yellow-green, and distant objects turn insubstantial. The sound of a boat's horn seems more palpable than the fuzzy rocks on the shore. By midmorning, however, the sun has burned through the fog, and that Fairfield Porter look of vacation weather has returned: flawless blue skies, shimmering water, dark-green spruces and firs. In late afternoon Fitz Hugh Lane returns to his easel. The low golden light, the mood of utter stillness, and the feeling of ripeness that fill his views of Somes Sound or Camden Harbor settle on a hundred coves and inlets from Kittery to Calais.

Inland has its appeal too, especially since the state has 2,200 lakes. But the mood is sharper. On the coast you can lull yourself into feeling that October will last forever. Away from the sea, however, by late August there are already signs that winter is approaching. It is more a matter of fading light than cooler weather, but the note of warning is unmistakable. By September the nights are decidedly nippier. By October there is a smell of Arctic air pushing down from Canada. But what a show the land makes. There is no putting it in words. It must have been one of the most remarkable sights to confront the earliest settlers, accustomed as they were to the brownness of the European autumn. Whether you are a "leaf peeper" on a chartered bus tour or a child running and leaping into a newly raked pile of them, the fall foliage, for a few short weeks, is the stuff of alchemy. And then, with one strong storm, it is all gone. The hills are left bare, and everyone goes inside again.

SUMMER SWIM

As children, play followed a rather fixed pattern through the year. In March we would take advantage of the high winds and fly homemade kites; in April we cut poles and built stilts so that we could walk high above the muddy roads; in May we played marbles, jumped rope, and rolled hoops which usually were the cast-off iron rims of old wagon wheels.

All summer we went swimming in the Mill Cove, which had sedge and cut-grass along its sides and mud in its bottom. On afternoon high tides, when the wind was southwest—as it usually was in fair summer weather—fifteen or twenty of us would show up for a swim. On these afternoons, the water was warm. All morning the sun had been pouring down on the mudflats, warming the slowly incoming water to about 70 degrees, and we were all there to enjoy it. We had no bathing suits. Some of the boys wore no underclothes in summer. Speed in getting undressed was somehow regarded as a great virtue. To shame the slow members of our gang, someone would shout, "Last one undressed got to f—— a leaf!" Although some of us were too young to understand what this desperate punishment meant, the threat would put speed into us and we would literally tear our clothes off to avoid the penalty.

–Wilbert Snow, *Codline's Child,* 1968

Campers in 1914 wade in the Great Pond, Kennebec Valley.

■ LEARNING THE LAND

Maine covers almost as much of the northeastern corner of the United States as the five other New England states combined, though relatively few visitors see more than about 10 percent of it—the coastal strip bounded on one side by U.S. 1, and on the other by the Atlantic. What immediately strikes people arriving from more thickly settled parts of the country is how green most of the state is. Since it is sparsely populated overall, none of Maine's cities is too far removed from the countryside. Maine seems to many people "from away" a land that the 21st century and its bulldozers have yet to touch.

Maine is actually greener today than it was a century ago. After the Civil War the state's agriculture went into gradual decline as the soil, thin to start with, became exhausted, and as Maine's more ambitious young moved west in search of better farmland or more prosperous economies. Much of the land that was cleared for farming in the 19th century reverted to forest in the 20th. The sight of a stone wall in the woods, or of a cellar hole surrounded by the hardy lilac bushes someone planted in the days before the young men marched off to Bull Run and Antietam—these are reminders of how transitory the human touch on the land can be. In the great North Woods, where, when seen from the air, the spruce and hemlock and white pines seem to stretch forever, the timber companies long ago cut down most of the virgin forest. What is left—save for a few inaccessible pockets or those preserved on purpose as "forever wild"—is a sort of industrial forest, its trees closely managed by the paper industry.

To understand this land, it helps to know about two events in geological history. Some 350 to 400 million years ago, molten rock from deep inside the earth was pushed up by heat and pressure and, intruding through the layers of bedrock that covered the eastern United States, formed ranges of mountains. The results of this complex upheaval can be seen all over the state in road cuts, at waterfalls where layers of rock suddenly point skyward, or where dikes of different-colored rock are exposed. Perhaps the most striking evidence of this great upheaval is to be seen on Mount Desert Island, where the famous pink granite—the color of poached salmon—has been exposed everywhere the older surface rock has been eroded away. About a million years ago, glaciers began to push their way south as far as Long Island, New York, in nine long cycles of advance and withdrawal. The last glacier began to recede around 18,000 years ago. At its coldest moment, ice about a mile thick—four times the height of Acadia National Park's Cadillac

Mountain—covered New England, compressing the land. Every Maine riverbed, lake, gravel pit, sand deposit, glacial erratic, and smooth-faced shelf of rock bears witness to the coming and going of the ice. On some mountaintops the scratches and grooves look so sharp they seem new—which, by a geological reckoning of time, they are indeed.

Maine's political geography is not so easily explained: at several points in its history things might have taken a different turn. Had 18th-century diplomacy between England and France worked out another way, French might be spoken today up and down the Kennebec. Had Massachusetts not been willing to give up its appendage in 1820, the District of Maine might still be paying its taxes to Boston. The long boundary dispute with Canada was not settled until the 1840s, and even today there are towns in northern Maine where the local economy seems to straddle the border. Sometimes "Maine" seems to exist as a well-defined entity more in the minds of people from outside the state than among its own intensely local citizens, whose strongest loyalties are often to their own town and their own kin.

■ LEARNING THE SEA

The Maine poet Robert P. Tristram Coffin (1892–1955) once wrote of two distinct Maines: one of "woods and lakes and mountains," and another of "woods and mountains and sea." He identified with the latter, as do most of the people who come each summer to eat lobster, watch the gulls, and stare at the eastern horizon. In truth, except perhaps in the potato fields of Aroostook County (something of a world of its own), much of the state is oriented toward the sea. This is more than a matter of romantic notions about sea captains and clipper ships. It is in fact a tribal memory of the days before the railroad and the interstate, when water carried commerce and ideas, when Maine timber floated downstream to the mills, and when Maine families traveled upstream from the seaports in search of rich valley land. However landlocked they might seem, both Augusta (the state capital) on the Kennebec and Bangor on the Penobscot are still accessible from the sea.

And while there is much of interest and beauty inland, and while I suppose a clever publicist for the state could do wonders with lumberjacks or snowshoes or moose, it is the legendary rocky coast of Maine that draws out-of-staters summer after summer, and it is the coastal mystique—part lobster bake, part spiritual retreat—that sets the state apart from the other 49 and that most defines the image of Maine in the American psyche.

Painter Fitz Hugh Lane's Shipping in Down East Waters *was part of the body of work that inspired the first wave of "rusticators" who came to Maine to escape the urban pressures of Boston, New York, and Philadelphia in the 1870s.*

The coast has many attractions. For one thing, there is so much of it. Although only about 250 miles separate Kittery on the New Hampshire border from the West Quoddy Head Light on the border with Canada, it would take you some 3,000 miles to trace the convolutions of the shoreline created at the end of the Ice Age, when the sea rushed into sunken valleys emerged from under the glaciers. (This would not include the shorelines of Maine's thousands of islands or the waterfront of Maine's 2,200 freshwater lakes and ponds.) As you travel "Down East"—that is, northeast along the coast—the shoreline grows wilder. And while there may be a very real problem of public access in many areas, at least the shoreline looks expansive in all but the most crowded parts of the state. (Looking is quite enough for many people; the ocean water is freezing.) Sure, there are scenic roads and overlooks, but if you don't go directly out on the water—even in the local mail boat or inter-island ferry—you haven't seen Maine. It is the view of the land from the sea—of dark fir trees against the sky, of safe little harbors, of surf crashing on the ledges—that meant "Maine" to the first three centuries' European arrivals, and that still draws their American descendants today.

■ APPRECIATING THE ARCHITECTURE

Maine has one of the greatest assemblages of distinctively American architecture to have survived from the 19th century. Because of the state's economic decline after the Civil War, there are many towns that have retained their pre-modern streetscapes, with houses ranging from simple late-18th-century Capes (one-and-a-half-story cottages) to stately Federal and Greek Revival mansions to Victorian fantasies where woodcarvers went on a spree. It is a tribute to the skill with which these houses were built—and pride of place so many Mainers exhibit—that such a large number of these 100- to 250-year-old structures still function successfully, in some instances inhabited by descendants of their original owners.

This guide pays particular attention to some of the buildings most characteristic of this Maine architecture, including both vernacular (or everyday) examples and a few high-style marvels that appear in architectural history books. The aim of such a tour is not to enjoy buildings simply for their aesthetic value, but rather to use them as a way of understanding the people who erected them—and who choose to live in them still. And there's an added benefit—in every Maine town some of the grandest houses are inevitably now bed-and-breakfasts waiting to welcome the curious traveler for the same price he would pay at a good but flavorless motel.

SOUTHERN COAST
& YORK COUNTY

What happens to me when I cross the Piscataqua and plunge rapidly into Maine at a cost of 75 cents in tolls? I cannot describe it. I do not ordinarily spy a partridge in a pear tree, or three French hens, but I do have the sensation of having received a gift from a true love.

–E. B. White, "Home-Coming," *The Essays of E. B. White,* 1955

The bridge no longer exacts a toll—though the Turnpike tolls more than make up for it—but many visitors still experience that rejuvenating lift of the spirit as they leave Portsmouth and the enclosed feeling of New Hampshire, soar high over the industrial-looking river, and reach the wooded shore of what for many Americans is a distinctly unusual place.

This immediate sense of being in "a place apart" was probably more striking to travelers of White's generation. They could make a leisurely journey by car through the landscape of saltwater farms and dusty villages as they followed U.S. Route 1A—an old colonial post road—on its meanderings along the coast northward from York. Today much of Kittery—the town that introduces Maine to the northbound traveler—is still a likable place, but many tourists come just to find a partridge or a French hen at Kittery's upscale discount outlet mall.

The notion of making a trip to Maine to go shopping may amuse the older residents—people who are more likely to seek out hunter's orange blaze or Arctic-weight underwear at Reny's in downtown Bath or Wiley's in Ellsworth than to try on blazers at Brooks Brothers in Kittery. And it probably horrifies those who've moved to the state in the past twenty-odd years to escape our consumer-dominated culture. So here's the question facing anyone who plans to visit York and Cumberland counties, Maine's densely populated southwestern corner: Is this the real Maine?

Well, yes and no. If your vision of Maine involves surf crashing on pink granite cliffs or loons bassooning on lonely lakes, you're bound to be disappointed. Most of the landscape is a continuation of the coastal plain that runs from Cape Cod

Children splash in the surf at Kennebunkport Beach.

almost all the way to Portland and Casco Bay. It is broken by the mouths of several slow-moving rivers, softened by long stretches of salt marsh replete with birdlife and shellfish, and enriched by miles of dunes and beaches. Sections of this coastal corridor are also packed with condominiums, shopping malls, motels, fast-food joints, and midsummer traffic jams. Plenty of people here commute, year-round or seasonally, to Boston, a couple of hours away. And the number is increasing now that train travel (on Amtrak), at least as far as Portland, is once again a Maine reality.

Typical of this side of York County is Ogunquit's famous Perkins Cove. Not too long ago it was a quiet, even seedy, collection of wharves and fishermen's shacks, much painted and sketched by summertime artists. But look around now and you'll see a cluster of condos and motels, boutiques and seafood restaurants, yachts and excursion boats—it's a kind of nautical theme park, where the smell of automobile fumes mixes with the aromas of lobster butter and bayberry candles. While most of the coastal corridor is intensely commercial, many of the farms farther inland, carved out in the past two centuries, have since reverted to fields and woodland. In recent decades this part of southern Maine has become a new exurbia—moderate to expensive houses on big lots in what would have seemed the middle of nowhere before 1980.

Pondering the sea at Perkins Cove, circa 1900.

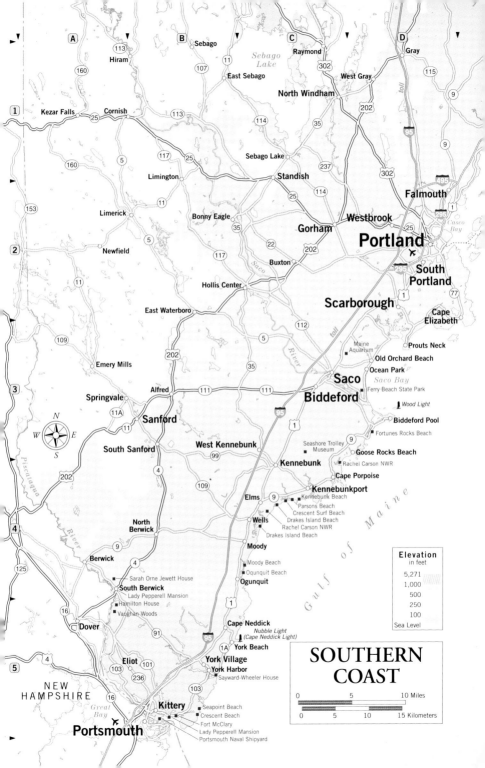

SOUTHERN COAST

■ SOUTHERN PISCATAQUA

The southern Piscataqua Valley was once the epicenter of a different exurban phenomenon: the invention of Colonial Revival America. For reasons commendable (the country was becoming too ugly) and deplorable (immigrants were "ruining" New England), many prosperous and well-educated people in and around Boston in the last decades of the 19th century decided that they preferred living in a place that at least looked like the America of their 18th-century ancestors. Since much of developed Massachusetts was already beyond saving, they looked farther afield and discovered, among other places, the sleepy backwaters of Portsmouth, Kittery, the Yorks, and the Berwicks.

This region had been anything but sleepy in the 18th century! A thriving lumber business (which started way upriver) brought prosperity to the Piscataqua Valley, and the merchant-princes of Portsmouth built splendid Georgian houses with the profits from sugar, slaves, timber, and rum. The home-grown timber and the imported sugar and rum were all grist for the mill, so to speak: cargo for the ship-owners' square-riggers and goods to fill the merchants' warehouses.

■ KITTERY *map page 27, B-5*

On the Maine side of the river, at Kittery Point, **Lady Pepperrell's mansion** of 1760—the finest Palladian house in the Piscataqua Valley—still stands on a hillside that once overlooked a river filled with tall-masted ships and flat-bottomed gundalows. (To get there follow Route 103 east.) Sir William Pepperrell, the richest landowner in early-18th-century Maine, led the combined British and Colonial forces that successfully besieged the French fortress of Louisburg, in Canada, in 1745—a military exploit that led to his becoming the first American baronet (a hereditary knighthood) and that helped persuade his Massachusetts militiamen that they could take on a professional European army, a lesson not forgotten in 1776. The year after his death, Lady Pepperrell (who even after the Revolution insisted on keeping her British title) built the imposing house, which shares numerous stylistic features with Longfellow's Craigie House in Cambridge, Massachusetts. (The house, privately owned, has recently been restored and can be seen if you can find the caretaker. The gardens are always open.) The 1730 First Congregational Church across Route 103 is also worth seeing; it was rumored to have been connected by an underground passage to the Pepperrell house.

Continue east on Route 103 and you'll come to state-owned **Fort McClary,** built in 1808 and modified several times—from this site the approaches to the Piscataqua River were protected from Revolutionary days through World War I. The stunning hexagonal blockhouse, built in 1846 of fieldstone, granite, and logs, rises from the hillside, dominating a windswept grassy expanse that continues down to ruined granite walls and the water. (This is a good picnic spot.)

In the 19th century, Kittery was best known for its Navy Yard (now the Portsmouth Naval Shipyard), where the 74-gun *Washington* was launched in 1815, and the *Kearsage,* which sank the Confederate raider *Alabama,* during the Civil War. The Treaty of Portsmouth, ending the Russo-Japanese War in 1905, was signed in the naval administration building.

■ THE ISLES OF SHOALS AND CELIA THAXTER

If there is any one spot where Maine can be said to have begun, it is on a cluster of granite outcroppings battered by the sea some eight miles off Portsmouth, New Hampshire. These nine small islands—five in Maine, four in New Hampshire— were inhabited by Europeans long before the coast was, and the distinction between the isles and "the mayne," or mainland, may have inspired the future state's name. Nobody really knows.

Salting cod for distant markets gave way to tourism as early as the 1840s, when to bored city dwellers the notion of a rocky island far out at sea began to seem less fraught with peril and more wildly romantic. A small hotel industry flourished, attracting both the well-to-do and the creative—among the latter Nathaniel Hawthorne, Mark Twain, Sarah Orne Jewett, Edwin Booth, Edward MacDowell, and Jan Paderewski. But once the hotels went out of fashion early in the 20th century, the islands would probably have faded from memory as surely as other vanished resorts had it not been for the happy collaboration between a woman of letters and America's leading Impressionist painter.

Celia Thaxter (1835–1894) was the daughter of a disappointed politician turned lighthouse keeper who opened the Appledore House, one of the first of New England's great wooden seaside hotels, in 1848. The solitude of her island childhood and her visits each summer back to Appledore inspired her popular verse, which placed her among the best-known writers of her day. In her essays, published as *Among the Isles of Shoals* (1873), she described both the pastoral side of the island life and the poverty and drunkenness of its longtime inhabitants. Best known is *An Island Garden*, written in 1893 and republished with its original illustrations. It's one of the grittiest garden books of its day, full of struggle against slugs, gulls, thin soil, and ceaseless wind.

Thaxter found a way to bring the world to her island. Each summer she conducted a salon on Appledore that attracted many of New England's artists, musicians, and writers. Among the guests there in the 1890s was a young painter who had recently seen in France the liberating effect that *plein air* had on the Impressionists. A splendid subject was at hand: Thaxter's flower beds. In the spirit of the Colonial Revival, she had attempted to replicate an old-fashioned English cottage garden of hollyhocks, poppies, dahlias, wallflowers, calendulas, nicotiana, sunflowers, and asters—all the more brilliant in their colors against the blue of the sea. The 400 or so paintings and drawings that Childe Hassam produced on his visits to Appledore are among his best work.

Visiting the Isles of Shoals today is a bit of a project. Appledore Island is now the home of Cornell University's Shoals Marine Laboratory, and Star Island is a religious center, so unless you're taking courses at the lab or you're attending a conference at the religious center there is no chance to stay overnight. (But you can take a day excursion in summer from Portsmouth, New Hampshire.) Thaxter's garden has been restored; you can visit it on Wednesdays from late June through August by making a reservation with the laboratory (prepaid, $36.50; call 607-255-3717). The Isles of Shoals Steamship Company (800-441-4620) takes you from the mainland to Star Island, where you can visit the small museum.

■ SOUTH BERWICK AND SARAH ORNE JEWETT *map page 27, B-4*

The winding coastal Route 103, probably the oldest road in Maine, passes many pretty old houses between Kittery and York, but this region's importance in American history lies upriver about 20 miles in South Berwick. This was the site, in 1631, of the first permanent European settlement in what would eventually become Maine. And in the last 200 years the town has ridden waves of modest prosperity— first as a shipbuilding center, then as a mill town, and finally as a center for the defense industry. Today the South Berwick Historical Society organizes lectures and house and garden tours, and supports the local Counting House Museum; people come from miles around to watch performances in the converted barn of the Hackmatack Playhouse (538 School St., 207-698-1807; www.hackmatack.org). Berwick, however, may be remembered more for its years of decline than for its successes, thanks to the town's author and elegist, Sarah Orne Jewett (1849–1909).

Emily Tyson and Sarah Orne Jewett in 1905.

   In her reminiscence "The Old Town of Berwick," Jewett's nostalgia for her New England heritage reaches near-epic proportions; her sentiments also reveal the motive behind the Colonial Revival—to reassert Protestant New England's role in defining what it meant to be American. While other writers and artists were busy searching barns and attics for discarded 18th-century paneling or collecting blue-and-white china, Jewett was busy transforming the human remnants of an earlier prosperity—the elderly sea captains, the village spinsters, the impoverished widows clinging to gentility—into a series of stories depicting Maine as a place where history stood still and the descendants of America's heroes lived dignified, hard-working lives. Her most famous locale—the Dunnet Landing of *The Country of the Pointed Firs* (1896)—is an imaginary place farther Down East (somewhere between Boothbay and Tenants harbors, she once said), but it was in the South Berwick of her childhood that she learned to listen to the quietness of Maine. It found its way into her sketches and stories, just as it did into so many twentieth-century depictions of Maine, literary and visual, all the way up to, say, Berenice Abbott's 1968 photographs of a state just on the verge of modernity.

There are two places to experience the world of Sarah Orne Jewett. The most elucidating is her family's house in South Berwick, the **Sarah Orne Jewett House** (5 Portland Street), now owned by Historic New England, formerly the Society for the Preservation of New England Antiquities (SPNEA), and open in the summer. Despite its location at a busy crossroads and flanked by two pizza parlors, the 1774 white-clapboard building has enormous dignity behind its picket fence.

In her own day Jewett was best known for her skill as a regional colorist, someone who could write charming and humorous stories about country folk, quoting them in their own dialect. Today her reputation is based more on the fact that she gave voice to the women of her time, both the village women who seem to make up most of the population of her fiction and the sensitive, upper-middle-class female summer visitors who, with great respect for local ways, serve as her narrators and observers. Aside from her father, a country doctor, Jewett's own closest emotional involvements were with other women, and she spent much of her life in what used to be called a "Boston marriage"—a shared domestic arrangement—with Annie Fields, the widow of Hawthorne's publisher.

Long considered one of the most beautiful houses in Maine, Hamilton House in South Berwick was a favorite excursion destination for Sarah Orne Jewett.

One of the most beautiful houses in Maine, **Hamilton House** (1787, renovated 1899), on a bluff overlooking the Salmon Falls River just outside town, was for many years a favorite excursion destination for Jewett. The house was in terrible disrepair, but Jewett brought it to the attention of her friend Emily Tyson's family, Bostonians with enough money to turn the property into a showplace of the Colonial Revival. The house, also owned now by HNE, is open in summer, and its garden is a popular setting for weddings and concerts. The nearby **Vaughan Woods State Park**, part of the original estate, has wooded riverside trails.

Also worth seeing in town is **Berwick Academy** (1791), the oldest secondary school in the state. In the 19th century, every Maine town of any significance had such an academy, a sort of finishing school for students whose parents could afford to give them more than a district-school education. They were either preparing for college or, as was the case for many women, learning enough to be literate wives and mothers. With some private endowment, academies like Berwick have survived as day or boarding schools; others have kept their historic names but have become part of the public system, and still others have disappeared. The campus, like its surrounding neighborhood, includes several attractive historic buildings, some of them open for house tours in summer.

From North or South Berwick—and before returning toward York and the coast—swing inland through the pretty towns of **Alfred** and **Limerick**. Alfred's courthouse holds records dating from 1636. You can get a good lunch or dinner at **Leedy's**, on the Square (207-324-5856). At Limerick, the **Peppermill on Main Street** (207-793-2500) does wonderful liver and onions.

■ **OLD YORK** *map page 27, B/C-5*

York and Kittery Point vie for the distinction of being the oldest settlement in what became first the Province, later the District of Maine. Both claim that their earliest settlers arrived in 1623. But York is unrivaled in Maine in the way it has preserved itself as an "historic" environment. Much of this was the work of Colonial Revivalists who not only rescued and "restored" a number of important 18th-century buildings but also did their best, in the days when zoning was unknown, to keep visual reminders of the early 20th century out of the center of town. Although today the look of it seems a bit contrived, it's still a pleasure to stroll through. There are enough sites open to the public to entertain you for at least a day's visit. York, as the highway signs remind you, is actually "the Yorks." The town's 66 square miles include four communities: York Village, York Harbor, York Beach, and Cape Neddick. If you're here for the first time, start with the historic Village to keep your sense of chronology, then move north along Route 1A, toward the more up-to-date diversions that the other Yorks and Ogunquit have to offer.

The area of **York Village** was first called Agamenticus, the Wabanaki Indian name for the river that creates York's harbor. An English speculator with the sumptuous name of Sir Ferdinando Gorges was granted a charter by James II in 1635 to create a "Province of Mayne," and chose this fishing village as his capital, chartering the town in 1640 under the name of Gorgeana (said to be the first such charter of an English town in the New World). His ambitious plans for laying out a great city in the wilderness were abandoned in 1652, however, when Puritan Massachusetts got control of the province, which was to remain part of Massachusetts until Maine achieved statehood in 1820. Renamed York after one of Cromwell's victories, the town was an important shipbuilding center and fishing port for more than a century, then was rescued from its post–Civil War decline by the arrival of summer residents and tourists.

Today more than 50 buildings from the late 17th and 18th centuries remain. A distinctive colonial building style in southern Maine and New Hampshire—the so-called "logg garrison" house, with its overhanging upper floor—was associated early on with York. According to legend, when the Indians or the French attacked, while the men fired their muskets, the women could pour boiling water from the projecting floor onto the enemy below. In truth, overhanging stories are a traditional European building style brought to America and adapted to log construction. But like the "borning rooms" (which were simply extra chambers) or "Indian shutters" (which were to preserve heat and privacy, not fend off arrows and tomahawks), "garrison houses" have entered architectural folklore. The style reappears, vestigially, in late-20th-century tract houses all across New England. (The threat from Indians was quite real until the 18th century. York still "remembers" the Candlemas Day Massacre of 1692. Colonial depredations against the "savages" were comparably barbaric.) The Old York Historical Society will welcome you at **Jefferds Tavern** (ca. 1750), which stands at the center of a well-maintained complex of pre-Revolutionary structures along Lindsay and York streets, each with explanatory exhibits. These include the **Old School House** (1745), the **Emerson-Wilcox House** (period rooms, 1750–1950), **The Ramsdell House** (a two-room workingman's house, 1740), the **Old Gaol Museum** (which housed prisoners from

Nubble Light on Cape Neddick.

1719 until 1860), the **John Hancock Warehouse** (owned by the famous patriot), and the **George Marshall Store** (a gallery of changing exhibitions).

But perhaps the most important place for anyone seeking to understand the Colonial Revival is the **Elizabeth Perkins House**, across the river where Lindsay Road ends. In 1898, when Elizabeth Bishop Perkins and her mother decided to buy a picturesque old house as a retreat from boiling New York City summers, they could have joined their fashionable friends on the ocean at York Harbor. Instead, they chose a decaying property on the bucolic York River. Over the next 37 years, the younger Perkins turned a rather simple mid-18th-century house into a showplace of the Colonial Revival, a process that involved many more disguised alterations (including a servants' wing and a garage) than the Tysons had found necessary at Hamilton House. But the final product—including a supposedly 17th-century dining room stripped down to expose its beams and timbers— looked exactly the way genteel house restorers thought the setting for domestic life in pre-Revolutionary New England should look. Despite its backwater location, the Perkins House became a social center for the York summer colony, a status enhanced in 1905 when its owners had the delegates from the Portsmouth Treaty negotiations to tea.

SPNEA tactfully declined Elizabeth Perkins's offer of the house (on the grounds that it had been altered too much) but in 1977 did accept another famous York Harbor dwelling, the **Sayward-Wheeler House** (ca. 1720), which had survived largely because of family pride, and which had welcomed respectful tourists since the 1860s. The white clapboard building at 79 Barrell Lane Extension is quirky and of no great stylistic importance, but its riverfront setting and its mementos of the town's leading pre-Revolutionary family (including loot from the capture of Louisburg) make it one of the most notable historic houses to visit in Maine. Jonathan Sayward, rich from the West Indies trade, lived there from 1735 until 1797—his reputation in the community being secure enough to protect him during the Revolution despite his Loyalist sympathies. His grandson, Jonathan Sayward Barrell, continued the family business, but like many New England merchants was almost ruined by President Jefferson's Embargo of 1807. His unmarried daughters, like characters in a Sarah Orne Jewett short story, remained in the house, living in genteel poverty yet keeping their ancestral possessions in place. In 1901 the house was bought by more prosperous relatives, the Wheelers, who made minor improvements but tried to keep the contents intact in honor of the family. The parlor in particular, with its ancestral portraits and Chippendale chairs against the wall just where the Saywards placed them, evokes the life of a rich provincial merchant's family on the eve of the Revolution. The room is low-ceilinged and cramped, but the furnishings are almost luxurious, suggesting that juxtaposition of comfort and primitiveness in which prosperous Americans of the 18th century lived.

Adding to the Piscataqua Valley's many literary associations, Sayward's grand-daughter—born in the house in 1759 and known as Madam Wood—was Maine's first successful popular writer, author of the Gothic novel *Julia and the Illuminated Baron* (1800). Years later, one of York's early parsons inspired Hawthorne's "The Minister's Black Veil." Today a mix of posh summer homes, hotels, and bed-and-breakfasts, **York Harbor** was a fashionable literary neighborhood a century ago, attracting writers as disparate as Mark Twain and Thomas Nelson Page; Kittery Point was the summer home of Boston's William Dean Howells (1837–1920).

Summer colonists a century ago thought of **York Beach** as a little too lively. Trains brought "the unwashed," presumably to wash on the splendid sand beach, and the genteel feared the outsiders might spill over into their neighborhoods.

Today there is still a distinct change in population density (and traffic) between York Beach and the more serene York Harbor, but York Beach has an attractively retro quality of its own, compared to the glitzier resorts farther along the coast. (At the famous **Goldenrod's,** for example, you can watch saltwater taffy being made.) Two landmarks appear on the northern side of the town of York: inland rises Mount Agamenticus, only 692 feet tall but a traditional navigational aid on this flat coastline. From the summit you'll get some memorable views of the White Mountains and the Atlantic. On a little island just offshore stands the much-photographed Nubble Light, also known as Cape Neddick Light.

■ OGUNQUIT   *map page 27, C-4*

Ogunquit is about as distinctive as any other resort town between the Gulf of Mexico and the Gulf of Maine—if you don't stray far from U.S. Route 1. But much can be forgiven when you see the three miles of beach: a broad, firm expanse of sand (it extends even farther if you add **Moody Beach** in adjacent Wells). There is nothing else quite like it north of Cape Cod. The town, remark-ably, has managed to protect most of it from development. Thanks to the inter-coastal Ogunquit River, several strategically placed parking lots, and the local trolleys, the beach itself is one of two places where you can escape from traffic. The other is the mile-long **Marginal Way**, an oceanfront path along the more dra-matic part of Ogunquit's shorefront. The developer of the property in the 1920s, concerned about complaints that summer people were buying up all the ocean frontage and blocking the public's view of the water, laid out a right of way between the house lots and the rocky shore and deeded it to the town.

Since the 1890s Ogunquit has been known as an art center, attracting such major painters as Edward Hopper (1882–1967), Walt Kuhn (1877–1949), and Yasuo Kuniyoshi (1893–1953), as well as lesser lights who produced studies of lobster traps and beached dories for the tourist trade. The **Ogunquit Art Association** was formed in 1928 in Charles H. Woodbury's studio, which over-looks Perkins Cove. The town continues to support several galleries, the **Ogunquit Museum of American Art**—with glass walls so you can see out to sea—and the well-regarded **Ogunquit Playhouse**. But the cultural side of Ogunquit tends to be swallowed up in the sheer mass of summer visitors, catered to by elbow-to-elbow motels, inns, and boutiques. Since World War II, in fact, Ogunquit has been the leading gay resort north of Provincetown.

A Childhood in Ogunquit

Ogunquit was a magic place for me as a child, when every summer beginning in 1917 for about ten years Lucy Stanton lent us her studio for one month. We ate at the old High Rock Hotel, so it was a real holiday for my mother. Both she and my father loved to swim, and we used to walk along the Marginal Way to one of the rocky coves, the charm being those jagged rocks standing up from soft white sand. I know of no other place that combines the two. I haunted the local library, and gradually borrowed and read through all the Waverly novels, taking them out one by one in a closely-printed edition with a musty smell, usually climbing up a pine tree and sitting there most uncomfortably. I wonder why reading in a tree is such a pleasure! There must be something atavistic about it—I can still smell the pine gum and feel its stickiness on my fingers. It is all so present to me that it is quite a shock to find old photographs and realize, looking at my father's stiff white collars and my mother's big hats, and her bathing costume which included long black stockings, how long ago it really was.

–May Sarton, *The House by the Sea*, 1977

■ WELLS *map page 27, C-4*

Ogunquit's neighbor, Wells, dates from the 1640s—Gorges named it for the English cathedral town—but strip development along U.S. 1 (also known as Route 1) has obliterated any sense of history in the place. What gives Wells some value, geographically speaking, is the broad tidal marsh that separates the busy commercial area from its beach.

Like barrier beach communities up and down the Atlantic coast, Wells faces the problem of whether to maintain its protective jetties with sand dredged from its harbor or to allow the free-roaming sea to wash against the beach, naturally eroding and replenishing the sands (which would erode many beachfront properties). The scale is small, but the problem of just how much development the beaches can tolerate is a very real one. And Wells is a town with an environmental consciousness, thanks in part to programs at its wildlife preserves. It's also a town with a sense of the past, evident at Wells's historical society and in some of the best antique shops and antiquarian bookstores in the state.

Sunny Beach, Ogunquit, by Gertrude Fiske, presents a nostalgic view of the summer beach resort.

If you're in search of sandy beaches you can find more at Kennebunk Beach, Biddeford Pool, and Old Orchard Beach, but the public beaches (in season) are crowded and have limited parking. Thanks to a court case involving Wells's Moody Beach, private beachfront is virtually off limits to the public, even between the high and low tide marks. If going to the beach is what you really came to Maine for, it's better to invest in a short-term shorefront rental or a room at a motel with access to the water.

■ RACHEL CARSON NATIONAL WILDLIFE REFUGE
map page 27, C-4

A beautiful estuary preserved as a refuge for migratory birds only a few minutes' drive from the clogged streets of Kennebunkport is a particular pleasure, especially as the stretches of uninterrupted countryside grow fewer. The Rachel Carson National Wildlife Refuge in Wells is hardly wilderness—you can glimpse houses

along the edge, and the distant roar of the surf has to compete with the traffic on busy Route 9. But it is a fitting memorial to perhaps the most influential writer on ecology in our time, a biologist whose early works *Under the Sea Wind* and *The Sea Around Us* reflected her summers on the Maine coast, and whose *Silent Spring* in 1962 alerted the nation to the dangers of DDT and other pesticides.

The Wells site is one of 10 saltwater marshes between Kittery and Cape Elizabeth that make up the refuge. These tidal estuaries and their upland "edge habitats" of woods and fields form a chain along some 50 miles of coast that offers migrating birds a place to feed, rest, and rear their young. Threatened by development in the 1950s and 1960s, this stretch of coastal wetlands was saved, at least in part, by the federal government's purchase of some 5,200 acres (eventually, about 7,600 additional acres will be included).

The Wells site is the most accessible to the general public, thanks to a well-explained trail laid out by the U.S. Fish and Wildlife Service. There are also trails at Brave Boat Harbor (Cutts Island, north of Kittery), Goose Rocks Beach (north of Kennebunkport), and Old Orchard Beach. While the marsh at Wells itself is too fragile for human traffic, you can admire it from several vista points along the one-mile trail. Perhaps at their tawny best on a sunny fall day, the tall marsh grass—saltwater cordgrass *(Spartina alterniflora)*—and the shorter salt hay *(Spartina patens)* form what is one of the most productive ecosystems in the temperate world. Migratory birds stopping here in the spring and fall include black ducks, black-bellied plovers, and thousands of other shorebirds. You can also spot scoters, mergansers, and eiders seeking winter protection in the marshes, followed in summer by egrets and herons.

If you want to know more about this environment, visit the nearby **Wells National Estuarine Research Reserve** at Laudholm Farm (207-646-4521), a historic saltwater farm accessible from U.S. 1 in Wells, on 1,600 acres of woods, wetland, and meadow. Nature programs and bird walks for children and adults take place year-round. (**Please note**: anyone walking in the country in southern coastal Maine should take precautions against the ticks that carry Lyme disease. Wear long pants and sleeves, use insect repellent, and stay on the trails. Most important, conduct a post-walk tick check.)

Rachel Carson National Wildlife Refuge in Wells.

■ KENNEBUNKPORT AND KENNEBUNK BEACH

map page 27, C-4

Kennebunkport has been so much in the news since the 1980s, thanks to George H. W. Bush and son W, that it's difficult to remember how much it owes its national profile to an earlier celebrity—the historical novelist Kenneth Roberts (1885–1957). His tales of colonial America were so well regarded that the village of North Kennebunk changed its name to one of his titles, and appears on today's maps as Arundel. Before the days of televised historical "docudramas," his novels, including *Rabble in Arms, Northwest Passage, Oliver Wiswell,* and *Arundel,* were not only hugely popular—earning Roberts a fortune—but they educated a large audience about colonial America in ways few contemporary writers have matched. A native of nearby Kennebunk, Roberts might have remained a journalist had he not befriended in the 1920s a well-established fellow writer who summered in Kennebunkport, Booth Tarkington. Roberts had little natural gift for narrative, but by reading his manuscripts aloud to the nearly blind older man and working out the problems of plot and characterization with him—he produced a series called The Chronicles of Arundel, which traced the fate of his characters from the French and Indian War through the Revolution.

In his later years Roberts cultivated a reputation as a crusty curmudgeon. His house at Kennebunk Beach did not shelter him sufficiently from the "twittery idle people" who wanted to meet him, or from the noises of modern resort life. His peeves ranged from lawn mowers to "squawking automobile horns" to "mentally deficient chauffeurs." His much publicized ability to throw a fit had some positive results, however: he was a pioneer in the eventually successful campaign to ban billboards from Maine's highways.

It would be amusing to know what a man who so loathed hearing Maine called "Vacationland" would make of his beloved Kennebunkport today. Many of the old sea captains' and shipbuilders' houses still stand on its shaded streets—a good number of them expensive bed-and-breakfasts—and the proximity along Ocean Avenue of the Bushes' ancestral Walker's Point, the little Gothic Episcopal St. Ann's Church on the sea, the Arundel Yacht Club, and the Kennebunk River Club might indicate that this was a last outpost of the Protestant Ascendency. But in the center of town, **Dock Square** and its neighboring streets are, all summer and on fall weekends, as packed and as democratized as any suburban mall. Kennebunkport

Canoeing along the shorefront in Kennebunkport.

itself, like Boothbay Harbor and Bar Harbor farther "down east," seems at times to be laboring under the weight of its touristic success.

The family of George Bush was already well established at Walker's Point in Kenneth Roberts's day. At the turn of the 20th century, efforts to turn the local shorefront into a fashionable summer resort—to rival Newport and Bar Harbor—quickly showed signs of succeeding. The Village Improvement Society had seen to it that the village had well-kept fences and hedges, clean streets and docks, roadside landscaping, and an "entire absence" of rubbish or unsightly advertising. The area's natural and man-made beauty was enhanced, in the eyes of its promoters, by the summer colony's busy round of teas, dances, regattas, fairs, and literary events. The villagers were startled, however, to learn in the summer of 1902 that a Cape Arundel peninsula variously called Damon's Park, Flying Point, and Point Vesuvius had been purchased by the Walker family of St. Louis.

The Walker family was well known in town; they had been summering there for some 20 years, either staying in one of the large wooden hotels that characterized the first stage of the summer people's arrival or renting a cottage. It was G. H. Walker who purchased Damon's Park from the Sea Shore Company, reputedly for $20,000, and during the winter of 1902–3 the local newspaper reported the arrival of 17 railroad cars of lumber for the two houses his family was building on the point. Nineteen carpenters worked through the winter, and by July one "cottage" was ready to be occupied, with the other completed by the end of summer. In 1903 the local summer newspaper *The Wave* published photos of Walker's son's cottage, comfortably stuffed with wicker furniture, oriental rugs, flowers, books, family photos, bibelots, and a Tiffany lamp.

There was nothing particularly unusual about this; the history of what soon was called Walker's Point is a familiar story on the Maine coast. From Kittery to Mount Desert Island, many vacant shorefront plots that were regarded locally as common property were bought up and divided into building lots for rich people "from away." But this story has a particular relevance. In recent times, most of the point has been owned by Walker's daughter, Dorothy Walker Bush, and her son, George Herbert Walker Bush, the 41st president, who now divides his year between Kennebunkport and Houston, Texas. (Plenty of people stop at a lookout point across the inlet to catch a glimpse of the famous family's summer retreat. You can actually have a front-row seat in solid comfort if you stay at the oceanfront **Cape Arundel Inn,** where Room 8 faces both Walker's Point and the inn's luscious garden.)

■ **KENNEBUNK** *map page 27, C-4*

Many Maine residents are particularly intrigued by the early 1800s, as they consider the decades from 1790 to 1860 to be the founding years of the modern state. That was the time when Maine's towns, industries, educational system, religious beliefs, and ways of life took shape. If you share this curiosity for Maine's beginnings, there are two places you ought to visit in southern Maine.

Kennebunk, a few miles inland from the more famous port, is by comparison a retreat. The meandering Kennebunk River, which seems hardly more than a stream, was in fact in the early 19th century a busy shipbuilding center, bringing a degree of prosperity still reflected in the handsome Federal houses that line Route

A view of the elaborate Wedding Cake House in Kennebunk.

35. The most spectacular of these is the famous **Wedding Cake House** (private), once a rather chaste Federal mansion from about 1825. In the 1850s, owner George Bourne encased his dwelling and barn with exuberantly Gothic filigree woodwork. The effect in no way resembles a wedding cake (except for its intricate icing). It's a fantasy—half ecclesiastical, half Sir Walter Scott. There is reason to believe that its creator—an otherwise conventional shipbuilder—found in its architectural details an escape from his problems. His once-booming shipyard started to decline in the 1840s; Bourne also experienced a series of family tragedies. In his final years he busied himself with his Gothic pinnacles, arches, and tracery, his crockets and quatrefoils and cusps, doing much of the woodcarving with his own hands. The work was completed in the summer of 1856, and by December Bourne was dead of typhoid fever. Subsequent owners have treasured his handiwork, on what must now be the most photographed house in the state.

On Main Street in town stands another local treasure, the **Brick Store Museum**, housed in an 1825 store but cleverly linking three other period buildings in a way that maintains the 19th-century street front and provides a series of intimate exhibition spaces and an attractive gift shop. The museum is noted for its furniture and portraits from the Federal period—the era of the town's great prosperity—and for rotating exhibits on local neighborhoods, writers like Roberts and Tarkington, and life in general in the early republic. The museum is a lesson in how a small, local institution can maintain scholarly standards and conservation practices while still appealing to the public. It offers walking tours highlighting local architecture, including the nearby **Storer House** (1758), where Roberts was born and where Lafayette was entertained on his American tour in 1825.

■ **SACO AND BIDDEFORD** *map page 27, C-3*

Saco and its neighbor Biddeford are distinctly unlike communities. The former is a classic New England town with old white houses, shaded streets, and a traditional academy. The latter is a redbrick mill town with one of the state's largest concentrations of citizens of French Canadian descent. In the mid-18th century, however, both towns became centers for the lucrative Saco River lumber trade. Portraits and possessions of two families that grew rich in that trade—those of Thomas Cutts and Daniel Cleaves—can be seen today at the **Saco Museum** (371 Main Street), another small museum of very high quality. Housed in a Colonial Revival building (1926) by the Portland architect John Calvin Stevens, the museum exhibits local art. Its collection of Brewster paintings is renowned. Several rooms displaying the decorative art of the Colonial and Federal periods—some of it locally made—are a reminder of the degree of luxury and sophistication that rich New Englanders enjoyed in the early republic.

In the basement is a re-creation of a "Colonial" kitchen, as typically interpreted by house restorers and museum curators of the Colonial Revival—an appropriate place to end this tour of York County's history. The kitchen as symbol of hearth, home, and family was an important and reassuring part of the Colonial Revival ideology, reinforced by such props as the musket over the mantel, the herbs hanging from the beams, the pewter mugs, the inevitable spinning wheel, and the crib close to the fire. It was a version of the past that glorified pre-industrial domesticity—and ignored the danger of flying sparks—and conveyed a romantic longing for the "good old days" when life seemed simpler. Unfortunately, inventories of actual colonial households do not suggest anything so cozy; an 18th-century kitchen was hot, dirty, smoky, and on occasion dangerous to those who had to labor there.

■ OLD ORCHARD BEACH *map page 27, D-3*

A popular, traditional warm-water port for French-speaking Canadians, Old Orchard Beach lies northeast of Saco on Route 98, off U.S. 1. In addition to a glistening crescent of sand, Old Orchard is a showcase of architectural styles. There are vestiges of its days as a fashionable Victorian summer resort as well as the more modest, almost toylike dwellings in **Ocean Park,** a small community southwest of town, where many religious camp meetings and conferences took place starting in the 1880s. Ocean Park also has several buildings, including an octagonal **Temple** from 1891, listed on the National Register of Historic Places. Through the Ocean Park Association (207-934-9068) you can even rent one of the little cottages. Much of the crowded beach area itself, with its fried dough stands, has a 1950s resort feel to it. In winter, when the pier-side carnival rides are covered with snow, the look is almost surreal, and at night strangely melancholy. Despite the high human density of the beachfront, and evidently in the absence of much in the way of zoning, all sorts of high-rise condos and motels have been squeezed into the "strip." Old Orchard Beach in summer is a suburb of Quebec. You may note, with amusement, beguilement, or alarm, that the skimpiness of the bathing suits, male and female, is a more immediate sign than the French being spoken that you have left the Anglo-Saxon world, at least for the time being.

P O R T L A N D
& E N V I R O N S

Continuing north from Old Orchard Beach and across the Scarborough River, you leave behind the overpopulated resorts of southern Maine and enter the more "year-rounder" townships of Scarborough and Cape Elizabeth. As almost every municipal sign will tell you, Scarborough was established in 1657, Cape Elizabeth in 1765. The hamlets were largely ignored until the 1970s and 1980s, when Portland's economy took off: condos and short blocks of two-bedroom houses sprang up in meadows and fields, accommodating commuters—especially young couples with families—to the re-energized city. Fortunately, development slowed down before any great damage to the landscape or historic architecture was done. Fields and ponds—many of them owned by the same family for generations—remain plentiful today, and the occasional early-19th-century connected farm building covered in faded yellow or gray clapboard still stands solemnly on its modest acreage. You'll find a few old pocket neighborhoods along quiet streets, but most of the larger Shingle Style and Colonial houses are visible only from the ocean, standing on jutting points of land or near the beaches in between them. Although much of the land and many of the beaches are privately owned, there are some public beaches and parks well worth visiting.

■ WINSLOW HOMER AT PROUTS NECK

About 10 miles south of Portland, in the town of Scarborough, Prouts Neck protrudes into Saco Bay—it's a triangle of land attached at one corner, as if about to float away. The grandeur of this shore was immortalized by the artist Winslow Homer (1836–1910), who spent many years in his salt-stained, shingled house painting the stormy seas, as well as the Mainers and summer colonists he saw on the neck. Returning to New York from Europe in 1882, Winslow Homer found himself at a crossroads in his career. His early work—as a Civil War illustrator and skillful watercolorist of outdoor scenes—had given little indication that he would become, relatively late in life, one of the greatest American painters of the century.

Portland's bustling downtown is filled with eclectic, fun shops.

But his two years in England, where he had studied the lives of fishermen in the North Sea port of Tynemouth, had revealed to him what would be his most powerful subject: the struggle of men and women with the brute force of the sea.

As early as 1875 Homer had visited Prouts Neck and been captivated by the wide beaches of fine white sand that fringe the neck's eastern side. In 1883 he and his brother decided to move there, in the hope of bringing the whole family, including their parents, to summer on the point—and eventually of subdividing their property to sell to other cottagers. The plan worked perfectly, and today Prouts Neck manages to be two things at once: a very comfortable summer colony of large houses and a cultural symbol of the wildness and implacability of the sea.

It is a familiar story on the Maine coast. A scenic locale attracts a few summer visitors who board in local houses or in quickly constructed wooden hotels. Some of them return to buy property and erect Shingle Style or Colonial Revival summer "cottages" in which they and succeeding generations of their families enjoy the

Winslow Homer's A Summer Night *depicts his family and friends dancing on a moonlit evening in Prouts Neck.*

GREATER PORTLAND

clean air and unspoiled ocean view while not really abandoning the comforts of urban life. Since the Homer family had bought up almost the whole neck, they could be very choosy about who was allowed to build.

Winslow Homer preferred to have few neighbors, for he enjoyed being left alone, either in the studio he built in the former stable of his family house, "The Ark," or during his long walks along the craggy shore. He also liked to be here well into autumn, weeks after the summer season had ended, because as winter approached, the North Atlantic pounded the rocks with 30- or 40-foot waves, sending "mare's tails" of salt spray into the air. Like Turner roped to the mast of a ship in order to study a storm at sea, Homer sat on the rocks, fascinated by the violence of nature. He also had an opportunity to observe more of the actual lives of seafaring people, for there was still a local fishing fleet. On his walks around the neck, Homer studied at different times of day and in varying weather the visual effects of waves as they struck the ledges and cliffs. After having worked in watercolor, Homer turned to oil pigments in 1884. One of the results was what is regarded as his first masterpiece, *The Life-Line,* in which a woman is being rescued from a wrecked ship—both she and her rescuer suspended from a rope over a foaming sea. Through the late 1880s and 1890s he went on to produce *The Fog Warning, Weatherbeaten,* and *Artist's Studio in an Afternoon Fog,* which cemented his international reputation.

Homer found plenty of other subjects, notably the lives of hunters and fishermen in the Adirondacks and of the people of the Bahamas and the Caribbean. But he always returned to Prouts Neck and the lessons of nature he learned there. In 1909, the last oil painting he completed before putting away his palette for good was *Driftwood,* a scene of a fisherman in oilskins trying to salvage a huge log from wave-beaten rocks. The setting, according to Homer scholar Philip C. Beam, is Kettle Cove, where 34 years earlier Homer had made his first drawing at Prouts Neck.

■ PROUTS NECK TODAY *map page 51, B-5*

A private beach club now occupies Prouts Neck, and access to the wide white sands is limited to members of the "P.N.A." (Prouts Neck Association), people who rent or own houses in the immediate neighborhood. Temporary membership is available if you're staying at the **Black Point Inn,** a rambling, shingled resort on nine acres just past the entrance gate to the beach. For a similar but free beach, try the public **Scarborough Beach,** northeast on Route 207, farther up the neck. You might notice that nothing prevents the sunbathers here from walking onto Prouts Neck territory, but they seem to recognize that Scarborough is every bit as beautiful and prefer to stay where they are. You can find a livelier scene, on the other hand, farther northeast along Spurwink Road (Route 77) at **Higgins Beach.**

■ CAPE ELIZABETH   *map page 51, C-2*

North of Scarborough on Cape Elizabeth is another public beach, **Crescent Beach State Park,** a scenic, sandy expanse along Route 77. Cape Elizabeth also has some of the state's most photographed lighthouses. Two of them can be found near Crescent Beach at **Two Lights State Park**: Cape Elizabeth Light—which functions—and its defunct twin. Afterward, a stop by the **Two Lights Lobster Shack** will provide you with more fried clams than you'll ever be able to eat.

Lemuel Moody's watercolor of the Portland observatory and signal flags that alerted merchants to their boats entering the harbor.

The Portland Head Light at Cape Elizabeth.

Maine's most photographed lighthouse is probably **Portland Head Light** (north on Route 77, turn right onto Shore Road), at Fort Williams Park. Commissioned by George Washington in 1791, the lighthouse has appeared on everything from U.S. postage stamps to cereal commercials. There's a small museum, where you learn that the poet Henry Wadsworth Longfellow (1807–1882) visited here often (he grew up in Portland, attended Bowdoin College and taught there). Gaze down at the surf crashing across the rocky crags and imagine the fear Maine's jagged coastline must have instilled in ship captains. On an ominous ledge nearby, white lettering tells the story of the Christmas Eve wreck of the *Annie C. Maguire* in 1886.

From Fort Williams it's a short jaunt into **South Portland** via Shore Road, which turns into Cottage Road; make a left on Broadway and follow signs to the **Casco Bay Bridge** to Portland. From this angle the Victorian townhouses of the Western Promenade stand on a hill straight ahead and to the left; behind them the Gothic Revival redbrick towers of St. Dominic's church rise elegantly over the gray rooftops. You'll then have to follow York Street to the right to get into town.

■ **PORTLAND** *map page 51, C-2, and map page 57*

Portland is by national standards a small city—but in a state with only slightly more than a million people its approximately 67,000 residents form the largest population in any one place. Portland has been Maine's largest community since the 18th century. Although only briefy the state's capital (1820–1836), it has dominated the state's economic and cultural life almost from the beginning. One way to look at Maine politics is as an on-going debate between Portland and the urbanized parts of southern Maine (more liberal than the rest of the state) and the northern towns and rural centers (Lewiston, Bangor) over how the state should be run.

Also an extremely attractive place to live, this small city inevitably appears on most of those "the nation's most liveable communities" lists. In part this is a tribute to its location—only two hours from Boston and much closer to some of the best scenery in New England—and its geography, a combination of hills, bays, and islands. But it's also a tribute to Portland's revitalization over the past 30 years, from a pleasant but somewhat run-down city living on the glory of its maritime past to a much livelier and more prosperous community enriched in both senses of the word by an influx of young, well-educated, civic-minded residents.

The city's promoters like to compare the place to San Francisco. True, there are parallels: views of deep blue water from steep streets, rows of wood-frame Victorian houses, an abundance of restaurants, an active cultural life, an interesting mix of an Old Guard Yankee society with a less conventional arts community, and even a politically active gay and lesbian presence. The comparison, however, is forced. Portland is nevertheless a very individual place, a thriving harbor town with a colorful past and a lot of rough edges beneath its veneer of sophistication.

■ **FINDING YOUR WAY**

There are two ways to orient yourself. One is to climb the octagonal wooden signal tower, the **Portland Observatory** (1807), on **Munjoy Hill.** Standing where anxious shipowners peered at the horizon nearly 200 years ago in search of familiar sails, you can take in a panoramic view of the city, its hundreds of neighboring islands, and its hinterland, with the White Mountains of New Hampshire far to the west. The center of Portland is a long, narrow peninsula bordered by **Back Cove, Casco Bay,** and the **Fore River.** The city's main thoroughfare, **Congress Street,** follows a ridge extending between Munjoy Hill on the east and

Bramhall Hill on the west, with the rest of the city spilling down from it on either side. In modern times the city has spread far westward, but the peninsula continues to define Longfellow's "city by the sea."

Another orientation technique would be to drive around the perimeter of this peninsula, perhaps starting at **Deering Oaks Park,** the wooded edge of the old city celebrated in Longfellow's poem "My Lost Youth." In the late 19th century, landscape architect Frederick Law Olmsted was commissioned to design a green-belt of sorts around downtown Portland, the most important elements of which survive. These include, in addition to the park, **Baxter Boulevard,** around the tidal flats of Back Cove, and the Eastern and Western Promenades. The Eastern Prom forms much of Munjoy Hill's Casco Bay frontage, and it is a curious twist of urban geography that this unfashionable part of town got by far the best view. Munjoy Hill was farmland in the 18th century, with a tiny settlement of free blacks. It became heavily Irish in the immigration of the 1840s and 1850s, with various other ethnic groups arriving as soon as local industries needed their labor and skills. Only today is this largely working-class neighborhood becoming gen-trified—were its Victorian row houses in San Francisco, say, they would long ago have been bought by yuppies. Portland's rich traditionally lived in the western part of town with its inferior view. Today the Western Prom overlooks the rather industrial Fore River.

There are four other older parts of the city worth examining. To the south is the **harbor,** still a vital part of the region's economy for both its fishing and shipping industries. In the 18th and 19th centuries, lumber piled on these wharves went to Boston or the West Indies. The waterfront has become a residential and tourist center, but it also continues to be a working harbor.

Across busy Commercial Street from the water, in what was not so long ago a semi-derelict warehouse district, is the bustling **Old Port Exchange** (also known as the Old Port), some 8 or 10 city blocks of late-Victorian commercial buildings converted to restaurants, offices, apartments, and boutiques. The area, particu-larly Exchange and Commercial Streets, continues to be the city's leading tourist attraction, the sort of place where visitors—especially those who like to shop—can be turned loose for an afternoon. The area's eclectic architecture is notable not so much for any particular building but for its imaginative reuse of some of the old warehouses and the pleasing mix of revival styles in brick, terra-cotta, and granite.

DOWNTOWN PORTLAND

2,000 Feet
1,000 Meters

Storey Millinery, on Congress Street, in 1914.

Somewhat more "real" (in the sense that more Portlanders spend their days there) is the traditional downtown along **Congress Street,** with its center running from the ornate Beaux-Arts City Hall past **Monument Square** up to **Longfellow Square.** In a pattern repeated in many Maine downtowns, this once-thriving center lost much of its liveliness when in the 1970s suburban malls began drawing retail business out of downtown (only to find, in the 1990s, that huge discount warehouses would do the same thing to them). Despite the presences of much of Maine's legal and banking community at one end of Congress Street and of its leading medical center at the other, the traditional downtown grew decidedly seedy at a time when the Old Port was being rediscovered. Today Congress Street is perking up as the culture industry—an expanded **Maine Historical Society,** the **Portland Museum of Art,** the **Children's Museum,** the **Maine College of Art** (housed in what used to be the street's largest department store), the **Portland Stage Company,** the **Portland Symphony,** various dance companies—gives new life to the notion that cities need centers.

The fourth neighborhood is less easily defined by streets than by chronology: it is residential Portland of the early 19th century. A good many blocks of it survive, scattered on the western side of town along such streets as Spring, Danforth, High, State, and Park. This is an area to stroll through at leisure; for an authoritative introduction, **Greater Portland Landmarks** (207-774-5561; *www.portlandlandmarks. org*), the city's leading preservation group, runs frequent walking tours of these and other parts of town and has booklets ($1.25 each), with pictures and historical information, about each area. You can pick them up at the Portland Observatory and at the **Convention and Visitors Bureau** (245 Commercial St.; 207-772-4994). Portland has its share of traffic and parking problems, but it is still a city in which one can work downtown, lunch in the Old Port, see a film, eat a lobster dinner on the waterfront, and go home to a handsome 19th-century row house—without ever having to drive.

■ PORTLAND HARBOR

There are any number of pleasant spots from which you can watch modern Portland pass by—the popular **Portland Coffee Roasters** on Commercial Street, the sidewalk in front of **O'Naturals** on Exchange Street, or the park beneath the huge *trompe-l'oeil* mural in the center of the Old Port. Or stroll down to the harbor, where island dwellers arrive on the mainland by ferry.

Lacking a boat yourself, you can at least take one of the ferries from Commercial Street to the various islands in **Casco Bay.** Several are home to thriving communities, though others are little more than ledges. The bay's islands were named the Calendar Islands by 17th-century explorer John Smith, who claimed there were 365 of them. Though more realistically numbering between 130 and 220, they are replete with legend, much of it involving pirates (like Captain Kidd), privateers, and islanders of varying degrees of respectability. Take Captain Keiff of Crotch Island, who was said to ride up and down the shore during a storm with a lantern tied to his horse's neck, hoping to lure a passing vessel onto the rocks—after which he would salvage the wreck.

Christopher Levett built a house on Richmond Island in 1624. Then, seeking to promote New England back home among his countrymen, he returned to England and wrote an account of his voyage lavishly praising the potential of Maine. Over the next century a trickle of English colonists joined the handful of fishermen already in Casco Bay, but early attempts at permanent settlement were

Already busy, Portland Harbor is evolving into a popular port of call for cruise vessels.

thwarted by the series of "wars" with the French and their Indian allies. The first of three great disasters to befall the future city of Portland took shape in the spring of 1690 on the islands of Casco Bay. By then some 40 English families had settled around Back Cove on what was called "the Neck" (the Portland peninsula), and the French and Indians, sailing from their hiding places on the islands, ambushed a company of soldiers on Munjoy Hill, burned all the houses in town, and laid siege to the garrison at Fort Loyall (at the foot of modern India Street), into which the terrified settlers had fled. Tricked into surrender by promises of safe passage, almost all of them were massacred on the spot.

The Neck remained uninhabited for another 26 years, but as the 18th century progressed what was then called Falmouth slowly grew into an important market and courthouse town, the center of commerce for a rapidly developing interior. (The French problem had disappeared in 1763 when the British won Canada; the Native Americans in southern Maine were slowly being eliminated, partly as a result of the large bounty offered for the scalp of any male Indian over the age of 12.) Enthusiasm for the American Revolution was much less intense on the Neck, which depended heavily on maritime trade, than in the more radical backcountry. Many of the more respectable citizens of Falmouth, for example, were horrified in the spring of 1775 to learn that the fire-breathing Colonel Samuel Thompson of Brunswick had captured the captain of a British sloop of war, the *Cançeau*, which was protecting a Loyalist shipbuilder in Casco Bay. Captain Mowatt was eventually released, at the insistence of the townspeople, but he left, furious at his humiliation, and he and the *Cançeau* were back in the harbor with other warships by October. According to legend, he was determined to teach the rebels a lesson; recent scholarship suggests that his mission in fact was to lay waste to all the coastal towns, and Falmouth simply happened to be, thanks to the wind and tide, the easiest to reach. In any case, he gave the townspeople a few hours to evacuate their goods before his guns leveled the town and his marines landed to set fire to the ruins. It is some indication of the confusion in which the American Revolution was fought that whatever Falmouth property the British had left behind, the militiamen from nearby Gorham soon looted.

When Mowatt sailed away, more than 400 buildings on the Neck lay in ruins. The destruction turned more Mainers against the British, and after the war Falmouth—renamed Portland—quickly recovered. The Embargo of 1807 was a disaster—grass grew on the wharves, vessels rotted—but again the economy picked up, especially after the arrival of the railroads. There was some hope that Portland might even surpass Boston as a major Atlantic port, thanks to its rail connections with Canada, but this never happened, partly because of Maine's smaller population, but also because Boston still exerted a good deal of control over Maine's economy.

The next great disaster was homemade. During the especially festive Fourth of July celebrations in 1866, marking the end of "the War of the Rebellion," someone threw a firecracker into a boatbuilder's yard on Commercial Street. Wood shavings caught fire, the wind was blowing hard, the water supply proved inadequate, and by the next morning 10,000 people were homeless. The fire, one of the worst in the country up to that time, destroyed much of the eastern half of Portland. Longfellow, who happened to be visiting, said it reminded him of Pompeii. The uniformity of style that redbrick and granite gives to so much of the Old Port today is due to the rapid rebuilding of the city in the 1870s and 1880s. After this disaster the city adopted as its motto *Resurgam* ("I shall rise")—a slogan it had more than once lived up to.

■ HISTORIC HOUSES

The 18th and 19th centuries brought to Portland a cast of characters who shaped the city into a center for commerce and art. For an understanding of Portland's development, architecture may offer the most accessible clue. There are four house museums in Portland of considerable interest, each representing a specific period in the city's development. In the little neighborhood of Stroudwater—a survivor of the 18th century incongruously close to Portland's busy airport—you will find, for example, the **Tate House** (1755) at 1270 Westbrook Street. In the days when Britain ruled the waves, the Royal Navy had to make sure it had a reliable supply of tall, straight pines to provide masts and spars for its ships. In the early 18th century, New England—particularly sparsely settled Maine—became a major source. A great deal of unpleasantness resulted when agents of the Crown started marking trees with the "King's arrow" and telling the colonials, who thought they owned this valuable timber, not to cut them. In the middle of this business, on the shores of Casco Bay, was George Tate, the mast agent. He obviously did well, for his house in Stroudwater, with its unusual stepped gambrel roof, is a luxurious dwelling (now maintained by the Colonial Dames) for the time and place— another glimpse of what a distance separated the elite and the common folk in pre-Revolutionary America.

The Federal style: Neal Dow House.

Stroudwater's position across the Fore River from the Neck meant that its dwellings survived both the cannonade of 1775 and the fire of 1866. Today at the Means House (across the street from the Tate House) you can get a leaflet outlining a walking tour to see the dozen and a half notable 18th- and 19th-century houses in the neighborhood, which has been classified as a National Historic Area. The **Fore River Sanctuary** (Congress Street at Stroudwater; 207-781-2330), an 85-acre Audubon preserve, has salt marshes, woodlands, a waterfall, canoeing, and crosscountry skiing trails.

Much of the elite that owed its prosperity and status to its ties with the royal government had to flee New England early on during the Revolution, and the post-war period enabled a new set of people—many of them lawyers whose fathers had been prosperous farmers—to rise to the top. Maine, and Portland in particular, was an especially promising place in the 1790s, when trade boomed and a flood of new settlers poured into the backcountry. A fine example of the fruits of this prosperity is the **Wadsworth-Longfellow House** (1785) at 487 Congress Street, the first brick house in Portland, built by the poet's grandfather, General Peleg Wadsworth, occupied also by his daughter and son-in-law, Stephen Longfellow, and maintained much as it was in the 1850s, during the tenure of the poet's sister, Anne Longfellow Pierce. The house, now part of the Maine Historical Society complex, is filled with mementos of Henry Wadsworth Longfellow's childhood and of the Wadsworth Longfellow family, and it serves as a reminder that Portland had a lively literary set in the early decades of the 19th century, including the lawyer-novelist John Neal and the satirist Seba Smith (whose "Jack Downing" sketches in backcountry dialect were the origin of later Down East humorous writing.)

The pre–Civil War generation in Portland is represented by two very different houses a few blocks from each other. One of the few remaining early-19th-century dwellings from Congress Street's residential days is the Federal **Neal Dow House** (714 Congress), a National Historic Landmark maintained—appropriately enough—by the Women's Christian Temperance Union. Dow, a controversial Portland mayor, abolitionist, and Civil War general, was the force behind the much debated Maine Law, passed in 1851 and not rescinded until 1934, that implemented the country's first large-scale experiment with prohibition. While Dow was honored by some, he was reviled by others—John Neal complained that the state motto *Dirigo* ("I lead") ought to have been changed to "Water, water, everywhere, but not a drop to drink."

Of a very different nature is the **Victoria Mansion** (109 Danforth Street), an imposing Italianate pile clad in brownstone (shipped from Portland, *Connecticut*). The rather severe exterior conceals a dramatic surprise, one of the best-preserved high-style interiors from the late 1850s in the country, a lush collage of stained glass, gilt, satin, walnut, mahogony, marble, and velvet, filled with Herter Brothers furniture and trompe-l'oeil murals. Named for a later owner's museum dedicated to the British monarch, the house was built between 1858 and 1860 for a Maine native, Ruggles S. Morse, who had made a fortune in the hotel business. Designed by Henry Austin, the house does suggest something of a luxury hotel of the Civil War era—in its skylit central hall, its massive gas chandelier, its grand stairway, its stately public rooms, and its state-of-the-art plumbing. Morse had many commercial ties with New Orleans; on the landing is a stained glass window in which you will find the state seals of Maine (the sailor and farmer) and Louisiana (the pelican). Like many Mainers with shipping and other business interests in the South, he was less than enthusiastic about the Civil War—which he spent in New Orleans. His house, the grandest in Portland in its day and intended only for summer use, remains in such a remarkable state of preservation because it has had so few changes in ownership.

■ MODERN PORTLAND

The city adopted its motto *Resurgam* as a tribute to its resolve in the face of earlier adversity, but it's also not a bad description of the city's renaissance in the last quarter of the 20th century. The quality of life in Portland long suffered for lack of a good college or university in town (an attempt in the 1790s to build Bowdoin

College on Bramhall Hill lost out, for political reasons, to Brunswick, half an hour to the north). This is changing with the growth, since the 1990s, of the **University of Southern Maine.** The new campus library, recycled from an old landmark bakery, can be seen from I–295; other USM features, such as the splendid Osher-Smith map collection and the distinctive New England Studies Program, are putting it on the national map.

The Portland Museum of Art is a well-established institution in new quarters downtown. The postmodern building, designed by Henry Cobb of the I. M. Pei architectural firm, with its echoes of Sir John Soane's house and his Dulwich Art Gallery in London, and its free use on the facade of highly stylized Renaissance forms, is one of the few contemporary buildings of any note in the state. The museum, however, seemed at first more building than collection; the gift of the Payson family's fine Impressionist and Post-Impressionist works now joins the museum's important State of Maine collection. The 2002 restoration of the Sweat Memorial Galleries (1911) and the adjoining McLellan House (1801) has created a fascinating complex of art and architecture.

A new passenger train service between Portland and Boston is having many ramifications on life in Portland. The comfortable (2 hours and 40 minutes) ride to and from New England's largest city might even, for some people, make Portland become, like Salem and Marblehead, a place to live if you work in Boston.

■ OUT AND ABOUT

Portland has by far the greatest number of restaurants in the state—and the greatest variety. The city's most sophisticated cooking can probably be found at **Cinque Terre** (on Wharf Street), or under the vaulted ceiling at the **Fore Street Restaurant**.

Restaurants of varying quality—and unpredictable longevity—are found throughout the Old Port in particular; and just beyond its limits, across Franklin on Middle, is a sort of restaurant row, from the award-winning **Hugo's Restaurant** to the very popular **Pepperclub,** with its innovative and largely vegetarian menu. The most successful "serious" restaurants in Portland seem to be those which manage to combine the new interest in relatively unadorned, almost home-style cooking with seasonal ingredients and considerable technical skill. Look for this style at the funky **Katahdin** on Spring and High streets (near the Museum of Art),

Fried seafood served with a smile at Gilbert's.

The Old Port is the city's most visited district.

Bibo's Madd Apple Cafe (next to the Portland Stage Company), and **Walter's** (on Exchange Street). **Friendship Café, Inc.** remains a favorite for breakfast; **Ruby's Choice** (Commercial Street) makes the best burgers, and **Norm's Bar and Grill** (Congress Street) the best chicken sandwiches in town; tiny **Silly's** (on the Munjoy Hill end of Cumberland Avenue) has the best Jamaican jerk chicken; and **Street & Company** (Wharf Street) is the place for seafood beyond the boiled lobster level.

The **Portland Public Market**—on Preble Street, one block from Congress— offers a visual feast of fresh foods from Maine and around the world in its 37,000-square-foot space; you can also buy café meals here. For picnic food you might also try **Micucci's** (an old-fashioned Italian deli) or **Foodworks,** both on India Street, or such Old Port shops as **Le Roux Kitchen** (which is primarily a kitchen goods store), **Stonewall Kitchen,** and the **Portland Greengrocer.** You might stop for a latté at **Coffee by Design,** on Congress. For a bowl of chowder to go, or just to look at the catch of the day on its bed of seaweed and ice, the **Harbor Fish Market** on Custom House Wharf gives you both a picturesque locale and a wide selection of fresh and smoked seafood. For the same fare fried or broiled, try the nearby **J's Oyster** or **Gilbert's Chowder House,** both of them intensely local eateries in a rapidly gentrifying neighborhood. Or go for the organic pizzas and great ales at **The Flatbread Company,** on Commercial Street. **Village Café** (Newbury Street) probably serves the best fried clams in town.

Neal Dow (*see above*) would quiver in his grave to know that central Portland today contains the state's largest concentration of places to have a drink. On warm nights the Old Port can turn a bit rowdy, though compared to most other American cities Portland is still a safe place to be after dark. **Gritty McDuff's,** a Fore Street pub, is a local pioneer in micro-brewing (as the owner likes to point out, its Best Bitter, Portland Head Light Pale Ale, Black Fly Stout, and Sebago Light Ale are made only 30 feet from the tap, along with various seasonal additions, such as Christmas Ale). **The Shipyard Brewing Company** (86 Newbury St.) sells its local ale and gives tours of the brewery, and at **Ri-Ra**'s Irish bar (above the **Flatbread Company**) you can admire the imported bar and adaptive reuse of the old warehouse. Try also the **Top of the East** penthouse bar in the Eastland Park; since the no-smoking rule took effect, it's a pleasure. Another local product to taste in Portland pubs is the widely distributed Geary's beer. On Fore Street you can get designer martinis at **Una,** a very chi-chi wine bar and cocktail lounge. Also lively after dark are **Brian Boru,** an Irish pub with a second-story deck; **Rivalries; Three Dollar Dewey's;** and **Bull Feeney's** in the Old Port, all offering progressive music and crowded dance floors to a youngish clientele.

For more laid-back activity, a few rather upscale pool halls can be found above the storefronts in and around the Old Port; try **Old Port Billiards** on Fore Street. Bargain entertainment after dark can be found at **The Movies** on Exchange Street (foreign, vintage, and non-commercial films) and the price-cutting **Nickelodeon Cinema,** at Temple and Middle, facing the lobsterman statue.

Large rock concerts and Portland Pirates' hockey games take place at the **Cumberland County Civic Center,** on Center Street, between Free and Spring streets. In summer the Portland Seadogs (a minor league baseball team affiliated with the Boston Red Sox) play baseball at Hadlock Field, on the southwestern end of Park Avenue.

Some of the best places to stay in Portland are in well-rehabilitated old buildings: the posh **Regency** occupies a medieval-looking, redbrick former armory in the Old Port; and the **Percy Inn** is in two 1830 row houses on Pine Street, with satellite suites in other old buildings in the neighborhood. On the other hand, many people swear by the new **Portland Harbor Hotel** in the Old Port and even the large, unlovely, but reliable **Holiday Inn**. The best-known hotel here is the **Eastland Park Hotel** (convenient to "Museum Row"), and the most talked-about B&B is the **Pomegranate Inn** on Neal Street.

Although most Portlanders now shop at the huge Maine Mall and its imitators, the center of town has lots of interesting specialty stores. If you're seeking stylish Maine-made crafts, including jewelry and pottery, you'll find them at **Abacus** and the **Maine Potters Market,** both in the Old Port. Portland's best bookstores include **Casco Bay Books** (Middle Street) and **Books Etc.** (Exchange Street), but the real treasure troves are in the city's second-hand and antiquarian stores, notably those of **Carlson-Turner** (on Congress, near the historic Eastern Cemetery) and **Cunningham Books**—a light and airy shop on Longfellow Square that looks just the way a bookstore of character ought to look.

The **Center for Cultural Exchange** on Longfellow Square has sparked a cultural and arts revival, with ethnic and domestic arts events every week. Portland's art-gallery scene is going strong, and the market for antiques remains stable— you'll find small items like estate jewelry at **Geraldine Wolf's**, in the Old Port. And when you get to **Scott Potter**'s, on High Street, if you find that the Sultan of Brunei has bought all his découpage plates and vases and other articles, be consoled that you might be able to get one at Bergdorf's or Harrods.

As you leave Portland going north on I–95, you'll get a splendid view of the city behind you: a few miles north, look across the tidal flats near the mouth of the Presumpscot River. In the distance, above the waters of Casco Bay, the eastern end of the city on a sunny day literally shimmers on its hilltop. Soon you'll be driving on one of the most stunning sections of the interstate in Maine. Across the Presumpscot estuary you'll see 60-acre **Gilsland Farm** (207-781-2330), a "gentleman farm" within sight of downtown Portland that is now the headquarters of the Maine Audubon Society. One of 15 Audubon sanctuaries in the state, it has two miles of nature trails and one of Maine's best museum-style gift shops.

If you're into geography, stop at the **DeLorme Map Store,** on Route 1 (also known as U.S. 1) in Yarmouth, midway between Portland and Freeport. The firm makes by far the best, most-detailed atlas of Maine, excellent if you intend to explore the state's byways. The store also carries an in-depth selection of travel guides, software, and maps—including the ones put out by Raven, which many cartophiles collect as works of art.

MAINE FOR KIDS

Children love Maine. What kid wouldn't be thrilled to cruise on a windjammer, run down a sandy beach, gawk his or her way through a country fair, or spot a moose feeding in a roadside marsh? Some parts of Maine, however, seem *made* for children:

AMUSEMENT PARKS AND WATER ACTIVITIES

Funtown Splashtown. It's the largest theme amusement park in Maine, with 18 major rides, 11 kiddie rides, 14 water slides, and many games and amusements on its 70 acres. *774 Portland Rd. (Rte. 1, about 20 minutes south of Portland), Saco, 207-284-5139; www.funtownsplashtownusa.com.*

Street fairs in Maine pack appeal for kids.

Lucky Catch Lobstering. This 37-foot lobster boat takes 14 passengers from Portland to various points in Casco Bay. You learn about lobstering, haul traps, and observe marine life in the live tank. You can buy your catch to eat later or have it shipped home. *170 Commercial St., 207-761-0941 or 207-233-2026; www.luckycatch.com.*

Old Orchard Beach. The town's three-mile strand is the center of the seven-mile stretch of beaches between Saco and Scarborough, and for almost a century the area has been built and rebuilt with amusements. It's hard to tell whether kids prefer those of the 471-foot wooden pier, or **Palace Playland** amusement park. Rides include the Sunwheel (at 75 feet, New England's tallest ferris wheel), the Galaxy Roller Coaster that drops almost 50 feet on a series of corkscrew turns, and the Power Surge, which spins you 360 degrees in three different directions. *1 Old Orchard St., 207-934-2001; www.palaceplayland.com.*

MUSEUMS

Belfast & Moosehead Lake Railroad. Steam-train rides ply between Unity and Burnham Junction (8 miles), and diesel-train rides travel between Front Street and Waldo Station (7 miles) in Belfast. There's also a roundhouse demonstration. *1 Depot Square, Unity, 800-392-5500; www.belfastrailroad.com.*

Children's Museum of Maine. This outstanding museum has a schooner/trawler in the backyard and "L.L.Bear's" Maine woods exhibit for adventuring. Among its exhibits—geared to all ages, from babies to preteens—is the amazing camera obscura, which gives a panoramic view of Portland rooftops. *142 Free St., Portland; 207-828-1234; www.kitetails.com.*

Maine Central Model Railroad. This large HO-gauge model has elaborate scenery, with buildings, bridges, people, animals. The privately owned attraction is still evolving—the latest project is night illumination. *668 Mason Bay Rd., Jonesport; 207-497-2255.*

Maine Discovery Museum. A large, self-guided children's museum occupies three floors, with such interactive exhibits as a two-story climber, animal habitats, and "Body Journey," where you can walk into the giant head and pedal in the huge heart. It's for ages 1 to 12. *74 Main St., Bangor; 207-262-7200; www.mainediscoverymuseum.org.*

Owls Head Transportation Museum. In addition to seeing an extensive collection of antique planes and vehicles, you can watch aerial performances on special-event weekend days through the summer. *117 Museum St., off Rte. 73; 207-594-4418; www.owlshead.org.*

Seashore Trolley Museum. Here you can see about 250 historic streetcars from all over the world (40 of them restored), and also take a ride in one. Then you can visit the restoration facility. *195 Log Cabin Rd., Kennebunkport; 207-967-2800 (recording) or 207-967-2712 (office); www.trolleymuseum.org.*

Southworth Planetarium, University of Southern Maine. Matinee and evening shows take place here throughout the year, including children's programs such as "Sky Friends," "ABCS of the Sky," and "The Little Star that Could." *96 Falmouth St., Portland; 207-780-4249; www.usm.maine.edu/~planet.*

Willowbrook at Newfield. This village museum has restored houses, a one-room schoolhouse, country stores replete with vintage artifacts and furnishings, a carousel, stagecoach, farm equipment, sheds, and workshops. *77 Elm St.,off Rte. 11; 207-793-2784; www.willowbrookmuseum.org.*

NATURE CENTERS
Maine Wildlife Park. Operated by the Maine Fish & Wildlife Department as a sanctuary for animals orphaned, recovering from injuries, or unable to survive in the wild, this facility has more than 25 species on exhibit in naturalized settings, including moose, black bears, mountain lions, wild turkeys, and bald eagles. *Rte. 26, Gray; 207-657-4977; www.state.me.us/ifw/education/wildlifepark.htm.*

Mount Desert Oceanarium. This marine education complex has two locations on Mount Desert Island, each with a different mission. **Oceanarium/Bar Harbor** displays lobsters and fish. *1351 Rte. 3, Bar Harbor; 207-288-5005.* **Oceanarium/ Southwest Harbor** has more than 20 tanks and many hands-on exhibits. *169 Clark Point Rd., Southwest Harbor; 207-244-7330; www.theoceanarium.com.*

Norlands Living History Center. Live-in programs and day visits to a 19th-century working farm teach you life as it was lived in rural Maine. Tours are also given during July and August. *290 Norlands Rd., Livermore; 207-897-4366; www.norlands.org.*

Wells Reserve at Laudholm Farm. This historic saltwater farm on 1,600 acres runs half-day children's programs and junior researchers' one- or two-week day camps. You can also take self-guided walks through the estuary, beach, and upland environments. If you buy a child's guidebook (10 are available, for different age groups and on different topics), you get the loan of a backpack containing a compass and binoculars to use while exploring. *Laudholm Farm Rd., off Rte. 1, Wells; 207-646-1555; www.wellsreserve.org*

ANDROSCOGGIN RIVER

As you leave Portland and head north along Casco Bay, you leave behind the towns first settled as outskirts to "Falmouth" (including present-day Falmouth), and arrive at places established around the falls of the Androscoggin River. While Brunswick (settled in 1628, incorporated in 1738) was initially this area's financial and cultural center, the town of Freeport (incorporated in 1789), with its countless discount shops and outlets, has become the area's major draw.

■ FREEPORT AND L. L. BEAN'S *map page 77, B-2*

For anyone attending a New England college in the 1960s and 1970s, the midnight trip to L. L. Bean's was a familiar ritual. You bought beer, jumped in the car, drove however many hours it took, looked for the big statue of the Indian chief on U.S. 1 (also known as Route 1) just outside Freeport, and at some odd hour of the morning arrived at the famous sporting-goods store, where you mingled with the hunters (in fall) or the fishermen (in spring) until it was time to begin a groggy drive back to the dorm. At the time, the journey mattered more than the purchases; nonetheless, by dressing in the L. L. Bean style—which seemed almost no style at all—you pledged your allegiance to everything Maine stood for. The heavy blue sweaters, leather-topped rubber-soled boots, khaki trousers, and plaid flannel shirts proclaimed that you were ready for the woods and the rugged shores of Maine, even if you were spending most of your time in Cambridge or New Haven.

■ BEAN'S BEGINNINGS

Born in Greenwood in Oxford County in 1872, Leon Leonwood "L. L." Bean grew up in a culture in which hunting, fishing, and trapping were not simply a pastime but a way of putting food on the table. He was good at it, and by age 13 or 14, as he recalled in his memoirs, he had sold his first buck to a pair of unsuccessful hunters for $12. Orphaned at an early age, he was sent to work on a farm, paid his way through Kent's Hill School in Readfield by selling soap, worked in a shoe store, married a Freeport woman, and in 1905 founded Bean Brothers, a Freeport clothing store, with his brother. His would have been an unremarkable story had it not been for a pet peeve: when out hunting in the woods, his feet always got wet. An avid outdoorsman, Leon had trouble finding a comfortable hunting shoe that

A 1915 photograph by Bertrand H. Wentworth captures a quintessential Maine coastal scene.

was both light and waterproof. So in 1911 he took a pair of rubber shoe bottoms from his store and asked a local shoemaker—Freeport's leading industry at that time—to stitch on a leather top. The idea seemed to work, but the first large batch was a disaster. The rubber was too flimsy to hold the stitching, and Bean had to take back 90 of the 100 he had sold. Undeterred, he borrowed $400 from his brother and convinced a Boston manufacturer to produce a light but sturdy rubber shoe with a heel low enough to attach a soft leather top.

From the start, he grasped two principles of successful marketing. First, money was to be made in a national mail-order business (his first mailing in 1912 went to holders of nonresident hunting licenses). Second, Bean insisted on a notably generous attitude toward returns, a policy that continues today. What came to be known as "the Bean boot" remained the company's best-known product, but Bean took advantage of the new and highly mobile leisure culture of the 1920s to offer a range of hunting, fishing, and camping products. When Freeport's most famous son, explorer Donald B. MacMillan, outfitted an Arctic expedition in 1923, he

Jennie Harrington stitching one of L. L. Bean's famous Maine hunting boots.

came to Bean's for footwear. In 1925 Bean introduced the trademark chamois shirt; in 1944 he added the popular canvas tote bag (known originally as the "Canvas Ice Carrier"). *Life* magazine ran a feature on the store in 1941, and during World War II the company advised the U.S. Armed Forces on cold-weather gear. In the meantime, the famous L. L. Bean's catalogue, with its nostalgic cover (probably one of the main reasons Americans picture Maine as an outdoor paradise) and homespun prose, carried the store's name across the country.

While mail-order remained the core of the business—the original store was on the second and third floors above Freeport's post office, with a mail chute going directly down—more and more customers took to dropping by to chat with L. L. Bean, who by the 1950s had become a popular Maine landmark himself. According to company legend, the store began staying open all night in 1951 because Bean was tired of sportsmen rapping on his window before dawn. Until his death in 1967, he could be found advising sportsmen on trout flies or duck calls and the like.

Then in the late 1970s, something unexpected happened. Already well known in hunting and fishing circles and frequented by old-time New Englanders, Bean's found a huge new market and a swarm of imitators as a result of the craze for "preppy" clothing. By the 1960s the preppy look—a remarkably long-lived, aggressively casual style—developed in East Coast boarding (or "prep") schools after World War II—had become the official leisure-time costume of upper-middle-class America. By the late 1970s it had been adopted far and wide. The requirements of the style—the slightly rumpled, well-worn feel, the use of conservatively colored natural fabrics, the suggestion that the wearer was socially secure enough to dress down—were all met with Bean's comfortable, traditional, and occasionally even frumpy clothing. The Bean "look" has since become a much-emulated American mode of dress: when the Pacific Rim leaders met at Seattle for a summit

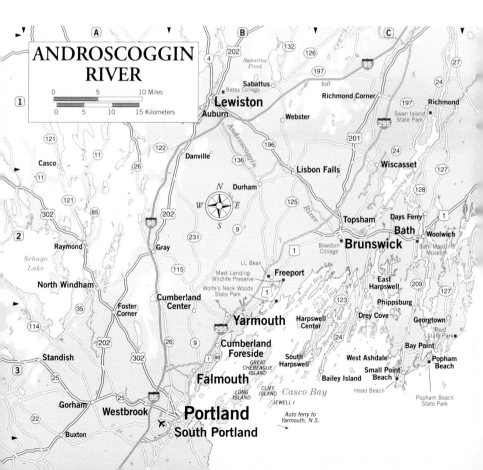

in November 1993, most of them followed President Clinton's informal lead in adopting what *The New York Times* called "today's L. L. Bean diplomatic dress code." To this day, L. L. Bean's is a place you have to visit if you want to understand Maine. The company is still owned by Bean's descendants, and the business continues to expand far beyond its founder's dreams. Nonetheless, the store still sells well-made, sensibly priced merchandise for use in the great outdoors. Despite the international scale of its operations and its immense floor space since a 1989 remodeling, Bean's signature products continue to be versions of that 1911 hunting boot. Much of what the store sells has not changed in half a century: fishing rods and flies, shotguns, canoes, and outdoor gear. Bean's also runs a series of "Outdoor Discovery" programs and lectures and workshops on everything from bow-and-arrow hunting to trail-bike maintenance to sea kayaking.

■ RETAIL CENTRAL

The success of L. L. Bean's brought an onslaught of retailers to Freeport, Maine. While Bean's folksy store had long been a landmark, the real business had always been in mail-order sales. But in the 1970s I–95 made Freeport seem even closer to Boston, and the crowds in the store grew larger. Savvy marketers began to wonder: if people detour from the interstate to shop at Bean's, would they linger if Freeport had something else to offer? The chance arose in 1982 when fire destroyed a commercial building across the street from Bean's. A Dansk "factory outlet store" was built in its place. The rest, as they say, is retailing history: as has occurred in many other American towns, shoppers and outlets continued to multiply. Dansk begat Laura Ashley, and Laura Ashley begat Ralph Lauren and Brooks Brothers, and they begat Coach, J. Crew, Cole Haan. . . . In 1981 the town had 55 retail businesses; by the dawn of the 21st century, there were more than 100. Even the local historical society has gone retail at its Harrington House, which is packed with gift items and reproduction antiques.

These upscale outlets line Main Street and spill down the hill (where Bean's itself has a factory outlet). Most of the stores are concentrated within easy walking distance of downtown, and it should be said that Freeport's streets, though sometimes as crowded as midtown Manhattan's at 5:30, are attractive and well tended. Only yesterday, it seems, Freeport was a sleepy town where most people worked in the local shoe factories; today, with an estimated 4 million visitors a year, it has probably surpassed Acadia National Park as the state's leading tourist attraction.

■ BEYOND SHOPPING

Whether people see Freeport as a destination or simply stop there on their way to some less commercial spot remains a matter of debate among Maine's tourism promoters. But the town is worth the short detour from the interstate. For one thing, local preservationists have tried to maintain some village flavor despite the boom (which, incidentally, local taxpayers are finding less of a windfall than was promised). One result is that Freeport must have the only Greek Revival McDonald's in the country: when the town refused to allow a 19th-century house to be demolished, the fast-food franchise did an adaptive reuse of the property. And anyone interested in seeing the complete line of Shaker-influenced furniture designed by **Thos. Moser Cabinetmaker** should stop by the company's Freeport store at 149 Main Street. The pieces, made in the company's Auburn factory, are classic examples of Maine craftmanship at its best.

If trying on all those sweaters and shoes gives you an appetite, you're lucky to be in downtown Freeport. Two blocks from L. L. Bean's, the **Harraseeket Inn** is highly praised for its kitchen's use of the best local and seasonal produce: Pemaquid oysters from Damariscotta, wild mushrooms from Mount Vernon, game birds from Warren, raspberries from Bowdoinham, organic herbs and greens from Lisbon. Visitors with a leisurely schedule might want to watch for the inn's wine-tasting weekends and seasonal festivals. The inn's **Broad Arrow Tavern** cooks up more casual, heartier meals, such as ribs and grilled fish; the popular Sunday brunch, on the other hand, is quite lavish. *162 Main Street; 207-865-1684 or 800-342-6423.*

Freeport, for all its crowds, is still a fairly intimate place—some very scenic countryside is only a few minutes' drive from downtown. Before the Civil War this was an agricultural area, with some shipbuilding. Many of its early-19th-century houses survive along the inlets of Casco Bay, notably in the very attractive town of **South Freeport,** which like the rural, coastal side of Freeport began to attract many affluent retirees and commuters in the 1980s. There are several spots where you can hike along the shore, including the **Audubon Society's Mast Landing Wildlife Preserve** and the larger **Wolfe's Neck Woods State Park. Wolf Neck Farm** is a popular place to take children to see the prize herd of Angus cattle.

■ FREEPORT TO BRUNSWICK *map page 77, B/C-2*

A few years ago, in response to complaints about traffic jams on coastal U.S. 1, the state put up a sign on the northbound side of I–95 suggesting in effect that motorists might get to Acadia National Park a lot sooner if they skipped the coastal route and traveled overland, so to speak, to Augusta and then by way of Route 3 to Belfast. This is still good advice—rarely crowded Route 3 crosses some beautiful lake and farm country—but the howl from chambers of commerce and motel owners from Brunswick to Camden could probably be heard in farthest Madawaska. So the sign came down. The innocent still take the Brunswick exit onto fabled U.S. 1 and, if they are patient, can enjoy some of the most interesting towns in New England. The town of Brunswick is about half an hour northeast of Portland—or 15 minutes northeast of Freeport—on I-95, and makes a wonderful jumping-off point for this corner of the state.

■ **BOWDOIN COLLEGE** *map page 77, C-2*

Brunswick likes to think of itself as a small college town, though in fact its U.S. Naval Air Station dominates the local economy. But it is Bowdoin College, founded in 1794, that has carried the town's name across the world. The college, on a slight hill beyond the wooden Gothic tower of First Parish Church at the end of the village green, is one of the cultural and intellectual centers of the state, with much to offer if you're curious about books, paintings, 19th-century architecture, Arctic exploration, or theater. Although in the last 25 years the college has grown increasingly national in its student body, Bowdoin's traditional role as late as the 1950s was training the state's social and professional elite. Educating the future leaders of the state is precisely what its founders, many of them large landowners in the district, had in mind two centuries ago, for they worried that Maine was an unruly place that would never prosper until it had stable institutions and an educated, civic-minded ruling class. Most of them also sought an educated—that is to say, Congregationalist—clergy: by the 1790s the backcountry of Maine was filled with itinerant Methodist, Baptist, and Universalist preachers whose reputations as radicals and evangelicals made them seem threats to the established order. (Though never officially Congregational, the college considered itself as "belonging" to that denomination throughout the 19th century, an allegiance that cost Bowdoin dearly when the new state government in 1820 turned out to be full of Baptists.) The college was chartered by the Massachusetts General Court in 1794. James Bowdoin III, an absentee proprietor of vast tracts of Maine land, became the

A typical storefront in Brunswick.

Henry Wadsworth Longfellow, Bowdoin College class of 1825.

new college's leading patron; with the other founders, he named the school for his father, James Bowdoin II, a merchant-prince and amateur scientist whose decisive action as governor in 1786 squelched Shays' Rebellion in western Massachusetts.

In its first century Bowdoin College rarely enrolled more than 200 students at any one time, but it has produced more people of note than any other college of its size in the country. The list is remarkable: writer Nathaniel Hawthorne and poet Henry Wadsworth Longfellow (both of the class of 1825) stand out, but they are joined by U.S. President Franklin Pierce, Sen. William Pitt Fessenden (Lincoln's secretary of the treasury), Congressman Thomas Brackett Reed (the most powerful speaker in the history of the House), Civil War generals Joshua Chamberlain and Oliver Otis Howard, Civil War Massachusetts governor John A. Andrew (who raised the famous black regiments), Arctic explorers Robert Peary and Donald MacMillan, U.S. Supreme Court Chief Justice Melville Fuller, the black editor and colonizationist John Brown Russwurm, and dozens of other writers and politicians famous in their day. In this century the list includes the expert on gall wasps (and human sexuality) Alfred Kinsey, poet Robert Peter Tristram Coffin, civil rights advocate Hodding Carter Jr., Olympic gold-medal marathoner Joan Benoit Samuelson (the college went coed in 1971), diplomat Thomas Pickering, and U.S. senators George Mitchell and William Cohen of Maine.

Although strong programs in the sciences and environmentalism have attracted students from far and wide, the school remains the quintessential Maine college, small (1,610 students) and traditional (fraternities dominated undergraduate social life until their recent elimination). The campus fits the New England stereotype, with a large, maple-shaded quadrangle surrounded by dignified, historic buildings of brick and granite. Perhaps at its most arresting early on a summer evening or after a fresh snowfall, the Bowdoin Quad offers a lesson in several architectural revival styles. Richard Upjohn's Romanesque chapel from the 1840s (a landmark in the history of "medievalism" on American college campuses) looks across the green to Henry Vaughan's Oxbridge-style Hubbard Hall (1903) and McKim, Mead & White's Renaissance Revival Walker Art Building (1894), which is probably the finest public building in the state. The oldest building on campus is Federal-style Massachusetts Hall (1802), which housed the president, the chapel, the library, and all eight students when the college opened, and which was later home to the now-defunct Medical School of Maine (an affiliate of Bowdoin, 1820–1921). Two other structures across Maine Street are of considerable architectural interest: the Carpenter Gothic Boody-Johnson House (Gervase Wheeler, 1849), whose design was published by A. J. Downing and widely copied across the country; and the Shingle Style Quinby House (John Calvin Stevens, 1900), an imaginative adaptation

Bowdoin College in the fall.

of a seaside cottage for a fraternity house, now student housing. Of the college's later 20th-century architecture, Hugh Stubbins's 16-story Coles Tower (1964) was for a little while the tallest building north of Boston, and the new Wish Theater (in Memorial Hall), the Searles Science Building's renovation into a state-of-the-art facility, and the new Druckenmiller Hall have all won awards.

The college's museums and library are worth a visit. The **Bowdoin College Museum of Art** houses an excellent collection of Colonial and Federal portraits; also in the museum are the Assyrian reliefs, six massive winged genii excavated by Sir Austen Henry Layard at Nineveh and sent by missionaries in Mesopotamia to various American colleges in the 1850s as proof of the historical accuracy of the Bible. The group of European paintings and Old Masters drawings (some of which were copies, as was accepted among collectors at the time) comprise what is probably the earliest public collection of European art in the country; the pieces were bequeathed in 1811 by James Bowdoin III, who believed strongly that the visual arts should be part of a liberal education.

Bowdoin's other tourist attraction, and a good one for kids, is the **Peary-MacMillan Arctic Museum** in Hubbard Hall, where you see the sled that took Peary and his colleague Matthew Henson to the North Pole in 1909. The navigational instruments with which Peary made his still-controversial calculations are also on display, along with stuffed polar bears, narwhal tusks, Inuit folk art, and other examples of material culture from the Far North.

■ OFF-CAMPUS BRUNSWICK

Brunswick has several other attractions. Sprawling across the open field where Hawthorne and his classmates picked blueberries and shot pigeons is the **Naval Air Station,** responsible for anti-submarine patrols over much of the North Atlantic and occasionally open for air shows. Maine Street (which, incidentally, is 12 rods wide, the widest street in Maine) runs north from the college to the late-19th-century Cabot Mill, which houses **Cabot Mill Antiques** (14 Maine St.; 207-725-2855; www.cabotiques.com). The mill, called Fort Andross, is named after the original garrison on the site at the time of the Indian wars. Until World War II the mill area near the river was working-class and Catholic—and largely French speaking because of the arrival of rural Quebecois workers, starting in the 1860s. The hill was "Anglo" and Protestant. Noisy brawls between Bowdoin students and boys from town ("Yaggers," in the local slang) were a regular feature of 19th-century Brunswick life. Up the hill, First Parish Church (1846) is one of three Medieval

Joshua Chamberlain

Although never forgotten in Maine, where he was a college president and four-time governor, Joshua Lawrence Chamberlain (born 1828 in Brewer) did not in his own day enjoy the national acclaim given such other Civil War generals as Lee, Grant, Sherman, Jackson, Sheridan, and Howard (another Bowdoin graduate, head of the Freedmen's Bureau, who founded Howard University in Washington, D.C.). There is no statue of him on a battlefield, and little mention is made of his heroism or his skill as a field commander in most of the standard accounts of the war. When he does appear in such works, it is usually in his ceremonial role of receiving the infantry surrender at Appomattox, and for his controversial gesture of saluting his defeated foe. Yet in recent years Chamberlain has emerged as one of the most exemplary figures of the Civil War era. It is now widely recognized that his decisive action at Little Round Top on the second day of the battle of Gettysburg (for which he was later awarded the Congressional Medal of Honor) may have saved the North from defeat: about to run out of ammunition, he ordered his Maine riflemen to fix bayonets and charge the Alabama troops who were about to turn the Union's left flank. His quick thinking under fire and his ability to inspire troops earned him a place in the modern U.S. Army's leadership training manual. The movie *Gettysburg* and Ken Burns' TV series "The Civil War" have done much to revive popular interest in Chamberlain, and in May 2003 Brunswick dedicated a statue of him on Maine Street.

After graduating from Bowdoin in 1852, Chamberlain became a professor of rhetoric and modern languages, and his colleagues at Bowdoin were not happy when, in 1862, he decided to go off to fight. But Chamberlain insisted, and, after writing the state's war-time governor to ask if any posts were available, he was asked to serve as lieutenant-colonel of the 20th Maine Infantry Regiment. On the long boat ride to Virginia he studied tactics. Despite his lack of training, Chamberlain had a dramatic career: 24 major battles and numerous skirmishes, six wounds (including, during the siege of Petersburg, a bullet through his groin—complications from which eventually killed him in 1914), near-death at Gettysburg when a Confederate officer tried to shoot him at close range (his pistol misfired), and several horses shot from under him. He was promoted to general on the field after Petersburg, and by 1865 was so admired by Grant that he was given the signal honor of receiving the surrender of the Infantry of the Army of Northern Virginia at Appomattox.

The place to which all Chamberlain admirers must make a pilgrimage is the **General Joshua L. Chamberlain House** at 226 Maine Street in Brunswick, which he occupied for much of his long life. Saved from being torn down for a fast-food franchise in 1980, the house has been partially restored after several decades of service as a

Joshua L. Chamberlain, 1865.

slightly seedy off-campus rental for Bowdoin students. The house, whose upper floors are still rented as apartments, contains a good deal of Chamberlain memorabilia, including his wartime saddle and his boots.

Built at 4 Potter Street, half a block away from its current location, the house started as a typical mid-1820s Cape house; the young Henry Wadsworth Longfellow and his bride lived there in the 1830s, and Chamberlain purchased the house just before the Civil War. When he returned to Brunswick after the war, he had the house moved to its current location (given enough oxen and rollers, wood-frame houses were not difficult to lift off their foundations and move in 19th-century Maine) and made major changes to it. In 1871 he had it jacked up and a new ground story built beneath it; the Greek Revival doorway that the Longfellows had entered became a decorative porch on the second-floor facade. He also added to the chimneys, which display the red Maltese cross insignia of the Fifth Corps, and had woodworkers ornament the house in a medley of Gothic and Italianate motifs.

Chamberlain's post–Civil War career had its share of disappointments. Although well respected as a Republican governor, Chamberlain found that civilian life lacked the clear-cut nature of the military. His marriage was not always happy, his plans to modernize Bowdoin were thwarted by the traditionalists, and he did not seem to share the skill (or absence of scruples) so many former Civil War generals had shown in making money. In 1914 he died in Portland—he was one of the last survivors of that dashing generation of young men who had gone off to command armies in the "War of the Rebellion"—and was buried in Brunswick's Pine Grove Cemetery.

On the Bowdoin campus, Hubbard Hall includes Chamberlain's portrait in the presidential gallery, and in Memorial Hall his name is on the bronze tablets listing 228 alumni who fought for the Union. Note, too, the smaller plaque on the west stair landing commemorating the college's 18 Confederate alumni.

Revival ecclesiastical buildings designed by Upjohn (see also the college chapel and St. Paul's Episcopal Church, on Pleasant Street). The First Parish interior is notable for its intricate complex of wooden arches, suggestive to some people of the hull of a ship, and for the pew in which Harriet Beecher Stowe had the "vision" of Uncle Tom's martyrdom that inspired part of her novel. In 1875 the church was also the setting for Longfellow's reading of "Morituri Salutamus," written for his 50th Bowdoin reunion. Stowe's house, at 63 Federal Street, was where in 1850–51, while her husband Calvin was teaching theology at Bowdoin, she wrote *Uncle Tom's Cabin*. Federal Street is lined with many attractive Federal and Greek Revival houses, several of them the work of the talented local housewright Samuel Melcher.

The Pejepscot Historical Society, at 159 Park Row (207-729-6606; www.curtislibrary.com/pejepscot.htm) overlooking the Mall (as the village green is called), runs not only the increasingly popular **Joshua L. Chamberlain Museum** (see essay "Joshua Chamberlain"), but a lesser known yet quite fascinating property at 159 Park Row, the **Skolfield-Whittier House**. Dr. Frank Whittier was a pioneer in forensic medicine in the state (his rather grisly tools are on exhibit), and his daughter Dr. Alice Whittier was the state's first female pediatrician. In 1983, a few years before she died, she turned the huge house and its contents over to the Society intact, and virtually nothing has been changed since then. The Society can give you directions for self-guided walking tours of Brunswick's African-American History Trail and Joshua Chamberlain's Brunswick.

As in most college towns, the arts scene is alive and kicking. The **Maine State Music Theatre** (207-725-8769; www.msmt.org) puts on four musicals during the season at the Pickard Theater at Bowdoin; free concerts take place on the Mall; and the **Bowdoin International Chamber Music Festival** (207-725-3875; www.summermusic.org) has concerts with guest artists each summer. Brunswick probably has more books for sale per capita than any other Maine community; aside from the commercial and college bookstores there is Gary Lawless and Beth Leonard's alternative **Gulf of Maine Books** (134 Maine Street; 207-729-5083), which has a good Maine poetry selection. The annual **Highland Games** (207-437-2355) has Scottish music, dancing, and singing, and there's a **farmers market** (207-666-3116) on the Mall, Tuesday and Friday from May through November.

■ TOPSHAM AND THE HARPSWELLS *map page 77, C-2/3*

The area around Brunswick also has a lot to offer. Across the river is the smaller town of **Topsham,** with a historic district along Elm Street that retains much of its early 19th-century look (the town, first named Pejepscot, was once an important lumber and shipbuilding center). The town's landmark, an 1860-ish yellow-brick mill that juts into the river, now houses a restaurant and small businesses.

To the south of Brunswick are three long fingers of rocky coastline known collectively as the **Harpswells.** On her excursions in this neighborhood while in the Brunswick area, Harriet Beecher Stowe gathered material for *The Pearl of Orr's Island,* a sentimental novel of coastal Maine life that helped popularize the use of local dialect in American fiction. Today the Town of Harpswell, which comprises Harpswell Neck, Orrs Island, Bailey Island, Cundy's Harbor on Great Island, and some 45 small islands, remains largely rural in feeling, though affluent retirees are beginning to outnumber the fishermen. The "heart" of the area is **Harpswell Center,** where a handsome 1757 meetinghouse overlooks the cemetery, a general store, and the 1843 Elijah Kellogg Congregational Church, named for a 19th-century minister and writer. Admiral Robert E. Peary's summer house (www. pearyeagleisland.org) sits on Eagle Island in Casco Bay, off the end of Bailey Island. You can take a morning excursion there through **Sea Escape Charters** (207-833-5531). On the south end of the neck and on Bailey Island you'll find several places to eat lobster, including the seasonal **Estes Lobster House,** with its view of Ragged Island—summer residence of Edna St. Vincent Millay—and **Cook's Lobster House**, sitting out on a peninsula just past the cribstone bridge.

■ MALAGA ISLAND

One other landmark deserves mention, though few people ever visit there (it is privately owned and accessible only by boat), and many old-time Mainers would prefer never to hear it mentioned. Malaga Island is as much a part of Maine's maritime history, however, as Bath or Wiscasset. A half-mile-long island near the mouth of the New Meadows River, between Harpswell and Phippsburg, Malaga was settled about the time Bowdoin College began—by a black fisherman-farmer, Benjamin Darling. He was one of several hundred blacks, some of them sailors, some of them descendants of slaves brought to New England, who lived along the

Environmentalist author Rachel Carson's cottage near Southport.

Maine coast in the decades following the Revolution. Darling's descendants inter-married with local white families and, like their neighbors, continued to eke out a meager existence through a combination of fishing, farming, and doing odd chores. The history of the island through the 19th century is obscure (residents of such remote places often escaped taxation, the draft, and the census). Other blacks may have joined the original settlers. According to local legend, sea captains from nearby Bath maintained mistresses and second families there, on an island where no one asked too many questions.

By the early 20th century, however, places like Malaga were highly desirable coastal real estate, and the island's impoverished, racially mixed population began to raise eyebrows. The rumor spread that the 50 or so islanders were "half-wits" and "degenerates." Local authorities began putting some of the islanders' children in state homes, and sentiment grew that this pocket of "shame" needed cleaning out. In 1912—in one of the most shameful incidents in Maine's modern his-tory—the governor himself supervised the eviction of the remaining settlers' descendants (none of whom could prove title to any land on the island, though their families had lived there since before Maine was a state). Even Malaga's ceme-tery was dug up and its contents hastily reburied on the mainland, at an institu-tion for the mentally "enfeebled." The "purification" was complete, and the island made safe for development.

■ **LEWISTON AND AUBURN** *map page 77, B-1*

The Androscoggin River is underappreciated today, even though it's much cleaner and less smelly than it was a generation ago. Nevertheless, its currents shaped the growth of much of west-central Maine in the 19th century. Brunswick, Lisbon, Lewiston, Auburn—all were built at falls on the river to harness its power for their mills (first lumber, then textiles). Today, if you stand on the Longley Memorial Bridge between the twin cities of Lewiston and Auburn at the time of the annual spring freshet, you can still get some idea of the river's strength as its floodwaters, fed by melting snow on the White Mountains, crash and explode over the falls of the Androscoggin.

Lewiston is not a city that appears on many tourist itineraries, other than being part of the popular Bates-Bowdoin-Colby circuit for parents and would-be stu-dents looking at Maine's best-known colleges. But Lewiston, the state's second-largest city and still an important manufacturing center, is as representative of the

The Bates crew team on the Androscoggin River at sundown.

French-American, industrial side of Maine's past as Wiscasset, say, is of the Yankee, maritime, Colonial Revival side. Lewiston's housing consists mainly of densely packed "three-decker" wooden structures. Settled in 1770, the city has been a textile center since 1819. From the 1840s through the 1870s its economy was dominated by Boston-owned factories and mills, whose massive brick buildings still line the riverfront and its adjacent canal and whose need for cheap, docile labor encouraged the migration of young people from Quebec. Lewiston in fact rivals Lowell and Lawrence in Massachusetts as one of the great assemblages of mid-19th-century industrial architecture, although the effect as you drive along the two miles of canals seems less Victorian Italianate than de Chirico–surreal.

The city is beginning to appreciate its remarkable stock of buildings; the Lewiston Mill System Project began in 1993 to survey the 654-acre mill and canal system (the earliest parts of which date from the 1850s) and make plans for adaptive reuse of its abandoned architectural marvels (it includes, for example, 26 historic bridges). The new **Riverwalk,** connecting the two cities by way of a pedestrian bridge and a meandering path along the river is a good example of this. Lewiston also has one of the finest 20th-century buildings in Maine: the soaring, twin-towered **Saints Peter and Paul Church,** built in 1936–38 of Maine granite in a modified French Gothic style. It's the second-largest church in New England. A drive on the downtown portion of Lisbon Street offers a slice of sociology, with rough-looking "social clubs" at one end and professional offices at the other. Lisbon Street is also the home of **L/A Arts** (207-782-7228), which brings world-class performers to what, in a brilliant if ambitious piece of marketing, is referred to now as the twin communities of "L-A" (meaning Lewiston and Auburn).

Bates College, one of the best small (1,600 students) liberal arts colleges in the country, was founded in 1855 by Maine's Free Will Baptists as the first co-educational college in the East. (It was later named for a local mill owner who liberally endowed it.) The pleasant leafy campus on the northern side of Lewiston blends into its residential neighborhood—many of the adjacent houses are now student residences or faculty offices—and has 19th- and 20th-century collegiate buildings in a variety of styles, perhaps the best of them being the **George and Helen Ladd Library.** Another attraction is the **Olin Arts Center,** which houses a concert hall and the **Bates College Museum of Art,** which has a fine collection of works on paper as well as works by Mary Cassatt, Walker Evans, and Lewiston native Marsden Hartley. Each summer the college sponsors the very highly regarded **Bates Dance Festival** (207-786-6381) as well as a **Lakeside Concert Series** (207-786-6077).

Although long non-denominational, Bates has preserved some of the earnestness and social commitment of its idealistic founders—Maine's antebellum Baptists were much more abolitionist, for example, than were Maine's well-established Congregationalists—while offering the curriculum of a progressive modern college. Moreover, unlike Colby and Bowdoin, it never welcomed undergraduate fraternities and thus avoided the problems those schools experienced in the 1980s in trying to figure out what to do with the "Greek" system.

Lewiston's early industrialists had high-minded ideals. In the 1840s they hoped to create a new Lowell on the banks of the Androscoggin, with Lowell's model factories, orderly tenements, and general air of paternalism. But by the time Marsden Hartley was born (1877), conditions had reverted to the Dickensian norm. As Hartley's biographer Townsend Ludington has written, "Much of the utopian atmosphere—if ever there had been one—had disappeared amid the huge, red-brick mill buildings, the increasing grime of industry, and the system of class and caste that prevailed among the growing population." The Anglos lived on "English

Hill" overlooking the river, the Irish in "Gaspatch," and the French in "Little Canada." A good deal of assimilation has taken place since then, although Lewiston—like Biddeford—still has a large bilingual Francophone community (as you drive into town from Lisbon, for example, you'll see the names on offices and shops change from Anglo to French). It was the enfranchisement in the 1960s and 1970s of this population of French Canadian and Irish Catholics that helped break the hold on Maine enjoyed by the Republican Party since the Civil War, and Lewiston remains one of the two cities (Portland being the other) that any successful Democratic candidate for governor or senator needs to carry.

The smaller town of Auburn, the Androscoggin County seat, had its manufacturing side as well (shoes, mostly), but still conveys the impression that this was where the managers lived, while the workers settled in Lewiston. Built on hills between the river and two large lakes, Auburn has a roomier feel. Neither community has much to offer in the way of hotels and restaurants, although Auburn's **TJ's** (2 Great Falls Plaza; 207-784-7217), in a newish glass and concrete office building, is an agreeable spot to dine. Auburn's Main Street along the river has several blocks of handsomely restored Victorian office buildings.

For all its early industrial air, Lewiston is not far from the country—after all, *The Farmer's Almanac* is published here, and a bumper sticker that reads "If the goin' gets easy, maybe you're goin' downhill" seems to proclaim a local homespun truism. A short ride out of town to the northeast will take you to the small lakeside town of **Monmouth,** whose ornate turn-of-the-century "opera house," Cumston Hall, houses, each summer, the repertory company known as the **Shakespeare Theater at Monmouth** (795 Main Street; 207-933-9999). Also in Cumston Hall is the Cumston Public Library. For thirty-five years the company has staged well-regarded productions of the classics at modest prices. The nearby cemetery is a thought-provoking spot to picnic before performances.

KENNEBEC VALLEY
& MIDCOAST

To today's Americans, the establishment of this country seems to have been so inevitable that they overlook how often the Europeans' first attempts at settlement ended in disaster or at least disappointment. In August 1607, for example, just three months after a similar experiment had taken root at Jamestown in Virginia, some 100 Englishmen led by Sir George Popham landed at the mouth of the Kennebec River in present-day Phippsburg, an area that Norsemen and some adventurous Europeans may have already explored. The glory of a late Maine summer had deceived them, quite cruelly it would turn out. The English held a service of Thanksgiving for having arrived safely and immediately set to work building a defensive palisade, which they named St. George, after their national patron.

Accustomed to the mild, damp winters of the British Isles, they were terrified when the harsh Maine winter arrived. Sir George himself did not live through it, and those who survived until spring were as disoriented as the shipwrecked sailors of *The Tempest*. But unlike the tobacco farmers at Jamestown, they had managed to cut and shape enough wood to build a sturdy little vessel, a pinnace they called the *Virginia*, which proved seaworthy enough to take them back to England. The Popham Colony was a disaster, but the *Virginia* made at least one more transatlantic trading voyage; it was the first in a long line of well-built ships to be launched on the banks of the Kennebec. There is a project now afoot in Phippsburg (mainesfirstship.org) to research and reconstruct her at the Maine Maritime Museum at Bath (for purposes of education and tourism).

History books may claim that the Kennebec River is one of those places that never quite lived up to the promises people constructed for it. In the 18th century, for example, its absentee proprietors in London and Boston, basing their claims on nebulous royal grants and bargains struck with the Indians, saw the great river as another Hudson or Potomac, carrying settlers, merchants, and soldiers far into the interior. Benedict Arnold saw the Kennebec as the back door to British Canada and military glory. William King, Maine's first governor and the Kennebec's richest merchant, ended his days in near poverty in the 1850s when his investments failed.

Fresh lobsters plucked from the sea off Southport Island.

Similarly, those sea captains and shipbuilders who could not make the transition after the Civil War from the age of sail to the age of steam were often to end their days sitting in some riverfront tavern. Even little Popham Beach, which tried in the 1890s to become another Bar Harbor, was doomed to relative obscurity.

Is it unkind to take some satisfaction in this long record of honorable failure? After all, it ultimately saved the beauty of the river. For much of the 150-mile passage of the Kennebec from its origin in Moosehead Lake until it flows into the sea at Phippsburg, the forests have reclaimed what used to be cultivated fields. How many other major rivers in the eastern United States have a landscape almost as pristine as the shore that greeted those ill-fated settlers in 1607?

The southern section of the river, navigable as far north as Augusta, was the site of considerable commerce during the 19th century. In fact, it's difficult to envision how much boat traffic there was on the Kennebec from Bath to the capital 150 years ago. The timber industry also contributed to river congestion in the 19th century: the stone pilings seen in several places in the river are not ruins of early bridges but supports to anchor log booms, a sort of holding area for the timber merchants' spring log drives. Nor did winter's freeze end the river's usefulness: rather, it began the season of ice harvesting, a major business before refrigeration. The river's ice blocks were cut with large saws, stored in warehouses in sawdust, and then taken by boat when the river opened in the spring—occasionally as far away as India, but more commonly to East Coast ports. Our counterparts in the 19th century could enjoy views of all this river activity from trains between Bath and Waterville. So if you're driving through this region, stop in some of the towns along the way to get a sense of the Kennebec Valley's history.

■ BATH, CITY OF SHIPS *map page 99, A-3*

There are many places around Bath to contemplate the river's history. The 19th-century houses on Washington Street—unquestionably still the handsomest residential street in the state—reflect the vast wealth that flowed through the city 150 years ago (and that reappeared at the height of the military build-up of the 20th century). **Sagadahoc Preservation, Inc.** (207-443-2174) has designed an excellent brochure for self-guided driving and walking tours of Bath's own historic district and the National Register Historic District. Ideas flowed here as well—on nearby

Schooners cruise into Boothbay Harbor.

Middle Street, for example, is the columned Swedenborgian Church, one of the purest exercises in the Greek Revival style in the country, a classical temple reinvented in wood. And you can see more precisely how present and past are linked as you note the contrast between the vessels docked along the waterfront at Bath Iron Works (B.I.W.) and those at the historic Percy & Small shipyard.

■ MAINE MARITIME MUSEUM

A good place to pull all these thoughts together—and to reflect on how powerfully water has shaped human lives and human aspirations—is at the southern end of Bath's riverfront, where you'll find the **Maine Maritime Museum,** one of two such museums and research centers in the state (the other is the Penobscot Marine Museum in Searsport). The museum includes a working boatshop, five buildings of the Percy & Small Shipyard, the site's original occupant, and various vessels (all of which can be toured), as well as Winton Scott's Maritime History Building (1988), widely regarded as the best example of postmodern architecture in the state. The stylized "Palladian" entry subtly echoes the neoclassical mansions erected by prosperous shipbuilders along the New England coast; behind that is the main hall, whose curved wooden ceiling suggests an inverted ship's hull.

Leading off from a series of small central galleries are larger rooms with exhibits telling the story of Bath's ships and sailors; the rooms' windows frame views of the swiftly moving Kennebec and the B.I.W. yard about a mile away. The exhibits range from a 19th-century sailor's ditty bag to huge maritime paintings, and a glistening black model of J. P. Morgan's 344-foot *Corsair,* the largest power yacht ever made (built at B.I.W. in 1929–30 for $1.5 million). Objects salvaged from wrecks include the main cabin door of the three-masted schooner *Joseph Luther,* which sank at sea but later drifted ashore at the mouth of the Kennebec in 1901. Several **Georgetown** houses were built from timbers salvaged from the wreck, while the cabin door served as the kitchen door of a modest dwelling for decades. If part of being a coastal Yankee was braving the dangers of life at sea, another part was being resourceful enough to pick up the pieces—and use them.

If you have kids, take them to see the exhibits on the Maine coast and on lobstering; they also may like seeing all the vintage craft moored on the river in the summer, just outside the museum. Some of the wooden boats you'll see there have been restored by participants in the museum's restoration apprenticeship program.

Among the more important exhibits in the museum are those that trace the history of **Bath Iron Works** (www.gdbiw.com), perhaps Maine's most famous company after L. L. Bean's. Originally a foundry for marine hardware and deck machinery, the company later expanded to the manufacture of steam boilers, and eventually found itself building ships for the U.S. Navy during World War I. Unable to readjust to a civilian economy, B.I.W. went bankrupt in the 1920s. Revived as yacht-builders in 1927, the company enjoyed perhaps its finest hours during World War II, when one out of every four U.S. destroyers was "Bath-built" and when a large number of women entered the shipyard's workforce. At the height of the war effort, B.I.W. launched a new destroyer every two to three weeks.

Today the state's largest employer, the company enjoyed boom times in the 1980s, then made the transition to the post–Cold War economy. It has now modernized to "land level" building and for the last 15 years has been building the Navy's Aegis guided missile destroyers. Closing or even significantly down-sizing

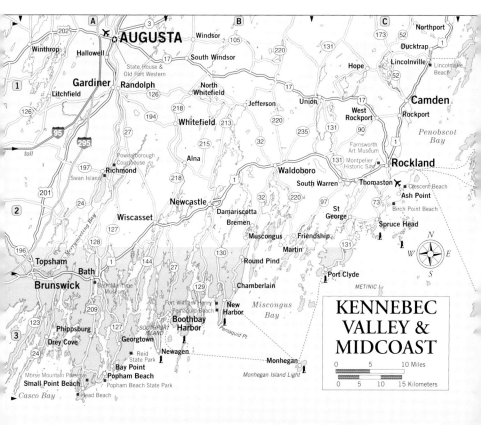

KENNEBEC
VALLEY &
MIDCOAST

Carroll Thayer Berry's painting of the Bath Iron Works during World War II.

B.I.W. would be a severe economic blow to south-central Maine, a reminder that however much Maine's image is based on a rural and self-reliant past, this part of the state, at least, has come to rely heavily on a military-industrial economy.

If your energy is flagging after taking in so much maritime history, you might repair to one of Bath's pleasant eateries. **Mae's** (formerly Kristina's), at the corner of Centre and High steets, is renowned for its pastries, and the **Kennebec Tavern & Marina** makes good use of the Bath waterfront. To refresh your soul, look into **The Chocolate Church Arts Center** (diagonally across from B.I.W.; 207-442-8455), which has a theater and gallery in the historic old Central Church and displays the work of artists and performers from far and wide.

It's easy to make excursions from Bath. Just north of town, at the Chops (an isthmus), the Kennebec joins **Merrymeeting Bay,** a traditional hunting and fishing area whose wild-rice marshes are an important stopover for many migratory birds. Merrymeeting Bay is also fed by the Androscoggin, which was a stinking sewer within not too distant memory, though it's now a relatively healthy river and people no longer refrain from eating its fish.

Directly south of town on Route 209 is an exceptionally beautiful drive, by way of the historic village of **Phippsburg,** to **Popham Beach State Park,** which has some of the best sand dunes on Maine's midcoast. At the point where the river flows into the Atlantic, and within sight of the early lighthouse (1795) on Seguin Island, stands **Fort Popham**, the rather grim, Civil War–era fort that controlled the mouth of the Kennebec.

■ BOWDOINHAM AND VICINITY *map page 99, A-2*

From Bath, take U.S. 1 (also known as Route 1) west to its junction with Route 24, then head north five miles to Bowdoinham. Situated on the marshy Cathance River, which also feeds into Merrymeeting Bay, **Bowdoinham** is a pleasant little town known for its contra dances (folk dances). **Richmond**, seven or so miles north on the Kennebec itself, has some gorgeous old houses (stop by the Railway Café at 64 Main St. to pick up information about a self-guided tour) and a Russian Orthodox émigré community described in the short stories of Willis Johnston. At **Richmond Sauna** (207-737-4752 or 800-400-5751) you can get therapeutic massage and use the heated pool, hot tub, and Finnish sauna. **Swan Island,** in the Kennebec River, is a slightly mysterious wildlife management area that includes the extinct 18th-century town of Perkins. In summer the state allows visitors, by appointment (207-547-5322), and provides a free five-minute boat shuttle from Richmond. You can also get there in your own canoe or kayak (there's no docking for power boats) and spend a morning exploring this National Historic District and its six standing houses, which are being restored. Across the river is historic **Dresden,** a hotbed of Loyalism on the eve of the Revolution, thanks in large part to its Anglican priest, the Rev. Jacob Bailey, whom the local patriots quickly expelled.

On the wooded bank of the river stands Boston architect Gershom Flagg's very simple but somehow moving **Pownalborough Courthouse** (1761), where the young John Adams, among others, followed the judges on circuit in order to practice law. The house, now on the National Register of Historic Places, is one of the great relics of 18th-century Maine. Lonelier looking today than it was when the river was a busy highway, the whitewashed courthouse stands as an ambiguous symbol of life on the Maine frontier. On the one hand, it represented the rule of law, the hand first of British and then of Massachusetts civilization bringing order to the backcountry. On the other, it was a hated symbol of authority for the farmers who had settled along the Kennebec after the Revolution, only to discover that some absentee landowner was trying to evict them for squatting on his land. Most of the land was owned by a group of Boston holders and investors known as "Proprietors of the Kennebec Purchase"; they had hoped to establish settlements in the valley and built the courthouse. A sort of low-grade civil war simmered in the backcountry from the 1790s until statehood in 1820. Settlers dressed themselves as "wild Indians" and harassed surveyors, threatened land agents, and burned records in order to protect the land they had settled on. The Pownalborough Courthouse is one of those undramatic, little-publicized historic sites that suddenly prove very powerful when you encounter them. The plain, three-story Georgian building, always a family residence, was also a gathering place, a tavern, and the Dresden post office. Upstairs you'll find a wonderful display on ice-harvesting on the Kennebec. And when a Public Broadcasting Service (PBS) documentary was made of *The Midwife's Tale,* Laurel Thatcher's book about local resident Martha Ballard (see below), the scene of Judge North's trial was filmed here.

■ **GARDINER** *map page 99, A-1*

Not all the great proprietors were absentee. One proprietor of the Kennebec Purchase, Dr. Silvester Gardiner of Boston, settled with his family in the town that bears his name; his son Robert Hallowell Gardiner succeeded the scientist-physician-statesman Benjamin Vaughan as "first citizen" of the Kennebec Valley. A landowner who for half a century encouraged the commercial development of the area, as well as a prominent Episcopalian, the younger Gardiner was a leading enthusiast of the new Gothic Revival style. **Christ Church** (1819), facing the town green in Gardiner, was one of the first churches in America to try to look medieval and English, an effect the architect Richard Upjohn achieved even more successfully at the Gardiners' 1835 home, "Oaklands." Glimpsed from the river road today, the crenellated, gray-granite manor house (private), with its sweeping lawn and its "hanger" of magnificent trees on a steep hillside, still looks more like a house in Northumberland, say, than in the middle of Maine.

The town of Gardiner was the childhood home of the poet Edwin Arlington Robinson (1869–1935), who seems to have disliked it, although his family

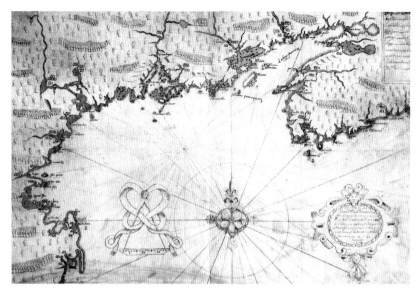

This map of coastal Maine was the result of two voyages that Samuel de Champlain made to America between 1603 and 1606. The Kennebec River and Valley can be seen in the upper left corner.

situation—his mother's painful death and his father's failure in the lumber business—could not have made life there easy for him. The town in that post–Civil War period was sharply divided between poorly paid mill workers who lived near the river (an area now largely cleared) and proper folk "up the hill." Robinson transformed this Gardiner into his mythic Tilbury Town, a troubling place inhabited by the likes of Minniver Cheevy and Richard Cory. His house near the green is marked by a plaque.

For years Gardiner has been a bedroom community for Augusta, but today its proximity to I–95 and it attractiveness are appealing to professionals from Portsmouth and even Boston. Property values are climbing, and during its bicentennial celebrations in 2003 the town, with much fanfare, cut the ribbons on nine new businesses. A well-organized self-guided walking tour of town—available at the public library (152 Water Street; 207-582-3312)—touches on all the notable

Mt. Tom, in Gardiner, is a popular place for kids to go sledding.

buildings, four of which are on the National Register of Historic Places. Gardiner is worth a stop not only for its 19th-century churches and houses but for an artifact of the early 20th century, the **A1 Diner** downtown on Bridge Street. Its Depression-era interior is virtually untouched, but the food is eclectic, international, and cheap (dinner costs less than $12). The menu one night might include Moroccan stew, Mexican chicken pie, Russian vegetable strudel, Thai crab and fish stew, and lasagne al forno, alongside meatloaf and bread pudding. **A1 to Go** (207-582-5586) next door does a great business in take-out meals.

■ HALLOWELL *map page 99, A-1*

Augusta and Hallowell were originally part of the same 18th-century settlement, the former known then as "the Fort," the latter as "the Hook," short for Bombahook, a local stream. Today they still flow together, although you can tell when you cross the line. Hallowell, perhaps because of a stricter sign ordinance, just looks neater. A granite and lumbering community for most of the 19th century, Hallowell was the area's social and commercial center, thanks in part to the presence of the Vaughans, Hallowells, Pages, Hubbards, and other prosperous families in the area. Along with the Gardiners, these families formed the well-educated, politically powerful gentry of the mid-Kennebec Valley.

What is now Augusta had a bridge over the river, and so it became the state capital in 1832. Today Augusta still has the liveliness and services of state government, but Hallowell has the charm—and the good restaurants, bookstores, the **Gaslight Theater** (207-626-3698; www.gaslighttheater.org), and numerous antiques shops—that Augusta in general lacks. Maine's smallest city, Hallowell is classified as a National Historic District. Attractive Water Street, whose redbrick buildings seem to have one foot dangling in the river, has interesting galleries and shops and the popular **Slate's**, which since 1979 has occupied three adjoining 1804 buildings. They serve good food and a famous Sunday brunch, and have frequent jazz and vocal concerts. A walk in **Vaughan Woods**, a 150-acre nature reserve right in town, will get you back in the fresh air—or go for a stroll along the river on the **Kennebec River Rail Trail** (207-623-4511; *www.krrt.org*), which is on the railroad right of way leading two miles north to Augusta. A section also connects Gardiner with Farmingdale, and another is planned that will soon run north to Hallowell, making six and a half miles in all.

■ AUGUSTA *map page 99, A-1*

If this is your first time in Augusta, the town may seem a nondescript city organized around two large traffic circles, one on either side of the river. Most of the state's bureaucrats are housed in buildings of Hallowell granite that do not look pompous or forbidding, just ordinary, which is an approach to government Mainers have traditionally endorsed. Even the **State House** (corner of State and Capitol; 207-287-2301) looks less imposing than many an American county courthouse, though it has been recently restored and is open for tours. The old riverfront downtown has a somewhat depressed look, despite its postmodern office tower. There are a few notable buildings around—the "Romanesque-Renaissance" **Lithgow Library** (1898), for example, and the château-esque downtown post office. And gazing serenely from the east riverbank across from the State House sits a group of cream neoclassical buildings that used to house the insane. Beautiful and crumbling, they are slowly being restored for use as state and municipal offices. Yet Augusta is more than a traffic jam on the quick route to Bar Harbor. An easy day trip from many of the midcoast resorts, the capital has three major attractions, all of which (along with many other places) can be reached on the **Augusta Summer Trolley** (50 cents). A new bridge, completed in 2004, now connects I–95 and West Augusta with the less developed east side of the Kennebec, and facilitates travel to and from the coast.

On a bluff overlooking the river is the oldest of these attractions, **Old Fort Western** (1754). It's the last of the original French and Indian War fortifications surviving in Maine, and is now a National Historic Landmark. The fort's two (reconstructed) blockhouses and the long 18th-century storehouse—divided into the comfortable dwelling of the Howard family at one end and a re-creation of their store at the other—summarizes the history of the fort. Built by the Kennebec proprietors as a supply station for British troops farther upriver, the fort eventually became the commercial center of the new community. When the town grew on the other side of the river, the buildings housed Irish immigrants brought in to work on the local mills and dams. The fort eventually declined into a tenement, until it was bought by the Gannett family in 1922 and given to the city. Today, thanks to a combination of showmanship and scholarly and archaeological accuracy, Fort Western is a major educational center for teaching people of all ages about life in Maine on the 18th-century frontier. Staff members in period costume give occasional demonstrations of the domestic skills needed for survival. While

Benjamin Hallowell, scion of one of Maine's early influential families, as portrayed by artist John Singleton Copley.

MARTHA BALLARD, HALLOWELL MIDWIFE

The "new" history has brought to vivid life a whole cast of Maine characters on the 18th- and early-19th-century frontier, people who did not have their portraits painted by Copley or Gilbert Stuart and who rarely left their names in the official local histories, but who shaped the future of the District of Maine. There is no better example than the story of the Hallowell midwife and healer Martha Ballard, who between 1785 and 1812 attended 816 births and enjoyed a higher reputation for safe deliveries than the local, university-trained physicians. No one painted Ballard's portrait, but she sketched a self-portrait of sorts in a diary she kept during those 27 years. In 1990 Laurel Thatcher Ulrich, a professor at the University of New Hampshire, found the diary, researched its historical context, and published it. Ulrich's richly annotated version won her a Pulitzer Prize, and guaranteed a virtually unknown woman in Hallowell an important role in our understanding of everyday life in the early Republic.

The diary entries are, at first glance, laconic and banal. They record visits with neighbors, births and deaths, weather, housework, the occasional odd event. A typical entry from 1788 reads:

> Clear. Mr Ballard gone to Mr James Pages on public business.
> Jonathan & Taylor went to see the execution of Oneal. I have been
> at home. The Girls washt. Gilbreath sleeps here. The wife of old Mr
> Springer Departed this Life this morn.

What Ulrich does with them, however, is near miraculous, one of the great technical and imaginative feats of recent American historiography. From these often cryptic diary entries, she brings back to life an entire community. Martha Ballard, it turns out, was not an obscure folk healer or a quaint village herbalist, but a strong-minded, independent woman at the center of a complex network of social, familial, and economic relationships. Neither from the top nor the bottom of local society, she and her husband (a surveyor for the Kennebec proprietors) played a mediating role in the communal affairs of Hallowell's 100 or so families. She could not only see a neighbor through a difficult delivery, but could perform in her own way a variety of healing tasks that in modern times would require the skills of a druggist, psychiatrist, and medical emergency technician. The local doctors respected her enough to seek her advice in difficult obstetrical cases and to invite her to attend autopsies and dissections, though both she and they knew that the age of the expert midwife was passing as the prestige of the trained medical profession grew. Both she and they probably knew, too, that a patient's chance of survival was sometimes greater given her gentle care and herbal remedies than it was from the so-called "heroic medicine"—which called for lots of purges and bleeding—of the medical-school graduates.

Anyone traveling along the Kennebec near Hallowell today will see much of the same scenery that Martha Ballard knew intimately, though in her time there would have been less forest and more open farmland, and much more traffic on the river. For eight months of the year Hallowell was a seaport, connected to the Atlantic trade routes. The Kennebec froze with startling rapidity in early winter, however, and, as Ulrich points out, "Hallowell folks remembered openings and closings of the river the way people in other towns remembered earthquakes or drought." One year the ice did not clear until May.

It was part of Martha Ballard's sense of vocation that she would take great risks to answer a call for help. As you speed in your car upriver from Gardiner to Hallowell, imagine her walking across the ice on a winter morning, or paddling in a canoe in April, a middle-aged woman breaking her way through the ice floes, then struggling to climb the steep and muddy bank to rush to someone's sickbed on the farther shore. Or imagine her tending her garden—the sound of the local sawmills in the distance—growing the food that sustained her family and collecting the herbs (camomile, catmint, pennyroyal, tansy, and two dozen others) that soothed the pain, killed the worms, cured the colic, and settled the bowels of her friends and neighbors. There is perhaps no other book since Thoreau's travel accounts that can so enrich a visit to the state. In short, *A Midwife's Tale: The Life of Martha Ballard, Based on Her Diary, 1785–1812* is the most important—and most readable—work on Maine history to appear in a generation.

you're here you can peer through the pickets and try to imagine keeping watch for the French and their Indian allies.

Just south of the Capitol is one of Maine's hidden treasures, the **State Museum** in the state capitol complex. Sharing a building with the State Library and State Archives, the museum is one of the most imaginative and intelligently organized examples of its kind. Exhibits are eclectic and varied, and range from the wonderful collection of domestic and household glass and a Norse penny found in Brooklin to "The Lion" (1846), a small steam-powered freight engine that carried lumber to the sawmills for 50 years. Here also is your chance to meet *Pertica quadrifaria,* the State Fossil, a plant that grew in the marshes of the Katahdin region 400 million years ago. The two major permanent exhibits focus on Maine pre-history, and on the products and industries of 19th- and early-20th-century Maine, complete with sound effects and period artifacts. There's also an important early view of Augusta by the painter Charles Codman from 1836; it shows Bulfinch's original Capitol (the columned facade was kept in later renovations). The almost brand-new neoclassical building arises from a romantic but thoroughly tamed wilderness—an image that reflected how Mainers thought about their state in its early years of independence. And before you leave the capitol complex, it's worth tracking down the historic dioramas of stuffed deer, moose, bears, and beavers on display in a tunnel between the State House and State Office Building.

The intimate, down-home quality of government in a small state is nicely captured in another Capitol Hill landmark, the 1830-ish **Blaine House,** which since 1921 has been the official residence of Maine's governors, and whose reception rooms are open to the public. It bears the name of the state's most famous politician of the immediate post–Civil War period, James G. Blaine, a successful journalist, congressman, and two-term U.S. Secretary of State who helped cement Maine's century of allegiance to the Republican Party. Despite his skills, Blaine ("the Plumed Knight") never got what he really wanted—to be president. In 1884 he lost decisively to Grover Cleveland, but he was always much honored in his home state, and his youngest daughter, Harriet Blaine Beale, gave the house to the people of Maine. Its current look owes much to Colonial Revival remodeling by John Calvin Stevens, but Blaine's study retains its Victorian style.

There are other things to see in and around Augusta—the Summer Trolley goes to the 200-acre **Pine Tree State Arboretum** (207-621-0031), for example, with its wooded trails, and you can easily walk from the capitol complex to the **Maine Military Historical Society Museum** (upper Winthrop St., 207-626-4483; open the first Sunday of the month).

■ WATERVILLE AND ENVIRONS

Relatively few tourists follow the path of the Kennebec beyond Augusta and farther north, into the heart of the Great North Woods, though it's an historic route. In September 1775 Benedict Arnold (still at that time on the colonists' side) and an army under General Richard Montgomery set out to capture Quebec from the British and persuade the French Canadians to join the rebellion. Arnold brought 1,100 volunteers from the Continental Army besieging Boston, and sailed up the

Kennebec to Gardiner, where he transferred his men and two women into 225 bateaux (large flat-bottomed boats), ill designed for the rigors of the trip up river. As winter set in, he crossed overland from the Kennebec to the north-flowing Chaudière, by which means he reached the St. Lawrence River after a very difficult trip. Some 650 men survived the trek and reached Quebec City in mid-November. The city refused to surrender, and on December 3 Arnold met Montgomery's army, which arrived from the west, as planned, having captured Montreal. Lacking the forces for an all-out attack, the Americans settled in for a siege, planning a surprise maneuver. On the night of December 31 they assaulted the city's fortifications under cover of a blizzard. But their plan had been discovered, the defense was fierce, and the Americans fell back. Montgomery was killed and Arnold wounded; 60 to 100 of their men were killed and 400 captured. (In the Battle of Quebec the defenders lost 10 men, including one French militiaman, and a few were wounded.) The ill-fated and quickly forgotten campaign is remembered today chiefly in those towns in the Kennebec Valley where Arnold and his men stopped on their way north. (And of course, in Quebec.)

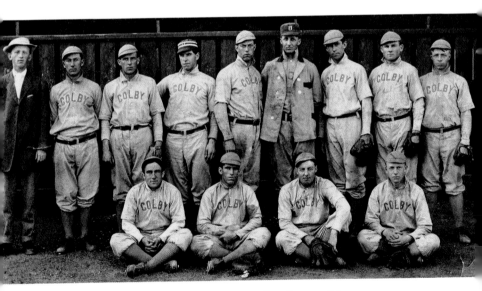

The Colby baseball team, in 1906, demonstrates the seriousness of the sport.

On the west bank of the Kennebec River stands **Waterville**, home of the Hathaway shirt (1847) and the Lombard Log Hauler, the forerunner of all caterpillar-treaded vehicles, including the tank. Today Waterville is no doubt best known as the home of **Colby College,** which was rebuilt in 1952 in neo-Georgian style on Mayflower Hill, at the edge of town. Founded in 1813 as the Maine Literary and Theological Institution, Colby was intended as a Baptist alternative to Congregationalist-dominated Bowdoin. The institution was chartered as Waterville College by a sympathetic legislature in 1820, but was renamed for a generous donor, Gardner Colby of Boston, in 1867. The original riverside campus was abandoned because the railroad tracks made the area noisy and dirty, and the site precluded expansion. Colby, a four-year liberal arts college of about 1,600 students, includes the martyred newspaper editor Elijah Lovejoy of the class of 1825 among its most famous alumni. A courageous and outspoken abolitionist, he was shot dead in Alton, Illinois, in 1837 while trying to defend his printing press against a pro-slavery mob. The attractive campus is worth visiting, especially for its **Museum of Art,** one of the state's best museums, particularly rich in 20th-century American painting and sculpture.

Off campus, a lively 21st-century spirit pervades Waterville—collegiate during the school year, and rather sophisticated in summer. The town is the center of civilization for the popular Belgrade Lakes region a few miles away. Local high spots include the **Railroad Square Cinema** (207-872-5111), which shows foreign and high-quality American films on three screens; **Jorgensen's,** a wine, cheese, and coffee shop (103 Main Street) downtown; and **Freedom Café,** a soul-food restaurant (207-859-8742; *www.freedomcafefood.com*). And for 10 days in July, Waterville's **Maine International Film Festival** screens more than 100 movies.

Colby's strength in the arts owes much to its proximity to the **Skowhegan School of Painting and Sculpture,** a few minutes' drive upriver. Founded in 1946 on a poultry farm, the school conducts summer classes that have attracted some of the nation's leading artists, and that lend a temporary flavor of Manhattan to the surrounding farmland—locals don't usually wear so much black. The other famous landmark in Skowhegan (aside from Bernard Langlois's enormous downtown statue of **Paul Bunyan**) is the **Margaret Chase Smith Library Center,** an extension of her house overlooking the river. It records some 40 years of public service, from her election in 1940 as a Republican congresswoman (replacing her late husband in the seat) through her career in the 1950s and 1960s as the first woman elected (a few had been appointed) to the U.S. Senate. Her finest moment came on the Senate floor in 1950 when she did what everyone around her had been afraid to do—denounced Senator Joseph McCarthy in what came to be known as her "Declaration of Conscience" speech. A moderate conservative herself, Smith opened a door for women into the mostly male world of politics. Wearing her signature red rose, she greeted visitors to her library until she died in 1995 at 98.

Skowhegan has another small treasure: **History House** (1839), a brick Cape cottage on the National Register (66 Elm St.; 207-474-6632), full of 19th-century furnishings and Civil War memorabilia.

Nearby **Norridgewock,** an attractive, historic town at a point on the old Indian trail linking the Kennebec and the Chaudière, is associated not only with Benedict Arnold's march north to Quebec but with the memory of Father Sebastian Rasles, the French Jesuit who composed a dictionary of the Wabanaki language and whose dealings with Native Americans showed great sensitivity to their culture. Rasles's accomplishments in Maine are celebrated in the essay "In the American Grain," by the 20th-century poet William Carlos Williams. After three decades of missionary activity in the upper Kennebec Valley (including training a choir of 40 young Norridgewock Indians to sing the Mass and make altar candles from bayberries), the scholarly Rasles was killed in 1724 by the British colonials, who pillaged and burned the Indians' village in what is now the pine grove at Old Point. Continuing upriver, you come to the town of **Bingham,** whose name commemorates the very rich Philadelphian William Bingham, who in the 1780s owned some two million acres of Maine land. The Forks, a destination for many hunters and fishermen, is a tiny community at the confluence of the Kennebec and Dead rivers. The next settlement of any size (meaning perhaps 1,000 residents) is the North Woods town of **Jackman** (*see* "Great North Woods"), after which you will very soon find yourself crossing into the Province of Quebec.

The province of Quebec and the state of Maine have cooperated to create a cultural trail, the **Kennebec-Chaudière International Corridor,** for the benefit of travelers, which follows the route taken by Arnold in the winter of 1775. It goes all the way from Quebec through Maine along Route 201 to the coast. A map outlining the history, culture, and activities of the region is available at www. kennebec-chaudiere.com.

Birdhouses for sale in Wiscasset, Maine's "prettiest village."

■ EAST FROM BATH *map page 99, A/B-2/3*

If after a trip up the Kennebec Valley you yearn for Maine's rocky shoreline, consider taking a trip east from Bath along midcoastal Maine. While there are plenty of places to visit in coastal southern Maine, there's something tame, even suburban, about much of that part of the state. But cross the new Route 1 bridge at Bath over the Kennebec and you'll soon see that you've entered the ideal Maine of so many people's imagination. The experience is only intermittently satisfying—the problem you face is whether to be content with commercial U.S. 1 and its succession of historic seaports, or to explore each neck of land along this much-fragmented coast. Not every fishing village or saltwater farm looks like the last one; the pleasure of wandering up and down the sea-pointed roads lies in finding the one that most meets your expectations.

If you decide to explore the area down toward the sea, cross the Sagadahoc Bridge to Woolwich and turn south on Route 127 toward Arrowsic and Georgetown islands. The very scenic drive ends at Bay Point and **Reid State Park,** and you certainly won't go hungry on the way. Two of the area's better restaurants are nearby: Michael Gagne's wonderful **Robinhood Free Meetinghouse** and the beautifully situated **Osprey,** overlooking remote Robinhood Cove. When you return to Route 1 on your way east again, keep your eyes peeled (if it's Wednesday or on a weekend) for the big **Montsweag Flea Market,** at about the town line between Woolwich and Wiscasset.

Wiscasset has long billed itself as "Maine's prettiest village," a title that several towns might successfully dispute, though the claim has certainly benefited from the shutdown and dismantling of the Maine Yankee Nuclear Power Plant that used to loom on the other side of the harbor. The fact that Route 1 goes directly through the center of town is also a mixed blessing, depending on the time of year you travel there, but plans to build a new highway slightly inland have been fiercely opposed by residents concerned about the rural beauty of the backcountry. At any rate, it's quite pleasant to get out of the car in Wiscasset and explore its mainly 19th-century side streets and its antiques shops.

Don't miss Wiscasset's two architecturally significant homes and its historic jail. Historic New England's **Nickels-Sortwell House** (1807–09), a magnificent dwelling at the corner of Federal and Main streets in the center of town, is literally a textbook example of Adamesque Federal design (its entrance was copied from Plate 30 of Asher Benjamin's 1806 architectural design book, *The American Builder's Companion*), though it conveys little of the personality of its builders (or its Colonial Revival rescuers). **Castle Tucker** (1807–08), on the other hand, a gorgeously sited Regency dandy across the cove, is still occupied by a descendant of the early owners and is full of the wonderful stuff—including an egg collection—that used to accumulate over the generations in an old seacoast house.

The **Old Jail** (1809) and adjoining **Jailer's House** (1839), on Federal Street, which are both on the National Register of Historic Places, are now the headquarters of the Lincoln County Historical Association (207-882-6817). Certainly come here if you want some fascinating insights about the early life of prisoners and their keepers. For lunch or dinner, try **Le Garage** on Water Street (locally called "the Le"), a converted 1920s-era garage. The restaurant's glassed-in porch overlooks the pretty Sheepscot River.

■ **BOOTHBAY HARBOR** *map page 99, B-3*

As you drive east, you'll have the chance to detour to several well-known places. Just over the river at North Edgecomb the road takes you to **Boothbay Harbor,** a famous sailing town that in July and August seems on the verge of sinking beneath the weight of its tourists. The café-lined streets are especially densely packed for three days during Windjammer Days, in late June or early July, when a dozen or so great sailing boats fill the harbor and the town celebrates. Thirty years ago Boothbay Harbor must have seemed a charming fishing village (60 years before that, it had been a bustling commercial and shipping center for the fishing and fertilizer trade). It remains a very popular destination for many tourists and recreational sailors, but, as Roger F. Duncan drily notes in his indispensable *Cruising Guide to the New England Coast,* "it is a port we are always glad to get into and delighted to leave." Clearly uncontrolled commercial and motel development along the narrow streets of the harborfront have given the town a circus atmosphere in high season. On the other hand, the view down the narrow harbor toward the sea is as lovely as ever, the confusion of all those boats coming and going has its Raoul Dufy qualities, and you will not have trouble finding a place to eat or (if you book ahead) a nice Victorian house turned B&B in which to stay.

The **Linekin Bay Resort,** about a mile from downtown, is a family resort with a fleet of sailboats, tennis courts, and cottages surrounding the 1909 main building. The **Boothbay Railway Village,** one mile north of town on Route 27, is delightful, especially for children who have never ridden on an actual train and for anyone who likes antique cars. The Maine Department of Marine Resources runs the **Marine Resources Aquarium** (207-633-9559), on McKown Point Road in West Boothbay Harbor, where you can picnic, pet a live shark, and get your hands wet in a touch tank.

Two peninsulas reach south from Boothbay Harbor in a pincer—the drive east on Route 96 past East Boothbay to **Ocean Point** is scenic and will be decidedly rewarding if your idea of Maine involves fewer people and ocean views. Nearby **Southport Island**—just south of town on Route 27—is also a welcome alternative. With its cove-indented shore, its little white Capes, and its stacks of lobster traps, it comes very close to being the *Down East* magazine version of Maine people so adore. For the moment, the mix of lobstermen and affluent retirees does seem to work—on Southport and in many similar Midcoast communities—although the inevitable increase in property values poses potential long-range problems. The place to enjoy Southport is the **Newagen Inn,** a complex of buildings at the tip of Cape Newagen, where you can still feel the timelessness of old-fashioned summers. Cape Newagen can be enjoyed, more briefly, in the winter, too: it is a superb place to watch the northern waters. The little tidal pool of a harbor is sheltered, almost toylike, especially in comparison to the Atlantic. Just beyond the barrier islands the Atlantic is churning—when big waves hit the distant ledges, white water explodes like a geyser at sea.

Back on Route 1, continue east, but before exploring Newcastle and Damariscotta, twin villages divided by the Damariscotta River, turn north to **Damariscotta Mills,** whose Kavanaugh Mansion (private) inspired one of Robert Lowell's poems. A few miles farther inland are the villages of Alna and Head Tide. **Alna** is the site of the **Old Alna Meetinghouse** (1794), with original ship-lapped clapboards, box pews, and raised hourglass pulpit, and the **Alna Center School House Museum**. And **Head Tide** was the birthplace of the poet Edwin Arlington Robinson.

Newcastle comes next, and down by the bridge to Damariscotta take a turn left on tree-shaded Glidden Street, along the river, to see the pretty old houses and the splendid half-timbered English Gothic architecture of **St. Andrew's Episcopal Church** (1893), which also has a peaceful memorial garden. **Damariscotta,** mercifully off the main through highway, somehow manages to be both a river and a seaport town. Nearby are the **Damariscotta Shell Heaps,** a shell midden left by Paleo-Indians 3,000 years ago (*see essay,* "Maine's Paleo-Indians").

On the seaward side of Damariscotta, Route 130 leads south down the Bristol/Pemaquid Peninsula (*pema* = "longest," *quid* = "finger") about 12 miles to the lighthouse at spectacular **Pemaquid Point,** whose thick strands of multi-colored volcanic rock seem in violent argument with the sea. About three miles north, off Route 130, are **Fort William Henry,** a replica of a 1692 structure built to defend the eastern English frontier; the **Colonial Pemaquid State Historic Site,** an important archaeological site and small museum for studying and understanding the area's 17th-century origins; the **Harrington Meeting House** (1773), with its cemetery and museum; and the **Old Walpole Meeting House.** To continue east, take Route 32 north from New Harbor to its junction with U.S. 1.

Back on U.S. 1, the next major historic town is **Waldoboro,** tucked into a fold at the head of the Medomak River's navigable waters. The town was settled in

Storefronts in Boothbay Harbor.
(following pages) Early morning at the Pemaquid Point Lighthouse.

The Clamdiggers, *an 1895 photograph by Emma D. Sewall, illustrates an activity along coastal tidal flats still popular among Maine residents.*

1748 by Germans who had been lured across the Atlantic by the promise of prosperity, but were confronted, as a tombstone in the Old German Cemetery laments, with "nothing but wilderness." This is one of several New England towns that "preserved" an old cattle pound, a slightly batty exercise in Colonial Revival nostalgia. Longings for a kinder, simpler, less diet-conscious America can also be fulfilled at **Moody's Diner**, a landmark known for huge helpings, a retro menu (which includes tripe), and creamy pies. If you take Route 220 south to the next peninsula down east, you'll come to **Friendship**, on Muscongus Bay, a town famous for the sloops bearing its name.

From Friendship, Route 97 takes you northeast back to **Thomaston,** which displays along U.S. 1 two long rows of splendid Federal and Greek Revival houses and the showroom and crafts shop of the Maine State Prison—one of the state's most unexpected retail outlets (it, too, attracts charter buses). Wooden objects made by prisoners are sold all over Maine—often under the "Woods to Goods" label. Take a tour down Knox Street to look at more houses. The

Thomaston Historical Society (80 Knox Street; 207-354-2295) and the Library and Town Office have collaborated on a "Museum in the Streets," with informative plaques outside noteworthy examples of local architecture. See if you can begin to identify the Italianate-style work of James Overlock (1840–55).

On a hilltop just beyond the town you'll find "Montpelier," a beautifully furnished replica of the mansion of the Revolutionary War hero and land speculator Maj. Gen. Henry Knox, whose unhappy business ventures in lumber, shipbuilding, lime-burning, and the like, combined with his personal extravagance, led to his ruin. His family's sudden decline and the legends that grew up about his heirs' land claims are believed to have inspired Hawthorne's account of the Pyncheon family "fortune" in *The House of the Seven Gables.* Side roads from Thomaston lead southwest to **Cushing** and Andrew Wyeth country on the west side of the St. George River, and, on the east side (Rte. 131), down the St. George peninsula to **Tenants Harbor, Martinsville,** and **Port Clyde**—the landscape Sarah Orne Jewett described in *The Country of the Pointed Firs.* The whale's hump of **Monhegan Island** can be seen in the distance; ferries to the island, a popular summer residence and artists' colony, leave daily from Port Clyde.

Driving back up the "Down East" side of the peninsula, you'll first come to **Spruce Head**, where the poet Wilbert Snow spent his youth on a farm (vividly and realistically portrayed in his 1968 memoir, *Codline's Child*). Next comes **South Thomaston**, with its wonderful **Old Post Office Gallery** (207-594-9396; www.artofthesea.com), displaying all things nautical, from ship models, prints, and paintings to navigational instruments and antique artifacts. And then there's **Owls Head**, home of the **Owls Head Transportation Museum,** with its vintage cars (that run) and planes (that fly). On your way to see the **Owls Head Light**, just at the turnoff from South Shore Road, you might stop at the **Owls Head General Store** (207-596-6038) for one of their famous hamburgers or a crab melt, or try the homemade soups and pies. From there it's only a few miles on Route 73 to the town of Rockland on West Penobscot Bay; these shores mark the end of "midcoast Maine," which began with one historic river, the Kennebec, and that here meets another, the Penobscot.

PENOBSCOT BAY & RIVER

No one knows how the name "Norumbega" originated, but as early as 1548 a map of the "Tierra Nueva" published in Venice indicates a "Tierra de Nurumberg" on the northeastern coast of what is now the United States. The term—applied variously to a river, a city, and a region—may derive from the Algonquian word meaning "where the river is wide" as transcribed by Giovanni da Verrazano, the Italian navigator who, in the service of the French, reached the Maine coast in 1524. By 1597, when Cornelius Wytiet published a map of "Norumbega et Virginia" in a Flemish atlas, the idea was well established in the European imagination that somewhere on the North American shore was a river that offered a passage to the Indies as well as a fabled city at the head of that river rich with gold. The mapmakers may have heard that in 1525 a Portuguese captain employed by the Spanish had sailed up the Penobscot as far as modern Bangor in search of that Northwest Passage, and soon various European explorers had followed, including Jean Allefonsce in 1527 and French geographer Thevet in 1556. David Ingram, an Englishman who survived a 1568 shipwreck in the Gulf of Mexico, returned home on a French vessel and wrote a colorful account of visiting the mythical city of Norumbega.

Although Wytiet showed Norumbega extending as far south as the Chesapeake, the imaginary land was reduced on later maps to what is now New England and, at the time of Champlain's voyages in 1604 and 1605, was identified with the headwaters of the Penobscot in northern Maine. Although the territory along the Penobscot was to be fiercely disputed by the British and French and their respective Indian allies in the early 18th century, no one ever found gold there, much less a route to Asia.

From a vantage point in **Penobscot Bay,** or even from the roadside overlook on Route 1 (also known as U.S. 1), just before the suspension bridge at Verona, it is easy to understand how a river like the Penobscot could have fired the imaginations of the first Europeans on the scene. More dramatic than the Kennebec, with steeper banks and fewer habitations in view, it cuts its way from the foothills of Mount Katahdin—with a western branch arising among the huge lakes of north-central Maine—and drains much of the eastern half of the state before flowing into the Atlantic at Penobscot Bay.

The view from Mt. Battie in Camden.

■ WEST PENOBSCOT BAY *map page 127, A-3*

Continuing on Route 1, you drive along the western side of Penobscot Bay, stopping by towns that serve as jumping-off points for some of the most beautiful islands on the New England coast. Between **Thomaston** and **Rockland,** the landscape abruptly changes; the cement plant and the hillsides torn up to quarry limestone seem out of place in this otherwise pastoral part of the world. While it is possible to bypass this section of coast by detouring onto Route 90 and driving inland for a short stretch until it rejoins Route 1 at Rockport, to do so would mean missing **Rockland,** a town with a mix of year-round working people and artists. To be sure, Rockland is at first glance plainly utilitarian, best known to tourists and summer people for its ferry boats to North Haven, Vinalhaven, and Matinicus islands in Penobscot Bay. But the city, a busy fishing port with a splendid museum complex and a popular farmers' market every Thursday from the end of May into October, is much more agreeable now than it was in the 19th century, when its skies were darkened by the smoke of the lime pits and when travelers approaching from the sea at night compared its eerie glow to the gates of Hell. It was the birthplace of

Louise Nevelson by the wood sculpture she donated to Westbrook College.

the poet Edna St. Vincent Millay (200 Broadway) and the composer Walter Piston, as well as the childhood home of the Russian-born sculptor Louise Nevelson, whose constructions from wood scraps surely owed something to the jig-saw Victorian carpentry of her Maine youth.

Nevelson's work can be seen at the town's leading attraction, the **Farnsworth Art Museum and Wyeth Center** (16 Museum Street), where you'll also find pieces by many other leading American artists who have painted in Maine. The Wyeth Center houses paintings by three generations of Wyeths, as well as the personal collection of Andrew and Betsy Wyeth. The Portland Museum of Art may one day outshine the rest of the state, but for the moment the Farnsworth shares with the Bowdoin College Museum of Art the distinction of being one of Maine's best art museums. Both museums offer high-quality collections small enough to be absorbed in a single visit. If you want to see how Maine has looked to artists over the past 200 years, the Farnsworth is the place to begin. The museum also owns two historic properties, both on the National Register: **The Olson House** in Cushing, the subject, with its inhabitants, of thirty years of Andrew Wyeth paintings; and the **Farnsworth Homestead** (ca. 1840), attached to the museum, which is preserved very much as it was during the long lifetime of Lucy Farnsworth. Having inherited a respectable fortune from her father, Farnsworth managed to increase it several times over through her shrewdness and frugality. In the dining room you can see the soup tureen in which her tenants are said to have placed their rent each month in summer—it sat in the window, they stood outside. When Miss Farnsworth died at age 96 in 1935, she astonished Rockland by leaving the city her $1.3 million estate to establish and endow an art museum and library and to maintain the family's homestead. Having spent a lifetime of monotonous stringency, one unrelieved (if the furnishings of her house are any indication) by literature or art, Lucy Farnsworth ended it with a magnificent act of largesse.

Before continuing north, stop at the Island Institute's store, **Archipelago** (386 Main St.), on the next block after the museum, to browse through the arts and crafts of Maine artisans, all in support of the communities of the state's islands and working waterfronts. Next you pass through Glen Cove and come to the stoplight at the Route 90 junction. If you turn right here, you'll enter into **Rockport** (of André the Seal fame) and reenter the world of summer people. Following the

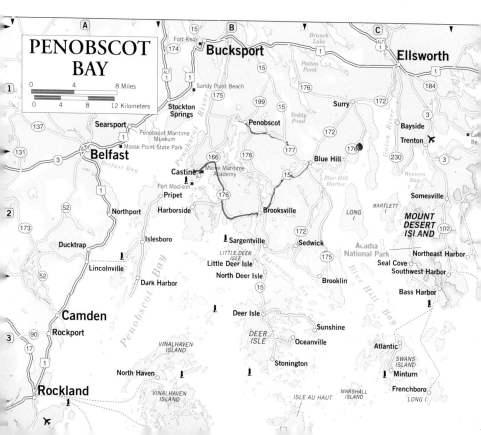

Her Room, *by Andrew Wyeth, shows the light-filled interior of the Wyeths' living room in Cushing, Maine. Through an open door and wavy-glass windows, the St. George River can be seen, lit by the diffuse, oblique rays from a solar eclipse. Nearby is the Olson House, made famous by Wyeth's* Christina's World, *and now owned by the Farnsworth Museum, which opens it to the public in summer.*

Born in 1917 the son of noted illustrator N. C. Wyeth, Andrew Wyeth had his first one-man show in New York in 1937. He is best known for his use of watercolors and tempera in muted grays and soft browns. These colors convey perfectly his vision of the rural life about him. For the most part, Wyeth painted the houses, hills, fields, and people of his home in the Brandywine Valley of Pennsylvania and of his summer home in Cushing.

winding street into the village center and then down the hill to the large red sheds at Rockport Marine will bring you to one of the loveliest harbors on the Maine coast. Unspoiled by commercial development, the long, narrow harbor is filled with sturdy lobster boats and classic wooden sailing vessels. If you come upon the scene at sunset, you'll understand why Charles Kuralt included Rockport Harbor on his list of the five most beautiful places in the United States. Up the hill, over-looking the harbor on the corner of Central Street, stands the redbrick building that houses the **Maine Photographic Resources Center**, which runs summmer workshops in photography, film, and screenwriting for professionals and talented amateurs. Across the street you'll find **The Corner Store**, a friendly spot where locals and students fill the booths during breakfast and lunchtime, and the **Rockport Opera House.**

Central Street becomes Russell Avenue, which leads via Bayview to the town of **Camden**, cutting through Aldermere Farm, where a herd of Belted Galloway cows from Scotland reside. Camden is an attractive place long teetering on the verge of being overrun by boats and cars in summer. It's one of the few towns north of Portland with a thriving year-round economy, thanks to the jobs (with benefits) provided by a large credit-card company whose president, a long-time summer res-ident, renovated the long-abandoned mill in town into a fairly dazzling office com-plex along a tumbling stream. The business's impact can be seen throughout the village, from the renovated opera house to the library's handsome addition, and even to the local galleries that supplied much of the art hanging on the company's walls. The credit-card company has moved on to Belfast, but its complex, now the **Knox Mill Center,** is filling up with shops, small businesses, and professionals.

Camden still functions as a lively coastal destination for visitors. The town is packed with restaurants, and has possibly more bed-and-breakfasts and inns per block than any other Maine town south of Bar Harbor. Among the former, **The Waterfront,** off Bayview Street, has the best combination of views and cuisine; among the latter, the white-clapboard **Maine Stay** on Hight Street is perhaps the most graciously comfortable. Look also for the **Owl and Turtle Bookshop** in the Knox Mill Center (32 Washington Street).

On the north side of town, U.S. 1 passes by some of the best Colonial Revival domestic architecture in the state, one of the finest examples being the historic **Whitehall Inn** (where Edna St. Vincent Millay was "discovered" in 1908). Famous

Sailboats docked at the picturesque Camden Harbor.

Skiers at Camden Snow Bowl, with a view of Penobscot Bay.

for its harbor, Camden is also remembered for its circle of hills, a combination celebrated in Millay's poem "Renascence" ("All I could see from where I stood/Was three long mountains and a wood;/I turned and looked the other way,/And saw three islands in a bay. . . .") Nearby **Lincolnville,** with ferry connections to Islesboro, was the retirement home of the great Brazilian soprano Bidu Sayao (1902–99); the little estuary of **Ducktrap,** once a famous hunting and fishing spot, today gives its name to superb smoked fish, seafood, and pâtés.

■ BELFAST *map page 127, A-1/2*

Knox County, with its pockets of wealth in places like Camden and Rockport, gives way, as you drive north, to Waldo County, once one of the poorest places in the state but growing faster than any other county. A case in point is the town of Belfast, which, thanks to the move up the coast of Camden's credit-card company, has had a wave of prosperity that is putting new life into the handsome Victorian downtown and its streets of superb Greek Revival sea captains' houses. It is well worth a visit, if only to fantasize over the real-estate ads or support its growing arts community. A walk down Main Street toward the waterfront will bring you to six galleries collectively called **Belfast Art;** it will certainly give you a feeling for the lively town. There might be a play on at the Belfast Maskers Waterfront Theater or a movie at the Colonial Theater. **The Clown,** a brand-new wine shop on Main Street, holds frequent tastings and also sells delicacies, fancy olive oils, ceramics, and some antiques. Two restored mansions, the **Alden House** and, just down the street, the **White House,** offer luxurious B&B accommodations at prices lower than those in neighboring Camden. **The Belfast Historical Society** (10 Market Street, 207-338-9229; belfastmus@yahoo.com) has recently started a "history out-doors" program, with architectural tours.

Leaving Belfast going north, you'll cross the Passagassawakeag River, and just over the bridge, come to **Perry's Tropical Nut House,** a landmark since the 1920s. It's a tourist trinket shop so filled with tchochkes and nuts that it tran-scends the genre.

■ SEARSPORT *map page 127, A-1*

Searsport is an under-appreciated town, and certainly a much quieter one than in the 19th century when some 600 sea captains lived here and the town's 17 ship-yards launched some 200 vessels. In 1850 a fourth of Searsport's population was in the maritime trade, which brought enormous bounty, both in artifacts and money, and made the town a very cosmopolitan place. Today it is the second-biggest shipping port in the state, and its modern prosperity is reflected down-town in an art gallery, bookstore, coffee shop, updated grocery store, and a boutique or two. The downtown is only a few blocks long; many of the large old Greek Revival and Victorian houses along Route 1 are bed-and-breakfasts, inter-spersed with antiques, flea markets, and malls. In one old farmhouse behind a tall hedge of evergreens, just across Route 1 from the Irving station, is the **Rhumb Line,** whose chef-owners use their considerable culinary imagination, tastes, and skills to good effect.

Above all, Searsport is known for its **Penobscot Marine Museum** (on Church Street at Route 1; 207-548-2529), which is older than the maritime museum in Bath, and stresses, instead of shipbuilding, the maritime trade and the lives of its

Wayne Canning unloads lobster traps in Belfast.

participants. The exhibits are divided among half a dozen historic buildings, including two captains' houses, and they do an especially fine job of explaining the history and ecology of Penobscot Bay. The museum has an important collection of marine paintings—including three rooms of Buttersworths, father and son. Boats displayed include wonderful North Haven peapods, a Herreshoff sloop that sailed Penobscot Bay, and even a smelt scow. Among the antique photos on view are scenes of domestic life at sea (including chickens roaming the deck), a reminder that many Maine captains took their families on their lengthy voyages.

About 10 miles north of Searsport, Route 1 offers one of Maine's most spectacular highway views: the "gorge" where the Penobscot makes a near right angle below the battlements of Fort Knox (begun in 1844 to defend against the possibility of an invasion from Canada). Nestled on the opposite riverbank, the small town of **Bucksport** would be the perfect locale for a David Lynch movie: innocent, with 19th-century houses and churches, green hills, and a majestically flowing river. Then you turn the corner and see the huge, steamy paper mill dominating the upper reaches of the riverbank. Closer examination of the town reveals the mysterious grave of Col. Jonathan Buck, the town's 18th-century patron. According to local legend, Buck presided over the condemnation of a local woman as a witch (this is quite a legend: no one was ever executed in Maine for witchcraft). On the scaffold she cursed him, saying she would yet dance on his grave, and to this day the shape of a leg and foot appears on the side of his granite obelisk.

The road to **Winterport,** Route 1A, on the west side of the river, crosses some grassy marshes, with Mount Waldo in the background. Winterport's 1831–32 **Union Meetinghouse** is a vigorous example of what Greek Revival church architecture could do on the right site. **Hampden,** birthplace of the reformer Dorothea Dix, is now a historic bedroom community for Bangor; **Brewer,** on the river's right bank, is the birthplace of Civil War hero Joshua Chamberlain.

■ BANGOR: QUEEN CITY *map page 209, C-5*

Not too many years ago a German tourist whose English was at best shaky booked an air flight to San Francisco on a plane that made a refueling and customs stop at Bangor's modest but international airport. Suffering a little jet lag, the German visitor got off the plane and headed downtown. He found a place

Bangor has for years been the center of the lumber trade and gateway to the North Woods.

GROWING OLD ON EAST PENOBSCOT BAY

I have become a member of a very small communion of Episcopalians who meet for services in the American Legion Hall in Blue Hill. Most of them are sturdy, healthy retirees, professionals who have left cities all over the country and moved to this peninsula to live out their lives. There is not a black, Hispanic, or Oriental face among them. Throughout this homogeneous church, the thirty or so families have become friends as well as parishioners. After Sunday-morning Eucharistic service, they stay to have coffee and cakes and to talk about the "outreach" programs many of them engage in. One works in an old people's home on Saturdays, another is active in a program to build houses for homeless families, one is concerned with helping Hancock's adult illiterates learn to read. On the whole, they are well-to-do and extremely active. I am of the belief that Maine residents live a long time because, unlike Florida retirees, they rarely sit down. They walk, sail, garden, shop, go to the library, the post office, the bookstore, visit and assist their friends, go to restaurants, movies, concerts, lectures, classes in crafts. Yesterday I heard a neighbor talking about a friend in Camden who had died, "prematurely," she said. Turned out the gentleman was eighty-one. Not to reach ninety up here is regarded as a disappointing act of carelessness or accident. The slogan here seems to be the old German saw *Rast ich, so rost ich*. When I rest, I rust.

–Doris Grumbach, *Coming into the End Zone*, 1991

to stay and was able to point to things on the menu and for several days happily wandered through the city—under the impression that he was in San Francisco. Promoters of Bangor love to tell this (true) story; when his mistake was revealed and widely publicized, he was treated as a visiting dignitary. Not every visitor may be that immediately enamored of Bangor, but the town is an important place historically—the self-styled "Queen City" of Maine's 19th-century lumber trade—and it continues to be the metropolitan center of northern and eastern Maine and even parts of eastern Canada.

Bangor may be best known today as the home of Stephen King, the thriller author whose bat-winged wrought-iron fence and Victorian lumber baron's house on West Broadway have been frequently photographed. Mr. King and his wife Tabitha are generous participants in their community; their involvement is evident in the newly renovated library downtown, in the pediatric facilities at the regional hospital on State Street, and in the spiffiest Little League field in the state. One word of caution: if you happen to see the writer lunching at a downtown restaurant or strolling the streets, do as the rest of Bangor does and leave him to it; he likes his privacy.

Much of Bangor's historic redbrick commercial district by the river was leveled by ill-considered "urban renewal" in the 1960s (about a decade before cities realized how such districts could be boutiqued and gentrified), though many splendid Victorian-era residences remain up the hill. The **Bangor Museum and Center for History** (6 State Street; 207-942-1900) concentrates on the city's history and culture, and also runs a 19th-century house museum, along with an overview bus tour and several walking tours. The **Penobscot Theatre**, at 131 Main Street (207-942-3333; www.penobscottheatre.org) puts on a sophisticated program September through May and runs two-week acting camps in the summer. The best place to see modern Bangor, though, is amid the sprawling acres of new buildings—office parks, mini-malls, franchise restaurants—out by the gigantic Bangor Mall (which is a social as well as commercial hub for much of northern Maine). If the summer retreats of Penobscot Bay are the version of an idealized Maine we are most accustomed to, here is the new Maine, and a harbinger of the future elsewhere in the state. It is all low, clean, orderly, spread out, relentlessly upbeat, and well heated indoors. And you'll drive, not walk, to get there.

■ EAST PENOBSCOT BAY *map page 127, B-1 to 3*

You perhaps should tour as far north as **Orono,** site of the University of Maine and its wonderful museums, and **Old Town,** home of the Penobscot Indian Nation (www.old-town.org) and the Wabanaki Arts Center Gallery (opposite the Old Town Canoe outlet; 207-827-0391). Stop first at the fascinating **Orono Bog Boardwalk** in Bangor and Orono (www.oronobogwalk.org) to take the mile-long loop trail through the bog.

Now you'll probably want to head south to the coast again; from Bangor take Route 15 along the east side of the river. Between Penobscot and Blue Hill bays lies a modern sort of Norumbega, a collection of villages and fields and islands as mythologized by 19th- and 20th-century writers and artists as the fabled Tierra de Nurumberg was by 16th-century mapmakers and explorers. The picturesque **Blue Hill Peninsula** has been celebrated by enthralled novelists, poets, and essayists who have lived in Brooklin, Blue Hill, Castine, and Deer Isle.

■ **BROOKLIN** *map page 127, C-1/2*

In 1933, *New Yorker* writer E. B. White came to North Brooklin and bought a Federal-period house complete with 40 acres of farmland and the barn that would eventually inspire *Charlotte's Web*. During the 1940s and 1950s White created a vision of Maine as a more perfect place than the rest of the troubled United States—provincial, slow-moving, set in its ways, to be sure, but gentle, thoughtful, decent, and eminently admirable. As idealized as this image might seem, White, a thoroughly sophisticated and deeply urban man, wanted to believe it, as did thousands of people who read his inimitable prose and shared his bucolic longings. All over his part of the country live newcomers, many of them retired from noisier places, who may have chosen to end their days on the Maine coast because they once read sentences like this one: "And when . . . I dip down across the Narramissic and look back at the tiny town of Orland, the white spire of its church against the pale-red sky stirs me in a way that Chartres could never do." White lived there year-round from 1938 to 1943, then retired to the farm for good in 1957. The author once described to a friend the "certain bleak, hard-bitten character which the sea gives to the land":

> Our woodlot is full of hemlock, spruce, birch, juniper, and all the aromatic sweetness of a Maine pasture; yet it dips right down to the tideflats, where gulls scream their heads off and hair-seals bark like old love-sick terriers. . . . Many days are startlingly clear and blue, many are thick a-fog. The fog shuts in fast, catching you short when you are sailing. It settles like a cloud down around the Hackmatack swamp and the frog pond, and makes the earth mysterious and enticing.

North Brooklin was also the home of Katharine White, though it seems at times she missed New York and the literary world in ways that her husband did not. Best known to her contemporaries as fiction editor of the *New Yorker*, she surprised many of them in 1958 with a book-review column under the subhead "Onward and Upward in the Garden"—a review of the spring's new garden catalogues and the first of 14 such columns she was to write over 12 years. In part to assuage her loneliness in Maine, she joined a long line of people who had struggled with the Maine climate, the salt spray, the slugs, the deer, and all the other hazards of the field to make their particular desert bloom. In illness and old age she did not stop.

In his loving introduction to the 1979 compilation of her columns, *Onward and Upward in the Garden,* E. B. White recalled his late wife's persistence in planting spring bulbs:

> As the years went by and age overtook her, there was something comical yet touching in her bedraggled appearance on this awesome occasion—the small, hunched-over figure, her studied absorption in the implausible notion that there would be yet another spring, oblivious to the ending of her own days, which she knew perfectly well was near at hand, sitting there with her detailed chart under those dark skies in the dying October, calmly plotting the resurrection.

Those wishing to make a pilgrimage to the Whites' North Brooklin should note that while the original Norumbega was an imaginary city that appeared on many maps, North Brooklin is a real town that does not. The community can be found, however, northeast of Brooklin on Route 175, and White's white-clapboard house, with shingled attached barn and neat outbuildings, is privately owned (but you can see it from the road).

As well as their writing, E. B. and Katharine White left another legacy. Their son, the late Joel White, was an M.I.T.-trained naval architect who specialized in designing, building, and writing about wooden boats. Indicative of his impact on the local culture is a sign, only half-kidding, on the side of the road as you enter Brooklin from Blue Hill: "Welcome to Brooklin, Boat Building Capital of the World." Joel's company, the **Brooklin Boat Yard,** is now owned by his son Steve, and sits at the head of Center Harbor, where you can find the most stellar collection of wooden sailing craft on the coast of Maine. On the first Saturday of August, the annual Eggemoggin Reach Regatta attracts sailors and sailboats from all down the East Coast, and the waterfront is packed with more than 100 wooden vintage and classic yachts. When the reach is not socked in with fog, the sight of these beauties—under full sail as they race to the finish line—is breathtaking, something out of another era. In addition to founding the boatyard, Joel persuaded *WoodenBoat Magazine* (209-359-4651) to locate in Brooklin, in an old mansion on Naskeag Road. (Look for the magazine's sign on the right as you head down from the Brooklin General Store toward Naskeag Point.) With its residential summer boatbuilding and sailing school and its catalogue store, the magazine is something of a magnet for wooden boat enthusiasts.

■ BLUE HILL *map page 127, B/C-2*

The Reverend Jonathan Fisher, a country parson in nearby Blue Hill (north a few miles on Route 175) from 1796 until his death in 1847, brought to this remote part of coastal Maine an essentially 18th-century conviction that a well-educated man (Harvard, class of 1792) could do just about anything he set his mind to. In 1814 he built, largely with his own hands, the house that stands today as the **Jonathan Fisher House,** Route 15 in Blue Hill. At five each morning, Fisher read his Hebrew Bible before giving lessons in Latin and Greek to young men. In the 1840s the tutor founded the Blue Hill Academy, which in 1898 merged with the **George Stevens Academy,** founded in 1803 by Baptist George Stevens; it is now one of Blue Hill's 75 buildings on the National Register.

Fisher was also a poet, wood-engraver, amateur scientist, farmer, furniture maker, and artist; his paintings appear in the house and at the Farnsworth Museum in Rockland. He was paid and, in his later years, unable to keep some members of his Congregationalist parish from straying into less respectable (yet more emotionally satisfying) denominations.

Fisher's parishioners hoped, of course, that Blue Hill and its harbor would become a thriving commercial center. Today almost everyone is glad it didn't. The blueberry-covered hill that stands behind the village (and for which it was named) is still a relaxing place to stroll—a delicious experience come August, during blueberry season. To climb to the top, well worth it for the view, look for the wooden posts that mark the beginning of the trail on Mountain Road. You can also refresh your soul at **Kneisel Hall**'s summer chamber-music concert series, put on by faculty, guest artists, and students at the music school that takes place there from June through August. The town may be best known for the craftsmanship of its potters, many of whom use unusual local glazes; you may be familiar with the wares of **Rowantrees** on Union Street and **Rackcliffe Pottery** on Route 172, but you can find small art potters here whose work is so impressive it's being sought by museums.

The **Blue Hill Inn** (1830), a restored blacksmith's house on a quiet street across from George Stevens Academy on Route 177, has 12 antiques-filled guest rooms. Creative fine dining can be found around the corner at **Arborvine,** in a renovated 1832 Cape, and at **The Vinery,** a bistro and piano bar in the same building. For a rural experience, **Blue Hill Farm Country Inn** on Route 15 offers 14 guest rooms on 48 acres.

Local shops in mellow Blue Hill.

■ CASTINE *map page 127, B-2*

About 12 miles west of Blue Hill is the town of Castine, which occupies a small peninsula connected to the Blue Hill Peninsula by a narrow neck. Who knows which is the more perfect Maine village, Blue Hill or Castine? Both places have a lot going for them: white Federal houses, soaring church steeples overlooking green lawns and blue water, and storefronts that look like old *New Yorker* covers. It would be hard to find a more placid and restful spot than either one on the Maine coast—it also helps that both towns are far off U.S. 1. Castine has by far the more colorful history. Battled over by the English, French, and Dutch in the 17th century, the town was named for the Baron de St. Castin, the young Frenchman who, after marrying a Penobscot princess, became a sort of feudal lord and Indian chief over Maine's eastern coast. In the Revolution, the town was so Tory that it welcomed the redcoats and the construction of **Fort George** on the town's highest point—even the 1,400 troops and marines sent by Massachusetts could not drive them out, and the Americans suffered the worst naval defeat in U.S. history. The British returned during the War of 1812, occupying for eight months Fort George and a number of houses in town; today, panels on posts around town detail events from the last four centuries. A walking-tour guide, available at any shop or inn, will also lead you through the local high points. At the **Maine Maritime Academy**, on the site of the British barracks (207-326-4311), you can use the gym and pool for a small fee.

If Blue Hill has Parson Fisher's artistic legacy, then Castine wins the literary honors. Robert Lowell inherited his cousin Harriet Winslow's house on South Street and summered there with his second wife, Elizabeth Hardwick, through the 1950s and 1960s; Mary McCarthy spent much of the last part of her life there; and the poet Philip Booth continues to live in a large house on upper Main Street. Several important Lowell poems including "Skunk Hour" and portions of *Near the Ocean* have Castine settings, as do Booth's "This Day After Yesterday" (an elegy on Lowell), "Thinking About Hannah Arendt," and "Mary's, After Dinner." While communing with writerly spirits past and present, you'll find several pleasant places to sleep and dine in this historic town: on Main Street there's the late Victorian **Castine Inn**, a B&B with large airy rooms; and the **Pentagoet Inn**, a turreted Victorian with cozy rooms and a popular restaurant; just off Battle Avenue is **The Manor,** a stately summer home on five acres.

To go south from Castine you must first go north around Northern Bay, and then at North Brooksville, if you choose to take Route 176 West, you can visit **Cape Rosier**, the home of one formerly urban couple who managed to set up a truly alternative way of life. The late Helen and Scott Nearing turned their house "Harborside" on Cape Rosier into a center of the rural homesteading movement and a witness to what they called, in the title of their best-known book, *Living the Good Life*. In his youth a controversial radical—he was fired as an economics professor by the University of Pennsylvania for having accused a rich trustee of exploiting child labor—Scott Nearing "dropped out" in the 1930s to try homesteading on a derelict Vermont farm. Their self-sufficiency, their reverence for music and art, and their Tolstoyan devotion to physical labor were greatly admired by the many people who came to pay the Nearings homage. Whatever their politics, they lived the lives of hardworking, old-fashioned Yankees, extremely rational and self-denying. Despite the success of the maple-sugaring business they ran on the Vermont farm, the Nearings were unable to fend off encroaching ski resorts and condo development. They sold out in the 1970s and came to Cape Rosier, where they turned to blueberries for their cash crop. Scott died at the age of 100, and Helen died a few years later. Their house continues, under the auspices of their foundation, to be a beacon on Penobscot Bay for admirers of their philosophy.

■ DEER ISLE *map page 127, B-2/3*

From Cape Rosier, the road takes you east toward and past Brooksville onto the suspension bridge over the Eggemoggin Reach to **Little Deer Isle** and then by causeway to **Deer Isle,** a place teeming with artists. Its eastern tip is home to the internationally known **Haystack Mountain School of Crafts** (end of the Sunshine Road; 207-348-2306; www.haystack-mtn.org), which runs two-week courses in 40 artistic disciplines throughout the summer and opens for tours every Wednesday. At Deer Isle's southern tip the fishing town of **Stonington** faces the sea, looking back on its boom days as a granite quarrying center. Today its restored **Opera House**, which is on the National Register of Historic Places (207-367-2788; www.operahousearts.org), draws people to play readings, movies, musicals, concerts, and Shakespeare. Boats depart from here to **Isle au Haut** (pronounced "I'll a hoe") and its section of Acadia National Park.

MOUNT DESERT ISLAND

One Fourth of July a few years ago, I hiked with two friends up the southern face of Cadillac Mountain, the island's tallest mountain. Starting at the trail just beyond Otter Creek, near the Blackwoods Campground, we steadily made our way up the 1,530-foot lump of pinkish granite, pausing at those occasional spots where the trail leveled out for a few yards, allowing us to turn around and see where we had been. Mount Desert (pronounced like "dessert") and Sutton Island glistened in the sunlight; The Eastern Way, the gray-green Cranberry Islands, the Baker Island lighthouse, and a broad expanse of Atlantic Ocean lay before us. Seabirds swooped below. The wake of tiny boats scratched the surface of the water. As we climbed, the tree cover at Cadillac's base gave way to blueberry-scrub, which dwindled until the glacier-marked rocks were bare of all but their crinkled lichens. This was the balding peak that French explorer Samuel de Champlain had seen from his ship 400 years earlier. What an extraordinary place to observe the nation's birthday, to rediscover an entire world as fresh and unviolated as the continent the first Europeans found.

As we neared the summit of Cadillac—named for another French explorer—a metamorphosis took place, startling even for an island whose weather is notoriously changeable and whose landscape shifts from hour to hour with the sun, wind, and fog. A phalanx of tour buses, hissing diesel, waited among many other vehicles at the top, spilling out people who, after a quick look from the designated viewpoints, crowded into the gift shop before returning to Bar Harbor. We entered this cloud of tourists, paused again to admire the view, and descended into the deep ravine that separates Cadillac from Dorr Mountain. A few minutes later the people and their buses were out of sight; soon they were out of hearing as well. On a steep, rocky face of granite we found a ledge, sunny but sheltered from the wind, where we unpacked our holiday lunch: sandwiches of local crabmeat, beer, and *tarte tatin* (an unwitting gesture of appreciation, I suppose, for the French role in securing our Independence).

Sunset in Bar Harbor.

That Fourth of July remains so strongly in my memory because it unexpectedly offered, within a few hours' walk, the essence of Mount Desert Island. This 100 square miles, Maine's largest island, is a place that has been ill-used by some but cherished by others, including that second mountain's namesake, George Dorr, the conservationist who, early in the 20th century, helped found Acadia National Park. Acadia is full of people, cars, and gift shops, but it is also, despite its millions of visitors each summer, an island of secluded glens and little-walked trails, of real fishing villages and even a few surviving farms. People are everywhere, but you can escape them easily. A century ago the name of the island's leading town—Bar Harbor—was synonymous with ostentatious wealth and shameless snobbery. The island still attracts the rich, from the comfortably affluent to the downright famous, at least some of whom now stay year-round. It is also one of the East Coast's most popular family resorts, whether you drive over from Bangor for the day or come from New Jersey to camp out in the Winnebago for a week. Democracy arrived on Mount Desert, not as local legend would have it, with the terrible forest fire of 1947, which swept away many of the huge wooden hotels and extravagant "cottages," but with the ending of the gas crisis of the mid 1970s, when the nation took once again to the highways in its campers and cars.

■ ISLAND HISTORY

In 1604 Samuel de Champlain discovered the island—or more accurately, ran aground on it. Champlain dubbed it the *Ile des Monts Deserts*—"Island of Bare Mountains"—none of them very tall even by Appalachian standards, yet *tout ensemble* a magnificent sight from the water. When the first French settlers arrived they encountered and later traded with Wabanaki Indians, who gathered shellfish on "Pemetic" (their term for the island) but lived on the mainland. French settlers traded with Indians on the island; in the 18th century, they used the island's harbors to hide their ships during the French and Indian War. After the British victory in Canada in 1760, English colonists were able to settle here.

By the mid-19th century the island had begun hosting summer residents; in 1858 the yachtsman-journalist Robert Carter commented on the growing number of "sea-side summer loungers" that M.D.I. was attracting. Over the next few decades the island became the scene of conflict over the degree to which nature should be tampered with. Carter himself believed the island needed the "hand of cultivated taste." Given the island's "mighty cliffs and sombre ravines and multitudinous ocean beaches," he noted, "it is impossible to conceive of any finer field for the exercise of the highest genius of the landscape gardener."

Carter had put his finger on a problem that was to animate luncheon conversation in summer cottages for the next generation: could—should—nature be improved? Did one approach the forest in a spirit of devotion, accepting as right whatever had naturally appeared there? Or did one treat nature with a gentle but firm hand, as if it were a willful child? When Percy Clark, for example, came to Northeast Harbor in search of a summer retreat in the early 1900s, he relished the wildness of the place and the physical challenges it offered the hiker and canoeist; the most that he and like-minded friends wished to interfere with the landscape was to lay out unobtrusive footpaths in the hills behind the village. Yet the very act of building rambling cottages along the shore had inevitably changed the balance of man and nature on Mount Desert Island.

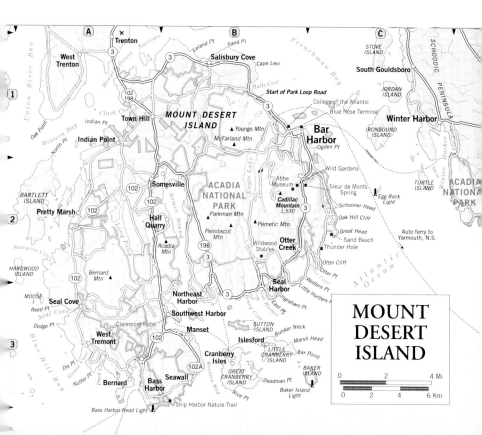

MOUNT
DESERT
ISLAND

■ NATIONAL PARK AND CARRIAGE ROADS

One person who realized this was oil heir John D. Rockefeller Jr., a summer resident of nearby Seal Harbor. Rockefeller helped George Dorr and Harvard University president Charles W. Eliot assemble pieces of land in the area—all donated by private citizens—and handed them over to the federal government. In 1916 that land became **Acadia National Park,** the first national park east of the Mississippi. Meanwhile, between 1913 and 1940 Rockefeller designed and built 57 miles of carriage roads on Mount Desert Island, some of them on his own land, others on publicly owned property. (About two-thirds, but not all, of M.D.I. is national park land.) Reserved then as now for hikers, equestrians, and horse-drawn carriages, they offered the best way, it seemed to him, to allow the public to discover and appreciate some of the island's otherwise hidden places.

Percy Clark and others were deeply offended. They saw Rockefeller as a "spoiler of the wild," for the carriage roads had opened up parts of the island's interior that had previously been the domain of the solitary hiker. Clark agreed with naturalists like John Muir and John Burroughs that nature ought to be kept pristine. Rockefeller disagreed, preferring the view of Gifford Pinchot, the first director of the National Park Service, that people could be trusted to treat nature gently. Ann R. Roberts, the granddaughter of both Clark and Rockefeller, writes in her 1990 book on Acadia—*Mr. Rockefeller's Roads: The Untold Story of Acadia's Carriage Roads & Their Creator*—that the dispute "reflected a deep division in approach to conservation, one that persists to this day."

Ironically, the roads may have helped save the park's wild lands in several respects. For example, during the great fire of 1947 that burned some of the island's loveliest scenery, the roads aided enormously in containing the fire. On a day-to-day basis, they probably curtail much potential damage to the environment by controlling and channeling the way people penetrate the park's more remote sectors. More than 80 percent of the park's visitors today walk on Rockefeller's trails and carriage roads; others cycle, or ride horses or carriages on them (from the **Wildwood Stables** near Jordan Pond). In winter they are popular routes for cross-country skiing and snowshoeing.

A national park road snakes through fall foliage along Jordan Pond.
(following pages) Bicyclists ride along one of many carriage roads that traverse Acadia National Park.

Otter Point in Acadia National Park on Mount Desert Island.

The network of carriage roads is distinctive in three ways. Although not always invisible on the landscape, the roads are carefully graded and their edges planted or terraced in ways that enable them to blend into the scenery. Rockefeller personally spent a great deal of time laying them out to open up vistas of the island's lakes and mountains that would otherwise be inaccessible to the casual visitor. And while the design of the various bridges and edgings is subtly varied, the roads are built of local stone (often the distinctive lichen-covered, pink Mount Desert granite) in a way that makes even the most elaborate of them seem always to have been there. As a design phenomenon, the complex system is unique to Acadia National Park and, though rarely studied, is surely one of the country's greatest achievements in landscape architecture in the 20th century.

Unfortunately, the system is showing its age, and the hard-pressed National Park Service does not have the money to restore the shifting stonework or eroding surfaces. It is a tribute to the importance of the carriage roads to the Acadia experience, however, that private groups, such as the Friends of Acadia and the Olmsted Alliance, are coming forth with the donations and the volunteer labor needed to ensure that this part of Rockefeller's legacy can be enjoyed by another generation.

■ GETTING TO MOUNT DESERT

There are several ways to approach the island. If you can manage it, come by boat. To see the Mount Desert Range from a few miles out in the Atlantic is one of the great American experiences. It is like the first time you see a whale close at hand. There is something so improbable, yet absolutely right about it, that you can find yourself in tears at the sheer beauty of the sight. (Without your own boat, you can experience something of this effect by taking one of the nature cruises offered in these waters, or perhaps the mail boat that chugs from Northeast Harbor to the Cranberries.) In the days of Bar Harbor's social glory, the approach was from the other side of the island: the overnight express train from Washington or New York delivered you and your servants early in the morning at **Hancock Point,** on the mainland, and a little steamer transported you across Frenchman Bay.

Today most people arrive by car over the bridge at **Trenton.** If you travel that way, the previous half hour possibly spent crawling through the commercial sprawl on the Ellsworth "strip" can be a troubling one. And the 10 miles of Route 3 from Ellsworth through Trenton, though still through some farmland and woods, is marred by several children's entertainment parks. But in the distance the blue hills of Mount Desert beckon you onward.

First you'll come to the **Thompson Island Information Center** (on a little piece, slightly detached, of the big island), where you can get both park and commercial information, and use hot-line phones (for direct reservations). Then you must make a decision: follow Route 3 into Bar Harbor, or continue on Route 102 toward the less busy part of M.D.I.

If you drive toward Bar Harbor, you see almost immediately the Bar Harbor branch of the **Mount Desert Oceanarium** (207-288-5005). Then you pass through **Hulls Cove,** whose cemetery holds the remains of the woman who once owned half the island. In 1688 Louis XIV granted all of M.D.I. to an officer named Antoine de la Mothe Cadillac. He never set foot on his island—he was busy settling Detroit—but his emigré granddaughter a century later pursued her claim and in 1786 persuaded the authorities in Boston to grant her the eastern half of Mount Desert (a letter from Lafayette is said to have helped). This Madame de Gregoire settled at Hulls Cove, where she died in straitened circumstances in 1811, a naturalized citizen who was also a final link in France's claim to this part of North America. Also at Hulls Cove is Acadia National Park's visitors center and the beginning of the **Park Loop Road,** a 20-mile circuit of some of the island's most spectacular scenery, including Cadillac Mountain. On the northern edge of

Bar Harbor you come to the Blue Nose Ferry Terminal, with its frequent service to Nova Scotia, and the small, bayfront **College of the Atlantic,** a center for environmental studies. The fast-moving 1947 fire stopped at Eden Street (Route 3 at this point), and the college campus incorporates several former estates on the water that escaped the fate of their neighbors up the hill. The most imposing of these, a château-like pile known as **The Turrets,** houses the college's **Natural History Museum.** This is one place where you can experience, at least spatially, what the cottage era was like, and the terrace offers a splendid vista of Bar Island and the bay.

■ **BAR HARBOR** *map page 149, B-1*

Henry James, returning to the United States after many years in England, declared upon visiting Palm Beach that it was a "hotel civilization." Bar Harbor presents a *motel* civilization, an effect amplified by the way the hostelries hang from the hillsides as you enter town on the poignantly named Eden Street. For the first century of its existence, however, Bar Harbor literally was the Town of Eden, a small fishing and farming community, the only remnant of which is the town cemetery with its Civil War monument. The post–Civil War years brought the sprawling wooden hotels, which became so popular with fashionable rusticators that they grew and grew, one of them covering most of what is now the Village Green. (Another was built on top of nearby Cadillac Mountain, reached in those days by cog rail; both hotel and train disappeared when the summit became national park land.)

The era of the hotels (1865 to 1885) was soon succeeded by that of the private "cottages," as beneficiaries of the country's great industrial fortunes arrived and began competing for status with their fellows. This was Bar Harbor's golden age, from the late 1880s to World War I, when J. P. Morgan's yacht *Corsair* was moored in the harbor, and the famous Mrs. Stotesbury of Philadelphia regularly entertained 40 at lunch in her palace by the sea. The less ostentatious of these cottages were constructed, sometimes quite fancifully, in the Shingle Style, which is now recognized as one of America's most pleasing contributions to vernacular architecture. The most ponderous of them were melanges of every European style. Some summer residents tried to transform the landscape by sculpting Bar Harbor's hillsides into Italianate terraces and gardens. Today, on the overgrown sites of estates destroyed in the 1947 fire you find traces of these elaborate schemes, in bits and pieces of wall and cyclopean blocks of dressed granite.

Remembering his childhood summers in Bar Harbor in the 1920s, the novelist Louis Auchincloss wrote of the "silly side" of fashionable life there and of his early realization that the summer colony's "big houses, their shining cars, tering yachts were designed to impress just such onlookers as myself. As recalled in *A Writer's Capital,* his Old New York parents were immune to this spectacle, even if their child was not: "Strong in their own innate decency, in their own high moral standards, they saw no reason why they could not live out a pastoral idyll in the very heart of Sodom or Gomorrah." Bar Harbor was still an idyllic place through the 1970s, despite the post-conflagration appearance of barracks-like motels and the slow erosion of the town's social cachet. It was not really until the 1980s that everyone realized that the place had turned into Lobsterland U.S.A. Some wailed and gnashed their teeth, others raked in the cash from the tourist herds.

Bar Harbor has received some bad press, "tacky" being one of the kinder adjectives used. Actually, the place is not that bad, especially outside the Fourth of July to Labor Day crush. The setting is still remarkable—the mussel-encrusted sandbar that allows you to walk at low tide across the inner harbor to Bar Island, the bristly-looking Porcupine Islands farther out in Frenchman Bay, the mountains standing like sentries along the southern flank of the town. And amid the modern clutter there are some survivors of an earlier day: **Butterfield's Market,** for example, with its air of the carriage-trade era; the **Bar Harbor Historical Society** (207-288-3807), housed in a former convent that's on the National Register and filled with photos and other memorabilia of the town's golden age and of the great fire; and the **Reading Room** (now the lobby and dining room of the **Bar Harbor Inn),** formerly the scene of much genteel tippling. One year-round pleasure survives from about 1880: the **Shore Path**, which runs south from the municipal pier for nearly a mile along the water's edge. It connects from time to time to residential streets, then back to Main Street, and is open dawn to dusk—no bikes allowed. At the Bar Harbor branch of the **Abbe Museum,** you can learn about pre-European life on the island, the Red Paint People, the contact experience of natives and Europeans, and such traditional crafts as bark-and-quill basketry.

Bar Harbor still offers the greatest range of places to sleep, eat, and shop while visiting Acadia National Park. It appears that almost every private house with more than two bedrooms has been converted into a bed-and-breakfast—but this at least assures an alternative to the more anonymous motels. (The hazard lurking in B&Bs is having to talk to people at breakfast.) The town also has more to offer you if you're here out of season; cross-country skiing on the park's carriage roads has been increasingly

(following pages) Despite Bar Harbor's reputation, the harbor itself still retains a scenic charm.

popular, for example, and as more innkeepers discover that they will entice more city dwellers to pay to sip mulled cider in front of a log fire on winter weekends.

Two on the list of local lodgings offer first-rate dining rooms as well as luxurious rooms. The **Bar Harbor Hotel–Bluenose Inn,** perched on the cliff above Eden Street, has the acclaimed **Rose Garden Restaurant,** as well as unimpeded views of Frenchman Bay and the Porcupine Islands. The intimate **Ivy Manor Inn,** a renovated French Tudor–style mansion in the middle of town, has a restaurant, **Michelle's,** that has earned rave reviews from the start. **The Tides,** a B&B reminiscent of old days in the Deep South, has a wide covered porch furnished as a living room (complete with fireplace) and open to the ocean view. A fine dinner can be had at the **Thrumcap,** on Cottage Street, and at **Havana,** on Main Street, both of which have imaginative menus a cut above the usual. The bookstore side of **Sherman's** is one of the island's cultural centers; the Art Deco **Criterion Theatre** is a good place to spend a rainy afternoon. Amid the tourist emporia on Main Street two stores stand out: **85 Main Street,** good for upscale souvenirs and resort wear; and **Island Artisans,** a cooperative selling the work of local craftspeople. The outskirts of Bar Harbor are still rural, thanks to the fact that the town is surrounded by national park land.

In an effort to reduce traffic on the island without discouraging visitors, the Friends of Acadia, the National Park Service, and the business community initiated seasonal free shuttle service. The **Island Explorer** (207-288-4573) serves Southwest Harbor, Northeast Harbor, Bass Harbor, the Hancock County/Bar Harbor Airport, some of the Schoodic Peninsula, and various points within the park (transport only; it is not a tour bus).

Leaving Bar Harbor on Route 3 South, you pass the **Jackson Laboratory** (call 207-288-3371 to arrange a free visit), an internationally renowned center for genetic research, which breeds genetically pure mice and sells them worldwide. Soon you reach **Sieur de Monts Spring,** where the **Wild Gardens of Acadia** (207-288-3338) maintain a botanical collection of native plants, demonstrating 12 habitats, and where you can visit the original **Abbe Museum,** in a 1928 building listed on the National Register of Historic Places. It's devoted to Maine's Native American culture and the history of the museum. Route 3 continues between the mountains to **Otter Creek,** whose cove was painted by Frederick Church in that first wave of rustication a century and a half ago (the actual cove can only be seen from the park loop road). The village itself has a landlocked air, however; its vistas of mountains make you feel you've visited the American West, not Maine.

MAINE'S PALEO-INDIANS

As recently as 18,000 years ago, Maine was covered by a sheet of ice as thick as a mile in some places. This was the last gasp of the Wisconsin Ice Age, and it took 5,000 years for its glaciers to loosen their clutches on Maine. Then, before the land surface could spring back from the weight of so much ice, nearly half the state was inundated by the sea, leaving marine clay deposits north of Bangor.

The prehistory of Maine began another 2,000 years later—about 11,000 years ago—when land surfaces had rebounded from the weight of ice and the sea retreated, establishing a tundra similar to present-day interior Alaska. Then wandering hunters now referred to as Paleo-Indians moved into the area, probably following such big game as caribou, and possibly mammoth, musk-ox, giant bison, and wild horse. They pitched camp on high, dry terraces that offered commanding views of the treeless landscape. These people, apparently well adapted to the cold, traveled long distances to follow game herds, and they carried with them beautifully made stone tools. Among these was the fluted spearpoint, distinguished by the long channel flake removed from its center, which is the hallmark of Paleo-Indian technology. They often crafted their spearpoints of chert, chipping this flint-like rock carefully to reveal its bands of color, usually shades of brown, blue, or red. The use of certain types of chert—types indigenous to New York, Pennsylvania, Vermont, Massachusetts, and northern Maine—indicates the great distances traveled.

The forest environment more familiar to us was established about 9,000 years ago, when a change in climate ushered in the Archaic Period. At their sites along rivers, streams, and lakes, the Archaic People left stone implements: spearheads, net sinkers, and woodworking tools. These artifacts, crafted from the local

Two slate spearpoints and an atlatl weight dating from the Late Archaic Period, about 3,800 to 5,000 years ago.

slate rather than chert, indicate that these hunter-gatherers traveled far less than their forebears. They migrated more narrowly, adapting closely to the local climate and to seasonal changes. Groups of hunter-gatherers moved up and down rivers, along the coast, and sometimes crossed water to off-shore islands. They fished in the spring and fall, when the rivers were filled with migratory species like salmon; hunted moose, caribou, and deer in the fall for their meat and skins; snared small fur-bearing animals; and probably collected a wide variety of seasonal plant foods and shellfish.

Porcupine quill over birchbark box.

During the early part of the 20th century, archaeologists were entranced when they discovered cemeteries of a Late Archaic hunter-gatherer culture along the Penobscot, the Kennebec, and other major rivers. They named the culture the "Red Paint People," for the red iron pyrite powder, or red ochre, that covered the numerous stone tools—probably left as ceremonial offerings—among the gravesite remains. Lacking other data, these archaeologists and their contemporaries romanticized the Red Paint People, describing them as a "vanished civilization" distinct from the Paleo-Indians before and after.

Modern research at living sites associated with the cemeteries reveals a more realistic picture of these people, who lived from 3,800 to 5,000 years ago. We know they hunted and fished, and probably relied on plant and other marine resources in season. At coastal and island archaeological sites, abundant swordfish remains have been found—surprising, since today swordfish are rare in the cold waters of the Gulf of Maine. But 5,000 years ago the climate had reached a post-glacial warming peak and the Gulf may have supported greater numbers. Archaic hunters probably traveled long distances from shore in large dugout boats to harpoon the fish—which can reach 15 feet and weigh nearly a ton—as they sunned themselves at the surface. The meat probably fed many people, and the bones and swords were used to make tools; swordfish bills were sometimes crafted into long daggers decorated with geometric designs.

The Archaic Period ended about 3,000 years ago, when the technology for making clay pots was adopted by Maine's native peoples. During the subsequent era, known as the Ceramic Period, people continued to hunt and gather the local flora and fauna—especially shellfish, as indicated by the many shell middens along the coast of Maine. The famous oyster heaps in Damariscotta, once mined for fertilizer but since preserved, are huge mounds measuring several hundred feet long and thirty feet thick. The piles of shells are conducive to the preservation of bone remains, providing us with detailed information about the variety of food resources during the Ceramic Period: in addition to the shells of softshell clams, mussels, and sea urchins, the mounds also contain the bones of various fish, birds, and mammals. Notable, however, is the absence of lobster shells; there is little evidence they were eaten by prehistoric native Mainers.

One of the earliest contacts between native peoples and European explorers on the shores of Maine took place in 1604–05, when Samuel de Champlain explored the coast and described the Wabanaki, meaning "Dawnlanders," in his journals. Beginning in the early 17th century, Indian tribes began losing their lands in a series of agreements that European explorers and settlers made and quickly broke. By the mid-18th century, the Wabanaki got caught in the middle of a conflict between European powers and found themselves designated allies of the French crown—and fair game for any British musket. Even after the European conflict ended, the Indians continued both to lose their land and to be wiped out from the diseases the Europeans brought with them. Meanwhile, heavy colonization destroyed much of the natives' resource base. In the latter 1800s a Wabanaki confederacy was formed, but after years of political tribal conflict, the alliance dissolved by the end of the century. Today, descendants of the Wabanaki still reside in Maine. The four federally recognized Indian tribes in Maine are the Penobscots, on Indian Island, Old Town; the Passamaquoddy tribe in Washington County; the Aroostook band of Micmacs in Aroostook County; and the Houlton Band of Maliseet Indians, also in Aroostook County.

–Rebecca Cole-Will, Curator of Archaeology, the Abbe Museum,
Acadia National Park, Mount Desert

■ THE QUIET SIDE

It is a not very well-kept secret that the nicest parts of Mount Desert Island today are on its "back" side: roughly the two-thirds of the island west of Bar Harbor and Park Loop Drive. Visitors who complain that Bar Harbor doesn't look like the quaint Maine fishing village they'd expected should make the half-hour trip to **Bass Harbor**, say, or **Bernard**. These working communities, not quaint in the least, are only lightly touched by tourism. But as they snuggle around their shared harbor, they certainly live up to the image, romantic or not, of the self-contained coastal village. The relatively low-key nature of life on Mount Desert Island's "quiet side," with its mix of fishing and recreational sailing, of "real" Mainers and summer folk, does not quite disguise the fact that hidden down many of those piney drives are some of the richest people in America.

This is perhaps easier to comprehend when the shoreline is seen from a boat; the huge new houses, almost ancient Roman in their opulence, on the high granite cliffs near **Hunters Cove** are as much a monument to the Age of Greenspan as their sprawling Shingle Style ancestors a century earlier were to the Age of Morgan, Gould, and Fiske. The same might be said of the new, quite controversial houses on **Schooner Head**, closer to Bar Harbor. But the authentic Mount Desert style is much more subdued, almost self-deprecating. Driving into Seal Harbor, for example—perhaps stopping at its small pocket beach or hiking to Jordan Pond for tea—you catch only glimpses of summer houses tucked into the woods. Long identified with the Rockefeller family, **Seal Harbor** may seem modest from the road, but its hillsides have magnificent views over the Eastern Way past Sutton Island and the Cranberries and out to sea: the waters celebrated by Samuel Eliot Morison and so many other yachtsmen.

■ NORTHEAST HARBOR   *map page 149, B-3*

Route 3 leads on, suddenly offering a dramatic view of **Northeast Harbor's** narrow, boat-packed anchorage, where in high season the boats may range from the converted lobsterboat that is someone's summer toy to yachts à la the late Malcolm Forbes, complete with helicopter and brace of motorcycles on deck. As you approach the head of the harbor, you come to Asticou Terraces, Thuya Garden and Lodge, designed by Charles Savage. The road turns sharply at the landmark **Asticou Inn,** which commands the head of the harbor, and just past the serene Asticou Azalea Garden (also by Savage) turns again into town.

For so famous a yachting center, the harborfront itself is rather bland, but a short walk uphill brings you to Northeast Harbor's **Main Street,** a very long block of modest yet festive shopfronts. The clapboards may look weathered, and no one really dresses up, but despite their almost exaggerated plainness, these little stores—the market, the fishmonger, Sherman's bookstore's other branch, the florist, the needlepointer, the paper store, the gift shop—have as much cachet in their own way as anything on Worth Avenue or Rodeo Drive. Try Fourteen Carrots, at No. 141, for Maine Indian baskets and elegant, locally woven silk and merino wool shawls. But it is not what they sell, it's who you see shopping there. Northeast Harbor is probably as fashionable an address in summer as any place you could find in North America. The town began as an obscure fishing village, was discovered in the 1870s and 1880s by college presidents and Episcopal bishops, and for much of the 20th century was regarded as a sensible, if slightly dowdy, alternative to the more glamorous Bar Harbor. (The Asticou, a classic Maine hotel, seems to have preserved this quality, like a well-used country club.) After World War II, however, the focus of social life shifted. Today, the grandchildren and great-grandchildren of those early rusticators—many of them having had the good sense to marry into a major industrial fortune—now spend their summers *en toute simplicité* in a part of Maine they have tried (fairly successfully) to keep from ever changing, at least in terms of the way it looks.

In the early 1950s the French writer Marguerite Yourcenar and her life-long friend Grace Frick bought a small farmhouse amid the summer cottages in Northeast Harbor and named it **Petite Plaisance.** For years, few people on the island realized that Yourcenar was one of the greatest French prose stylists of the century—until she made headlines in 1981 as the first woman to be elected to the French Academy. *This house is open mid-June through August; call 207-276-3940.*

■ SOMES SOUND   *map page 149, A/B-2/3*

Northeast Harbor needs to be seen from a boat, but the corniche of Sargent Drive, just to the north, offers remarkable views of one of Mount Desert's most interesting bodies of water, **Somes Sound.** Said to be the only fjord in the Lower 48 (a claim disputed by admirers of the Hudson River), Somes Sound cuts almost all the way through the island. On the opposite shore you can see, at the foot of Acadia Mountain, a stream of water dribbling down the granite—**Man o' War Brook—**

where in Revolutionary times naval vessels took advantage of the deep water of the Sound to funnel fresh water aboard by means of sail cloth. Farther south is **Fernald Point,** today a handsome meadow, and in 1613 the site of St. Sauveur, the first Jesuit settlement in New England. It was quickly destroyed by the English, who buried one of the French priests they killed somewhere on the point. In the words of Francis Parkman—himself an early rusticator on the Sound—"In an obscure stroke of violence began the strife of France and England, Protestantism and Rome, which for a century and a half shook the struggling communities of North America, and closed at last in the memorable Triumph on the Plains of Abraham."

At the head of the Sound today is the remarkably peaceful-looking village of **Somesville,** so picture perfect that people get out of their cars in the middle of the road to photograph the little white footbridge next to the Higgins's antiques store. Somesville is a triumph of the Colonial Revival. For its first century and a half no doubt a scrappy outpost smelling of fish guts and drying cod, from the late 19th century on the village has been re-created and preserved as a reminder of how the country might have looked, with a little care. Admittedly, the location helps. One place to appreciate it is **Port in a Storm** (207-244-4114 or 800-694-4114; www. portinastormbookstore.com), surely the most strikingly situated bookstore in America; the store has a resident eagle, and one day, a few feet from the tiny waterfront parking lot, I saw a loon swimming.

■ **SOUTHWEST HARBOR** *map page 149, B-3*

Driving south from Somes Sound on Route 102 you pass Echo Lake—a good, occasionally even warm, freshwater swimming spot—and soon reach **Southwest Harbor,** the commercial center for the western side of the island. It's a town in perfect balance—working port, Coast Guard base, just enough tourists, a friendly Main Street, a world-famous assortment of boat builders. Out-of-scale condos, however, already loom over part of the harbor. (If one notes that the huge 19th-century wooden hotels were just as obtrusive, the only reply is to ask if we've learned nothing since.)

If you're here in 2005 for Southwest Harbor's 100th anniversary, check out the **Wendell Gilley Museum,** devoted to the works of a local plumber turned famous bird-carver. It's a migratory stop for many birders, and will also interest anyone curious about modern techniques of making buildings energy efficient. In the

Kids fish off a pier in Southwest Harbor.

The Claremont Hotel has long been one of Mount Desert Island's most evocative resorts.

center of town you'll find **Rue Cottage Books** (on the Green; 207-244-5542), a small, cranky shop that shuns technology, avoids efficiency, and sells books to those of a Luddite bent, to paraphrase. On opposite sides of Route 102 are **Sawyer's Market** (207-244-3315) and **Sawyer's Specialties** (207-244-3317). The former, from the street, looks like a mom-and-pop grocery store; on the inside it's a gastronomic landmark: it sells hand-picked vegetables from local farmers, fresh local fish, the succulent local crab clawmeat, superb focaccia from the island's **Little Notch Bread** (which is now also a popular café), and the old-fashioned canned goods— aspic, hearts of palm, Indian pudding, and the like—that used to be found in every summer-house pantry. On Clark's Point, near the Coast Guard station, you can dine outdoors on the day's catch at **Beal's,** in an authentic dockside setting.

Southwest Harbor's most memorable landmark, however, is the vintage **Claremont Hotel** (on the National Register of Historic Places), which has looked out over Somes Sound and Cadillac Mountain for more than a century. It is one of the few wooden hotels in Maine to have survived, and it won't be to everyone's taste: there are no TVs in the rooms, and the furnishings are not the last word in design. But in terms of restful surroundings—the only public excitement comes from its famous croquet tournaments—superb views, good food, human scale, and a lightly worn sense of nostalgia, it cannot be equaled in the state. Actually a complex of old hotel and surrounding cottages, the hotel is usually booked well in advance for much of the summer. But you can always have a drink or lunch down at its boathouse and enjoy the scenery, directly across from Greening Island (private), the locale of May Sarton's novel *The Magnificent Spinster.*

Go to neighboring **Manset** to the **Hinckley Boatyard and Ships' Store** (130 Shore Road; 207-244-5572 or 888-446-2553), to browse through the nautical gear and clothing and see a video on how the dark, sleek yawls and sloops that fill the harbor are made. Continuing on 102A from Manset, you drive around the southern tip of the island, passing the natural barrier at **Seawall**, where the Western Way (a body of water) enters the Great Harbor of Mount Desert, and the **Ship Harbor Nature Trail** (where you can take a short hike). Land ends at the **Bass Harbor Head Light,** after which you can visit the little villages of **Bass Harbor, Tremont,** and **Bernard** (at Bernard, drop in at the tiny, picturesque Family Lighthouse, on Steamboat Wharf Road, which now contains **Island Astronomy** [207-244-9477] and its collection of telescopes). Then you'll rejoin Route 102 to drive up the quiet western side of the island, perhaps stopping at the **Seal Cove Auto Museum** (207-244-9242) to see the antique cars, or at **Pretty Marsh** to hike in good seal-spotting territory.

Mount Desert can also be circumnavigated by small boat but not by sailboat, though getting through the tidal flats near the Trenton Bridge can be tricky even at high tide. For most visitors, a more practical excursion is to take one of the many whale-watching cruises offered from the island or to take the little mail boat that regularly plies the waters between Northeast Harbor's town dock and the islands known as Sutton, Great Cranberry, and Little Cranberry (where the fishing village of Islesford has restaurants and a museum). For the more ambitious, a nature cruise to **Baker Island** and its lighthouse (part of Acadia National Park)—or to the Audubon Society–owned **Duck Islands** about five miles out to sea—offers one of the greatest visual experiences on the North Atlantic coast. Don't look back until you are far offshore. Then turn around and look at Champlain's "Ile des Monts Deserts" rising from the sea, and imagine yourself a passenger on the Frenchman's ship—a man who, as F. Scott Fitzgerald wrote of another explorer, "must have held his breath in the presence of this continent . . . face to face for the last time in history with something commensurate to his capacity to wonder."

D O W N   E A S T

A few miles east of Ellsworth on U.S. 1 you enter another time. The landscape isn't unspoiled, but has an oddly pristine quality you don't associate with other coastal neighborhoods. It seems a place where people had begun to leave their mark— some of it raw and ugly, some slight and unobtrusive—then stopped. It's a bit like the Maine of the 1950s: a simpler, friendlier place, a world without fast food or shopping malls, traffic congestion or urban ills. Much of it is a very poor place— recalling the world of Carolyn Chute's novel *The Beans of Egypt, Maine*—a place that seems not only to have missed the prosperity of the 1990s, but to have never quite recovered from the Great Depression. Nonetheless, the allure of its lakes and coastline and the almost toy-like quality of some of its towns (Steuben, say, with its postage-stamp of a post office and a few old houses and a church) make this east-ernmost corner of Maine especially fascinating. Fall is the best time to visit: the first touch of frost turns the blueberry fields all the shades of red of a Bokhara carpet.

Although some of the region might be seen on a day trip from Bar Harbor, to really appreciate eastern Hancock and Washington counties you'll need at least a few days. Starting at Ellsworth, where many roads converge, going on to Hancock and Sullivan—with their stunning views across Frenchman Bay—and continuing east, you will encounter the series of fishing villages and blueberry towns that represent what "Down East" means today.

■ ELLSWORTH   *map page 173, A-3*

The biggest town for miles around, **Ellsworth** is the region's commercial hub. Routes 1 and 3 enter from the west, and after passing some pleasant old houses, including **Woodlawn**, a historic estate and house museum, they turn south onto the Ellsworth "strip," for which the town has had much bad press—it's no worse than thousands of similar crowded stretches in other states, but it seems more offensive in coastal Maine. A couple of miles along the strip, the road splits: Route 3 becomes the Bar Harbor Road, and you come to the **Stanstead Homestead** and the adjoining **Birdsacre Sanctuary**, both commemorating a 19th-century ornithologist. Route 1 continues down east along the coast.

Harvesting of wild blueberries Down East

■ HANCOCK TO COLUMBIA FALLS *map page 173, A/B-2*

Stop in the town of **Hancock**, nine miles east of Ellsworth, around dinnertime: the understated **Le Domaine** restaurant serves a traditional French menu and has five beautifully appointed guest rooms done in Provençal style. Hancock is also where you'll find the highly respected and long-established Pierre Monteux School of Music, which holds concerts in summer.

Route 1 turns left and crosses the bridge over the Taunton River, separating Hancock from Sullivan. Just before the bridge, if you turn off right and drive a mile on Eastside Road you come to the **Tidal Falls Lobster Restaurant** on the Frenchman Bay Conservancy, overlooking the spectacular reversing falls at the narrows connecting Taunton Bay to Frenchman Bay. It's particularly dramatic at low tide, when the cascade effect is most pronounced. After you cross the Sullivan Bridge, keep an eye out for **Sullivan Harbor Farm Smokehouse** (207-422-3735 or 800-422-4014), on your left, where you can buy some of the best smoked salmon on earth.

From Route 1, Route 186 loops along the edge of the Schoodic Peninsula, through **Winter Harbor**, past the tiny fishing villages off **Birch Harbor** and **Prospect Harbor**, and then back toward Route 1. The old Gerrish's variety store in Winter Harbor has metamorphosed into **J. M. Gerrish Provisions** (207-963-2727), where you can buy wine or elegant picnic makings of all sorts, and at dinnertime try the stunning **Mama's Boy Bistro.** Another loop road leads off to the tip of the peninsula, where **Acadia National Park** owns a stunning outpost of forest and bold, bouldered shore. It's an adventure to stand on the ledges there with the surf pounding all around you and, in storms, blasting high in the air. A ferry service (207-288-2984) takes passengers daily (except in winter) between Bar Harbor and Winter Harbor, and also rents bikes to ride around the park; the Island Explorer bus meets the ferry, making stops at Frazer Point, Schoodic Point in the park, Birch Harbor, and Prospect Harbor. The peninsula people use this bus as a jitney.

As you head back on the loop toward Route 186, consider stopping at **Bunkers Wharf** to have a meal right on tiny **Bunkers Harbor**. In Prospect Harbor the **Oceanside Meadows Inn,** in a sea captain's house and big farmhouse at the head of Sand Cove, has agreeable summerhouse–style bedrooms from which you can watch the fog roll in over the beach; the inn also presents a lecture and music series in its renovated barn. From here Route 195 takes you to the end of the road, to **Corea**, where it's said they make the fog and where writer Louise Dickinson Rich lived when she wrote *The Peninsula*, a varied, evocative description of this less-visited part of the world.

In Gouldsboro, the local fruit comes in an enticing form at the **Bartlett Maine Estate Winery** (Chicken Mill Rd., off Rte. 1; 207-546-2408; *www.bartlettwinery. com*). The dry Blueberry French Oak Reserve wine is highly recommended, and the tasting room is open to the public. Close by on Route 1 is the tiny town of **Steuben,** just over the border into Maine's easternmost county, Washington—or more colloquially, "Sunrise"—County, which is bigger than Rhode Island and Delaware combined but has fewer than 50,000 people. The village is named for Baron Friedrich von Steuben, who served as inspector general of the Continental Army and was granted this land for his service in the American Revolution.

Washington County's major industries are well represented in **Milbridge,** home to one of the oldest wild blueberry processors, one of the few remaining sardine canning factories, and a considerable Christmas wreath industry. During the

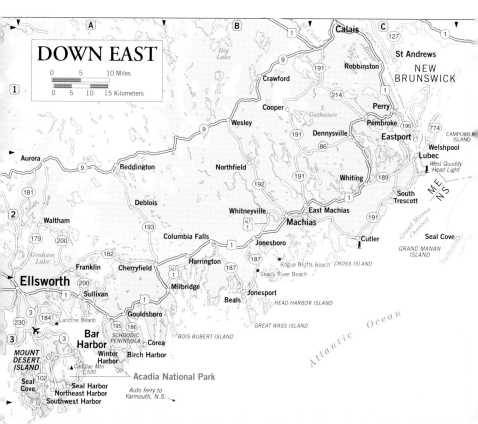

Puffins on Machias Seal Island.

annual **Milbridge Days** festivities, held in late July, the town also hosts an improbably competitive codfish relay race, in which a greased codfish is used as the baton. Ten miles northeast is **Columbia Falls,** which has a collection of 18th- and 19th-century houses well worth seeing. Most are privately owned, but the **Ruggles House** on Main Street is a must. Lumber dealer Thomas Ruggles built this one-room-deep Federal-style mansion with its elegant flying staircase and palladian window in 1818, only to die soon afterward. According to legend, the Massachusetts woodcarver Alvah Peterson lived in the house for three years completing the intricate woodwork with only a penknife.

■ JONESPORT AND BEALS *map page 173, B-3*

About 12 miles southeast of Columbia Falls on Route 187 are the towns of **Jonesport** and **Beals**, fishing villages with eastern Maine's largest lobstering fleet. Jonesport, at the end of the peninsula, is a long, skinny, low-key village with a few antiques shops; here you can take a puffin-watching excursion or go kayaking. The town of Beals comprises two islands joined by a bridge: the more inland Beals

Island, connected to Jonesport by a bridge over the Moosabec Reach; and Great Wass Island, the site of **Great Wass Island Preserve,** a 1,540-acre tract maintained by the Nature Conservancy. With hopes of spotting eiders, scoters, razor bills, ospreys, and bald eagles, birders flock to the preserve's coastal peatlands (no dogs are allowed). The island's jack-pine stands support several warbler and chickadee species, and its shores are visited by black-backed and ring-billed gulls, especially in August. The island is the largest of those within the Great Wass Archipelago, which the Nature Conservancy guidebook describes as being "in an unusual oceanic microclimate, where islands are colder and more moist than on the mainland, yet are buffered from the year-round temperature extremes of the interior." Because island weather is generally hard to predict, be prepared for various conditions.

■ MACHIAS   *map page 173, B-2*

In 1763, settlers from Scarborough in southern Maine were exploring the coast in search of grazing land for their livestock when they discovered the site of present-day Machias and squatted there. It was not clear to them at first whether they were in Massachusetts or Nova Scotia—some indication of how vague a concept "Maine" was, even on the eve of the Revolution. This group, like most groups of new settlers at the time, erected a sawmill; by 1774 there were 46 such mills between Cherryfield and Ellsworth alone. Within a year of its settlement, Machias had produced a million and a half board feet of lumber.

The last river drive in Machias took place in the 1960s, but the town remains prosperous-looking by Washington County standards—thanks in part to its wild blueberry industry—and it is in fact a very attractive community, with a branch of the University of Maine, a good bookstore, two good restaurants, a famous old academy (in East Machias), and a beautiful situation overlooking the Little Bad Falls of the Machias River. In Machiasport (3 miles south) you can visit the **Gates House** (1807), with its period furnishings and ship models.

The historic, gambrel-roofed **Burnham Tavern** stands on a slight bluff overlooking the river in the center of Machias. Thought to be the oldest building in the state east of the Penobscot and one of the most important sites in Maine to be associated with the War for American Independence, the tavern—today operated as a museum by the Daughters of the American Revolution—was in its first century not only a

Lobster boats unload the day's catch.

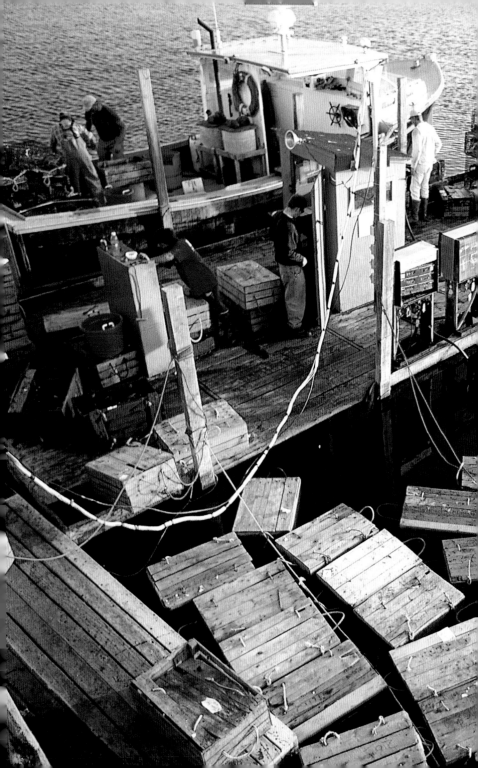

hostelry but an important meeting place in which much of the social and political life of the region was conducted. (The original sign over its door read: "Drink for the thirsty, food for the hungry, lodging for the weary, and good keeping for horses.") It was in its public rooms that citizens gathered in 1775 to discuss the battles at Lexington and Concord and resolved to erect their own Liberty Pole in the village. More importantly, it was in the Burnham Tavern that the patriots of Machias planned the daring venture that turned into the first naval battle of the Revolution.

In the early summer of 1775 the state of affairs in the Machias Bay region paralleled that in Casco Bay in one important respect: a local Tory sympathizer, Ichabod Jones, was supporting the British war effort by shipping desperately needed firewood and lumber to the royal troops occupying Boston. When the local Whigs threatened to destroy his vessels, the British naval commander in Boston sent an armed sloop, H.M.S. *Margaretta,* to protect Jones's business, just as the *Cançeau* had been sent under Captain Mowatt to protect the Tory shipbuilder at

Buildings at Passamaquoddy, *by Nellie Augusta Knopf.*

Falmouth. The leading citizens of Machias proved more determined, however, than their Casco Bay counterparts. On the banks of a small stream later named "Foster's Rubicon," the local patriot Benjamin Foster, after a long debate over whether the town should furnish wood to the British in return for badly needed provisions, leaped across the stream, inviting those who agreed with him to follow him on his symbolic gesture. One after another, beginning with other fervent Whigs, followed by those who had wavered, and finally joined even by the would-be loyalists, the entire community crossed over.

The patriots first tried to capture the British commander and his local allies when they attended church, but they failed. The British quickly sought the protection of the sloop and its four guns. That night, Hannah and Rebecca Weston, two young women from nearby Jonesboro, became local heroines by carrying 50 pounds of gunpowder and lead through 16 miles of woods to aid the rebel cause. The next morning, June 12, 1775, some 40 men under the command of Jeremiah O'Brien sailed downriver in a sloop they had captured from Jones and were joined by Foster and about 20 more men in a small schooner. Poor sailing had delayed the *Margaretta* from reaching open sea; the Americans came alongside, attacked and boarded the British vessel, and mortally wounded the officer in command (he died later in the tavern). The crew quickly surrendered. Soon after, the rebels also surprised and captured the schooner *Diligent* and its tender and converted the three prize vessels into a small squadron to defend their river. It was on a mission to avenge this humiliation that Mowatt happened to burn Falmouth that autumn.

Punishment of the Machias rebels came in 1777, when Sir George Collier, with the *Ranger* and three other vessels, routed the local militia from their breastworks along the shore at Machiasport and burned several buildings. The British feared—correctly—that Machias itself was a staging point for a planned invasion of Nova Scotia and intended to destroy it, but for some reason withdrew when their goal seemed within reach. One explanation is that the British commander, who had easily broken through a log boom placed to block the river and overcome the defenses of the port, thought his vessels were being lured into a trap upstream. Another factor was the presence of a large number of Penobscot, Passamaquoddy, and Maliseet Indians at Machias, some of whom helped fire on the British. (Overall, Indian support wavered between British and rebel forces during the Revolution in Maine, depending on local conditions and the Indians' sense of self-interest). History was repeated in 1814, when Fort Machias (now Fort O'Brien) at the mouth of the river was seized and its barracks burned by another British raiding party.

■ CAMPOBELLO ISLAND

Continue on Route 1 from East Machias and take in Campobello Island first, before returning to Route 1 for Eastport. So at Whiting, head east on 189 to reach the town of **Lubec,** Eastport's sister city, and the easternmost town in the nation. In truth, the easternmost *point* is the piece of land on which the candy-striped **West Quoddy Head Light** stands, about four miles southeast of town. In Lubec you can visit the **West Quoddy Biological Research Station** on South Lubec Road to watch a movie or see an exhibit on whales, or tour the **Sardine Village Museum** and learn about the industry. Then drive across the FDR Memorial Bridge over the Lubec Channel to Campobello. This involves entering the Canadian province of New Brunswick; if you're a U.S. citizen you'll need to present picture identification. Once you are on the Canadian side of the bridge, you are in the 2,800-acre **Roosevelt-Campobello International Park,** which occupies the southern fourth of the island. Established in 1964 under an agreement by President Lyndon Johnson and Prime Minister Lester B. Pearson, this unique international park commemorates the great World War II leader in a manner he would particularly have appreciated, for Franklin D. Roosevelt spent some of the happiest hours of his youth at the family's Campobello summer home, which was said to be second only to Hyde Park in his affections. The **Visitors Centre,** opened by Queen Elizabeth the Queen Mother in 1967, offers a brief introduction to FDR's life at Campobello and various exhibits related to the establishment of the park.

It is only a short walk from there to the **Roosevelt Cottage,** with its views of the islands and shores of Passamaquoddy and Cobscook bays, and to the four other summer cottages (used now by the park commission for international conferences) formerly occupied by friends and neighbors of the Roosevelt family. The rest of the park is worth exploring, either by car (a round trip of about eight miles) or, better, on foot, for it includes a remarkable variety of scenery, including several distinctive bog habitats. If you have more time, explore the inhabited parts of the island, including **Wilson's Beach**, the golf courses, and the village of **Welshpool;** despite its proximity to Maine, the island has a distinctly English feel, very different from nearby Lubec and Eastport. The old tales about why Campobello fell on the Canadian side of the border—most of them involving Daniel Webster's being drunk during the treaty negotiations in the 1840s—are doubtless exaggerated. The

West Quoddy Head Light in Lubec.

actual reason has more to do with the fact that the Lubec Channel was the most important navigable waterway in the immediate area and as such had to be shared.

The broad outline of the role the island played in FDR's life will be familiar to anyone who saw the 1960 film *Sunrise at Campobello,* a dramatization of his struggle to overcome the crippling effects of the polio that struck him in the summer of 1921. James Roosevelt, the president's father, had joined a number of other New York and Boston families in purchasing land and building a summer house on the island in 1883 (in the days when the trains ran as far as Eastport, Campobello did not seem quite so far away). The house, which stood just north of the surviving Roosevelt Cottage, was the family home each summer, and the athletic young FDR learned to sail in the tricky tidal waters of the bay. His mother, Sara Delano Roosevelt, purchased the cottage in 1910 and later gave it to Franklin and his bride.

The day that changed FDR's life, August 10, 1921, was a typically vigorous one for the future president and his five children. Roosevelt, having just campaigned unsuccessfully in 1920 as the Democratic vice-presidential candidate, had settled in for a career as a New York banker—an occupation leisurely enough to allow a long summer vacation. In the morning the family went for a sail on the *Vireo,* and after lunch they helped put out a forest fire elsewhere on the island. Hot and exhausted upon his return, FDR ran with his children across the island to swim in Lake Glen Severn, followed by a quick dip in the chilly waters of the Bay of Fundy. "When I reached the house," he wrote later, "I sat reading for a while, too tired even to dress." He developed a chill, went to bed, and awoke with a fever. What seemed at first just a cold developed into a paralytic condition, which within two weeks was diagnosed as polio. In mid-September, local fishermen carried him by stretcher to a waiting boat, and 12 years passed before he saw Campobello again.

The cottage is filled with mementos of the president: the room used as his office during his 1933 visit, the large frame chair used to carry him after he was crippled, his fishing rod and canes, and a huge megaphone used to hail boats or call the family in to meals. The 34-room house, which faces Eastport, is also one of the few summer cottages of its era to have survived with its original furnishings intact and to be open to the public. Given the family's wealth and social and political prominence, it is striking how simple—and sensible—the furnishings are: wicker chairs and tables, plain brass beds, birch-bark Indian crafts. Nonetheless, a pervasive sense of luxury is created by the large, airy rooms and the sweeping view down the lawn and across the bay—and by the undeniable proof that this family must have enjoyed extensive leisure time.

For all the reminders of FDR here, one should remember that Eleanor Roosevelt lived here too. While the summer house provided both recreation and escape for her husband, Campobello allowed Eleanor to form her own identity. As her biographer Blanche Wiesen Cook writes, Campobello was her first real home of her own (in New York City, the domineering Sara Roosevelt lived next door, in a connected townhouse). "Her romance with its rugged rocky shores, its intense mists and chill grey days, had much to do with the fact that on Campobello she and Franklin lived in a cottage that was well separated from Sara's by plantings and privets." Amid so much physical exertion, she welcomed the many foggy days when she could simply sit and read. Like many people who traveled "Down East" to spend their summers, she found the experience a healing one. To this day, opinions about Mrs. Roosevelt remain polarized—occasionally you'll overhear park visitors angrily disparage her advocacy of social programs and women's rights—but her reputation among admirers and historians seems to grow with each year. Although neither Roosevelt spent much time on the island during their busiest years, Campobello enabled them both to find a refuge from the cares of public life.

■ COBSCOOK BAY TO EASTPORT *map page 173, C-1*

From the bridge, drive west on 189 through Lubec and West Lubec back to Whiting and Route 1. Turn right and make a swing north to go around Cobscook Bay and you'll arrive at **Cobscook State Park** on the bay's western shore. The park has shoreside campsites, and there's always plenty of space available; few Maine visitors make it as far as Sunrise County, let alone its easternmost parts. Head south on Route 190 at Perry. A few miles farther is Pleasant Point, homeland of the Passamaquoddy. Formerly occupying the region around Passamaquoddy Bay and the St. Croix River, the Passamaquoddy by 1866 were restricted to the Perry area by the pressure of white settlement. The 100-acre reservation hosts a traditional Ceremonial Day, with canoe races, traditional dances, and a pageant recounting Passamaquoddy history. The celebration is usually held on the first weekend in August; call the reservation office for information (207-853-2600). Just beyond Pleasant Point—on the right near the causeway to Eastport—stands a redbrick ranch-style house containing a fine basket shop that's worth visiting, both to see the wares and to chat with the Passamaquoddy proprietor, Joe Nicholas. Mr. Nicholas is curator of the **Waponahki Museum & Resource Center**, across the road, where a written version of the Passamaquoddy language is being developed in order to help preserve it.

Maine's American Indian Crafts

The cultural distinctiveness of Maine's Wabanaki—meaning "People of the Dawn," composed of the Maliseet, Micmac, Passamaquoddy, and Penobscot tribes—is on the verge of disappearing. Although some of the tribal groups now enjoy a degree of prosperity (and public respect), thanks to settlement of their land claims with the federal government in the 1970s, their traditional culture seems increasingly fragile. Fewer people speak the tribal languages, and fewer young people in the tribal communities resist the urge to join mainstream, non-Native America.

One aspect of culture does show signs of survival, however: the traditional craft of basketmaking. While the number of people practicing this craft is small—probably only a few dozen skilled practitioners scattered through northern and eastern Maine from Presque Isle to Eastport—public interest has revived. Even some non-Native craftspeople are learning the techniques and reproducing motifs the Wabanaki developed over several centuries.

This trend actually marks a second "revival." About a century ago the craft flourished, when rusticators (city folks with Maine summer addresses) on the coast encouraged the efforts of the basketmakers. Each summer, members of the tribes would appear by canoe at shorefront cottages or at village fairs to sell that year's supply of baskets. To meet the domestic needs of their late Victorian customers, these Indians wove the baskets in special shapes and sizes; for example, they made thimbleholders,

Opal Nelson of the Penobscot tribe with her baskets.

pillboxes, and picture frames. Examples surviving from that period can frequently be found in older summer cottages along the coast.

Wabanaki basketmaking and its related crafts require two things: a supply of ash wood, sweetgrass (a tough, flexible, aromatic plant), and/or birchbark, and skill (an unusual degree of patience, manual dexterity, and hard work). The brown or black ash tree *(Fraxinus nigra)* provides the splints, or thin strips of wood used to make the larger, sturdier "rough" baskets—the all-purpose containers traditionally used in harvesting potatoes and hunting and fishing. The best trees for this grow in damp areas throughout northern Maine (although in modern times acid rain and clear cutting of forests has reduced the supply). A length of tree trunk is trimmed, peeled of its bark, and pounded with the blunt edge of an axe until the wood shatters into long, flexible strands that can be trimmed into strips for weaving.

Although today the distinction between male and female crafts is less rigid, customarily, "rough" baskets were the domain of men in the tribe, and "fancy" baskets were women's work. Centuries ago, Indian women collected sweetgrass on islands where their tribes stopped during the summer migration down river to the coast. Dried and twisted into strands, sweetgrass can be woven into intricate shapes and incorporated into "fancy" baskets for the tourist trade. Both ash and sweetgrass, which turn various shades of brown when aged, can be tinted with vegetable dyes for more complex work. While the antique boxes and baskets become dusty-looking and faded on the outside, if kept closed they often retain their brilliant color on the inside.

Birchbark, best known for its use in canoes, was also rapidly adapted by traditional craftspeople into merchandise for the rusticator market. Both the white outside bark and its reddish-brown inner layer were sculpted into popular items ranging from folding screens to children's toys. The craft survives today mostly in the form of wastebaskets, letter pouches (to hang on the wall), and other small receptacles.

Selling baskets and other household items to the tourists was a way of cking out a few dollars at times of the year when no work was available raking berries, trapping, or guiding hunters and fishermen "from away." Quite intricate work went for a pittance, and even today, when baskets sell for $25 to $125 or more, the earnings are modest given the number of hours spent.

But basketmaking represents more than commerce. As Kathleen Mundell, an expert on the subject, writes, "Making baskets sustains and renews an individual's ties to family and tribe. Like the growth rings of the ash tree, the weaving tradition connects contemporary basketmakers to past and future weavers, joining them as a people and a community." Today, Wabanaki baskets are sold through weavers' cooperatives in tribal communities and through a few high-quality craft shops around the state. Older examples can be found, in small numbers, in antiques shops.

Across the causeway, historic **Eastport** stands on Moose Island, whose proximity to the Canadian border allowed the city during the Embargo (1807–09) to become a center for extensive smuggling between America and Canada. Meanwhile, the British insisted that all of Moose Island actually belonged to them, claiming it had been granted them by the Revolutionary War peace treaty in 1783. Consequently, the British army took Eastport during the War of 1812 and occupied the city for four years, a story you'll hear told at the **Barracks Museum** on Washington Street. A survivor of that era, the 1810 **Weston House** hosted John James Audubon when he stayed in Eastport en route to Labrador in 1833. (The Weston House continues to operate as an inn.) Just as the road turns left on the way into town, definitely stop at **Raye's Old Stone Mustard Mill** (800-853-1903; *www.rayesmustard.com*), the only working one in North America, to see the four-foot quartz grindstone and take a tour. **The Pantry Store** out front holds tastings and sells the mustards and other goodies.

In 1875 the town became the birthplace of the sardine industry, when Julius Wolfe invented the canning process here, and at one time Eastport claimed 18 sardine canneries. After years of decline and an almost eerie quiet, the old town of Eastport is showing definite signs of revival. The island's economy has benefited from the new port, built on the western side of the island, which handles large cargo ships. But there's another force apparent in the somewhat zany mix of stores and restaurants along Eastport's Water Street, one that's almost startling after the long and sometimes featureless miles of Route 1. Eastport may be a community long dependent on fishing and shipping, but it's also a sophisticated arts outpost with a good sense of humor about itself. Maybe Provincetown was like this a very—*very*—long time ago. The resulting mix can make for some odd juxtapositions, as well as delightful surprises—the **Milliken House** bed-and-breakfast is furnished with massive Victorian antiques and huge oil paintings of nudes; a mysterious shop *appears* to rent bizarre costumes, but it's hard to say for sure; and **La Sardina Loca,** a Mexican restaurant, is wildly decorated and serves fabulous and authentic food. Even the local motel is different—**Motel East** has big rooms furnished with executive-style Federal reproductions, knock-out views of Passamaquoddy Bay from private balconies, and rates that will make you grateful the rest of the world has yet to discover the charms of Eastport.

The **Tides Institute and Museum of Art** contains area art and archives, a library, a buildings collection, and early printmaking equipment. It's housed in the restored Eastport Savings Bank Building at 43 Water Street, and its aim is to aid local artists. One special place to visit is **The Commons Eastport** (*www.thecommonseastport.com*)**,** a cooperative artisans' shop at 51 Water Street that displays their work and promotes arts events.

Eastport claims the country's highest tides, which, although generally ranging from 12 to 27 feet, have been measured at 40 feet. (You can get a demonstration of this at the **Waco Diner,** whose dockside views let diners see just how far the water level drops.) Between the city's shores and Dog Island, the St. Croix River and the extreme tides churn against one another, creating one of the world's largest whirlpools. Called "Old Sow," the whirlpool can sometimes be seen from the ferry that runs between Eastport and Deer Island, Canada.

Back on Route 1 North after leaving Eastport you'll see on the left, after a few miles, **The 45th Parallel**, a large emporium of antiques, home furnishings, nautical gifts, and jewelry. A large blue globe marks the entrance, with a sign stating, "You Are Halfway Between the Equator and the North Pole."

About seven miles farther on you'll reach **Robbinston,** with, on your left, the beautiful Greek Revival **Brewer House** (1828), on the National Register of Historic Places. It's now a bed-and-breakfast, owned and run by an artist and her violinist husband, a faculty member of the Pierre Monteux School of Music. Continue, and look on your right for the **Redclyffe Shore Motor Inn,** which overlooks the St. Croix River and has extraordinary views from all its rooms and from the dining solarium in the Gothic Revival main building (1861–1863). Twelve miles farther are **Calais** (locally pronounced "Callas") and the bridge across into Canada. In 2004, along with St. Stephen across the river in New Brunswick, Calais celebrated the 400th anniversary of the first French settlement in the New World. In 1604–05 Samuel de Champlain and the Sieur de Monts visited the St. Croix Valley and attempted to establish a permanent settlement on small St. Croix Island. A third of the settlers died in the first winter, and although the survivors were helped by the Passamaquoddy, they left the island and moved to Nova Scotia.

WESTERN LAKES
& MOUNTAINS

Born on the coast himself, poet Robert P. T. Coffin once wrote that there is a Maine that is "woods and mountains and sea" and another Maine that is "woods and lakes and mountains." The former, of course, has received the more glory; the artists and poets, the summer people and the vacationers flocked there, creating an image of Maine that has the distinct tang of salt water to it. But the other Maine—freshwater, inland, often less dramatic, certainly less celebrated—also has plenty to offer. For one, it's rarely crowded, with the exception of a few aggressively promoted ski resorts on winter weekends and the southernmost lakes on summer weekends. Although not exactly untouched by tourism—thanks to now defunct railroads, parts of it were once as popular as the coast—today the region is far less known than the state's coastal locales. Western Maine is full of inns and rustic hotels; those in the southern part tend to be family oriented and those in the northern part cater to hunters and fishermen. But all seem to operate with a degree of friendliness not always in ample supply on the coast. And however astonishingly beautiful in autumn, this region is unfortunately not as well appreciated as comparable territory on the other side of the White Mountains. The western hills are an odd mixture of picture-book New England villages and grim paper-mill towns, of lush intervales and abandoned fields.

Much of this area is within a day's round trip from Portland (a rather long day, in the case of Rangeley). But to hurry through it—as many people do on their way to the outlet shops in North Conway, New Hampshire—is to fail to savor the one part of Maine that has probably changed the least, visually, since the Civil War. There is no one highway that will give you a slice of it all, at least not the way U.S. 1 "delivers" the major coastal towns. And there's no single compelling destination to draw tourists, although places like the Shaker community at Sabbathday Lake and the Norlands "living history" complex at Livermore are like nothing else in the country.

One option for visiting here is to stay at one of the region's distinctive rustic resorts. These "camps" offer accommodation in guest cabins with wood-burning stoves, screened porches, dining in a separate pine lodge, and outdoor facilities ranging from hot tubs to rowboats.

Kicking back in Bethel, the largest town in the northern part of Oxford County.

■ SOUTHWEST HILL COUNTRY *map page 191, A/B-5*

The hinterland of Oxford and western Androscoggin and Cumberland counties, a verdant region of forests and lakes, lies within an hour or two of Portland and Lewiston. This makes it the destination of choice for many Mainer day-trippers, as well as for the parents all over New England (and beyond) who send their children to the hundreds of summer camps here. Many of the 19th-century towns have some claim to fame and merit a visit. While exploring the area, you might use one of Oxford County's pleasant old hotels as a jumping-off point.

Your choice of "base camp" depends not only on personal taste but also on the season. The towns and villages are widely scattered, the roads meandering, and the recreational possibilities sufficiently mixed to render no single route or destination clearly better than another. Two seasonal resorts on Kezar Lake near Center Lovell, for instance, are the Adirondack-style **Pleasant Point Inn**, which has tranquil views from its spacious rooms, and **Quisisana**, where opera concerts are performed by the talented singers-in-training staff. If you prefer to stay in a town in slightly more formal digs, try the **Lake House**, an 18th-century stagecoach inn at Routes 35 and 37 in Waterford, a lovely crossroads village full of white clapboard—most of it on the National Register of Historic Places. The inn is renowned for its food and wine.

Once comfortably settled, you can explore villages like **Bridgton**, full of antiques shops, or **Paris Hill**, which has one of New England's handsomest ensembles of early-19th-century houses, including that of Hannibal Hamlin (1809–91), who was Lincoln's first vice president. An endearing story about Hamlin concerns Molly Ockett, the famous Pequawket Indian daughter of a Wabanaki chief, whose name (in many spellings) is seen and heard throughout southwestern Maine, especially on July 17th, when Molly Ockett Day is celebrated. She was, for her time, a true Renaissance woman, at home in both the white and Indian worlds. Affable and outgoing, she was a healer, midwife, storyteller, weaver and basketmaker, and worker in other crafts; she also taught people to hunt for food, medicinal herbs, and furs, and lent them money when they needed it. She was born near Saco in the second quarter of the 18th century and died in 1816. Late in her life she was wandering one winter night through Snowfalls, a valley below Paris Hill, looking for shelter, but no one gave her refuge. Cursing Snowfalls (to whom bad things began to happen), she went up to Paris Hill, where a family with a sick child took her in. She cured the child with cow's milk and predicted great things for him—he was none other than Hannibal Hamlin.

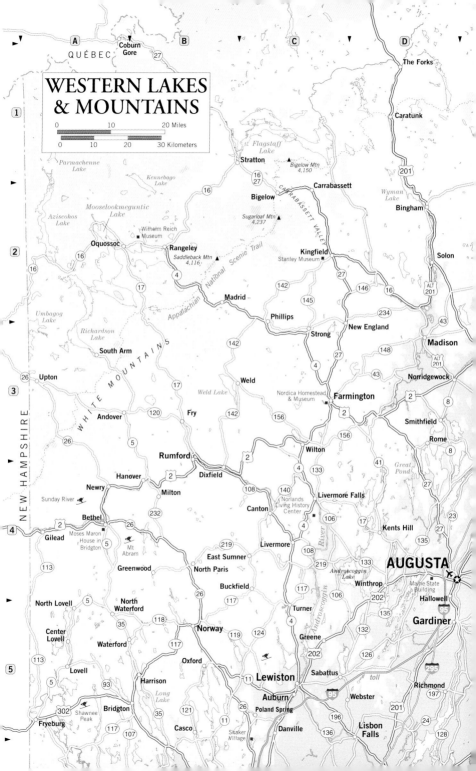

Close to the New Hampshire border is **Fryeburg**, with an academy once run by Daniel Webster and a countryside painted by Eastman Johnson. The town is most spectacular in the fall, when Fryeburg holds its famous country fair. **Cornish**, on the county's southern border, has splendid views across the Ossipee River toward the White Mountains. Southwest of the Oxford County border lies a chain of lakes, the largest of which is 46-square-mile Sebago Lake. **Sebago Lake State Park,** at its north end, is a popular day-trip destination for locals as well as a prized vacation spot for out-of-staters. The lake is known to fishermen for its land-locked salmon. Coastal dwellers come for a swim in water that's cool enough to be refreshing but not cold enough to turn their lips blue. The park can get quite crowded in July and August. Since Sebago and its neighboring lakes provide water for the city of Portland, water quality is closely monitored.

An alternative to the water might be a trip to one of the historic towns situated between the lakes. **Poland Spring**, near **Range Ponds State Park** (pronounced "Rang"), internationally famous for its mineral water, was once the sprawling Poland Spring Resort, where presidents and potentates and movie stars vacationed,

Baldpate Mountain is in the Mahoosuc Range near Andover and, at 3,812 feet, ranks among the highest peaks in the state.

and whose enormous main building burned in 1975. It's still worth a visit. Nowadays the Inns at Poland Spring (which bills itself as a "stress-free zone"), is a popular economy resort on about 800 acres, using the golf course, pool, tennis courts and buildings of the earlier resort. Next door, the **Maine State Building** (207-998-4142), a wonderful relic of the 1893 Columbia Exposition in Chicago, contains a museum and art gallery and is a national landmark, as is All Souls Chapel across the road, where weddings are often held. And in the adjoining **Preservation Park** you can visit the restored original bottling house and source building, where Sadie's Place serves pastries, quiches, salads, and sandwiches.

About seven miles southeast of Poland Spring on Route 231 is **Lower New Gloucester**, itself a gem of a village, and two miles south of Poland Spring on Route 26 is the **Sabbathday Lake Shaker Community and Museum**. The community was established in 1794, and today, with fewer than 10 "sisters" and "brothers," is the last remaining Shaker community in the country. Four of its 17 buildings are open for tours, and serve as illustrations of Shaker life and Shaker design. You can buy locally produced herbs, yarn, seeds, and a Shaker cookbook; you can even attend a Sunday service.

Bethel is the largest town in the northern part of Oxford County. The community straddles the Androscoggin River not far from where the Appalachian Trail passes through scenic Grafton Notch on its long march toward Mt. Katahdin. Bethel is a center for hiking in the White Mountains, which spill over into Maine from New Hampshire, or for skiing at the **Sunday River** ski resort (about six miles north of town), at **Mt. Abram** (about six miles southeast), and for the determined, at **Shawnee Peak** (about an hour south). The Mountain Explorer, a free shuttle service that runs from Thanksgiving until the first weekend in April, has buses that take you in and around Bethel and to Sunday River.

When Bethel was founded in 1774, it was named Sudbury Canada for its original grantors—citizens of Sudbury, Massachusetts, who had fought to conquer Canada in one of the early Anglo-French skirmishes. In 1781 it was the site of the last foray into Maine by hostile Indians, who came down from Quebec, plundered the town, and carried off two residents for the duration of the Revolution. Near Bethel you can relive history at the Newry and Andover covered bridges, as well as at Bethel's own **Moses Mason House**, a Federal-period dwelling noted for its gorgeous Rufus Porter landscape murals in the front hall. While in town you might stay at the landmark **Bethel Inn and Country Club**. William Bingham II and four other wealthy and grateful patients built the inn in 1913 to house patients of the famous Dr. John George Gehring, whose program to treat mind and body advocated a strict regimen of physical therapy and strenuous exercise, including wood-chopping and gardening. Today the inn offers golf, tennis, boating, swimming, snowshoeing, and cross-country skiing.

Bethel has really become a four-season resort town. Sunday River is planning a new golf course, which will probably be open in midsummer 2005, and the Bethel Inn offers monthly memberships for access to its other outdoor sports. Sunday River and **Sugarloaf**, both now owned by American Skiing Company, sell lift tickets that are good at both resorts. Visitors from out of state in particular should not expect too much off the slopes—however, the après-ski scene in Maine grows livelier every year. In Bethel there's something of a social "scene" at the Bethel Inn, and a slightly less family-oriented party atmosphere at Bethel's Sudbury Inn (the "Suds Pub"). Closer to the slopes, the **Sunday River Brewing Company** draws them in, as does the chef at the new **Phoenix House & Well** on the Sunday River access road (207-824-2222).

■ RANGELEY LAKES *map page 191, A/B-2*

The heavily wooded countryside around the seven lakes and innumerable ponds that make up the Rangeley Lakes region may seem familiar territory to anyone who has read Louise Dickinson Rich's popular *We Took To the Woods* (1942), a sort of domesticated version of *Walden* written near Lower Richardson Lake. Doubtless greeted as a diversion during the strain of World War II, the book was more prophetic than its author may have anticipated; in the next generation, vanloads of people would be moving to the Maine woods to escape "civilization" and try to establish some sense of harmony with the natural rhythms of the world.

Today the area still has more preserved land than any other part of the state. You can experience its serenity by canoeing through the chain of contiguous lakes all the way from Rangeley to New Hampshire. People in Rangeley like to point out that they are halfway between the equator and the North Pole, although to a new arrival the scenery seems so remote and coniferous that the Pole will feel much the closer of the two. At **Saddleback Mountain,** the nearest ski center, the resort's new owner has bought new grooming and snow-making equipment, and is planning big changes to the slopes. Saddleback overlooks the Rangeley Lakes, and the Appalachian Trail runs right over its peak.

A quiet dell along one of Maine's many interior rivers.

■ WILHELM REICH MUSEUM

Between the towns of **Rangeley** and **Oquossoc**, overlooking Dodge Pond and with a distant view of Saddleback Mountain, is one of Maine's least-known house museums. Its distinction is both architectural and biographical. Designed by the New York architect James Bell in 1948, the angular structure employs stones found on the property, but with a Bauhaus modernist effect that is all the more striking in this region of rustic camps and Victorian farmhouses. This was the home and laboratory of the controversial psychiatrist and writer Wilhelm Reich.

Born in Austria in 1897, Reich was an early associate of Sigmund Freud's and a well regarded figure in Viennese psychoanalytical circles. Soon he went far beyond Freud, however, in attempting to link neurosis with a failure to achieve sexual satisfaction. He produced a theory of "biological energy," to which he added an attack on the patriarchal social order of his day. Forced to flee from the Nazis in 1933, Reich first settled in Norway, then in 1939 accepted an invitation to teach at the New School for Social Research in New York City. Thanks to a sympathetic American colleague who owned a summer house on Mooselookmeguntic Lake, the émigré doctor discovered the beauty—and solitude—of western Maine, and in 1942 he purchased the 200-acre farm where he built his house. Reich's investigations into the psycho-biology of sexual stimulation led him to claim that he had discovered a hitherto unknown type of natural energy which he called "orgone," and so he named his property Orgonon.

Whether Reich was a genius or a crackpot is still debated, but he might very well have lived out his life peaceably in the Rangeley Lakes region had it not been for the zeal of the U.S. Food and Drug Administration. Determining that his "orgone energy accumulators" (the devices which were to concentrate sexual energy into a usable resource) were fraudulent, the agency sought to ban or destroy works Reich had written and block interstate shipment of his apparatus. Reich, denying the government's authority to judge his scientific work, lost in court in 1954. He left Maine and went off to study desert weather formations in the Southwest. But when one of his students transported some energy accumulators from Maine to New York (without Reich's consent), the doctor was charged with criminal contempt. He was sentenced to two years in a federal penitentiary, and in 1957 he was found dead in his cell. Perhaps his great tragedy was the fact that he did not survive into the 1960s, when he would have been celebrated for the same views on sexual repression that in the 1950s brought him into such disrepute.

Before entering prison, Reich set up a trust that today owns and operates the **Wilhelm Reich Museum,** and which is gradually publishing the doctor's writings. The museum was Reich's idea; he wanted to preserve for his students and future researchers his library, some 25 of his paintings, his unpublished findings, and his scientific instruments. The house, in other words, looks much as it did in Reich's lifetime. Reich is buried nearby, on a ledge with a panoramic view of the countryside.

After visiting the museum, consider driving south from Oquossoc on Route 17, and stopping at **Height of Land,** from which there are stupendous views (call the Rangeley Chamber of Commerce for information, 207-864-5364).

■ KINGFIELD *map page 191, C-2*

Between Rangeley and **Kingfield**, 10 miles northeast of Saddleback, rises **Sugarloaf** (4,237 feet), Maine's second-highest mountain and the site of its most fully developed ski resort—with plenty of lodging on the slopes, above-the-tree-line skiing, and a golf course. Named for William King, its early proprietor and Maine's first governor, Kingfield is a lively town and a good point from which to explore the ski-obsessed Carrabassett Valley to the north (between Sugarloaf and 4,150-foot Bigelow Mountain) or the rural towns of **New Portland** and **New Vineyard** to the south. The town itself is worth visiting during any season. The Bangor Symphony Orchestra comes to Kingfield in the summer, and the town also has, in winter, what is widely regarded as the best restaurant in western Maine, **One Stanley Avenue**.

A small museum in Kingfield commemorates the inventiveness and skill of the late-19th-century Stanley family, notably the twin brothers Francis Edgar and Freelan Oscar, who developed the Stanley Steamer, and their sister Chansonetta Stanley Emmons, who was a pioneer documentary photographer. The twins were enormously inventive from youth; before perfecting their jaunty little cars they had already developed the dry photographic plate process (whose patent Kodak later bought) and invented the artist's airbrush. In 1896 they built the first Stanley Steamer, a vehicle whose lightness allowed it to achieve phenomenal speeds (unofficially, as high as 190 mph). F. O. Stanley astonished the world in 1899 by driving one up the dirt trails to the 6,288-foot summit of Mount Washington in New Hampshire. By tragic irony, F. E. Stanley was killed in 1918 when he crashed into a pile of cordwood in order to avoid hitting two farm wagons traveling side by side down the road. It was perhaps also a tragedy for succeeding generations that, after

E.E. Stanley at the wheel of his 1908 Stanley steam car.

the Stanley Motor Carriage Company closed in 1925, few other people showed any interest in perfecting a steam-powered automobile. On view at the Stanley Museum are three of the twins' horseless carriages (models from 1905, 1910, and 1916) and the country's principal collection of Chansonetta Stanley's photographs and glass-plate negatives.

Both New Portland and New Vineyard were settled by farmers forced out of the Kennebec Valley in the early 19th century by absentee proprietors who disputed their land titles. One of New Vineyard's early settlers was Capt. Nathan Daggett, who, as chief pilot for Admiral d'Estaing at the battle of Yorktown, was responsible for positioning the French fleet so as to prevent the British fleet from coming to Cornwallis's aid. New Portland owes its name to the fact that the township was given to the citizens of "old" Portland by the Massachusetts General Court to indemnify them for the losses suffered when the British burned their town in 1775. Before you reach New Portland, and while you're going south on Route 27, stop at **Nowetah's American Indian Museum and Store** (207-628-4981), which exhibits Indian art of North and South America and a large Maine Indian basket collection.

A little farther along, consider making a short detour to see the historic **wire suspension bridge** (1866), the oldest and smallest of its kind in Maine. Sixteen yoke of oxen hauled the imported Sheffield steel cable from Hallowell to New Portland. Back on Route 27, not far from the turnoff to the bridge, you might stop for an excellent seafood meal at the popular **Wirebridge Diner** (207-628-3663).

■ CENTRAL HILLS *map page 191, C-3/4*

The lake-splattered hills north of Lewiston offer many hours of pleasant drives— say, from Monmouth (home of ornate Cumston Hall, circa 1900, an "opera house" now occupied by a much-praised Shakespeare theater company), north to such inviting country towns as Winthrop (center of the state's apple industry), Kents Hill (site of a well-known academy), and Mount Vernon (remembered by some as home of Elizabeth Arden's "Maine Chance" beauty spa). Beyond the Belgrade Lakes and to the northwest is **Farmington,** an important agricultural and educational center for much of the state's history. Today it houses a branch campus of the University of Maine that has particularly good teacher education programs. Farmington was the home of Supply Belcher, who wrote *The Harmony of Maine,* a tune book published in 1794 that stands at the beginning of the state's musical tradition. It was also the birthplace of perhaps the most famous singer the state has yet produced—the toast of two continents in the 1890s—the soprano Lillian Nordica.

Overlooking the Sandy River Valley is the **Nordica Homestead and Museum**, the 1849 farmhouse in which Lilly Norton was born in 1857. The family moved to Boston when Lilly was six years old—but she liked to think of herself as a child of the Maine countryside. Lilly was trained as an oratorio singer, a more respectable pursuit than opera in the Boston of the 1870s, but one day she squeezed through a grating at the Boston Music Hall and heard her first opera, *Il Trovatore,* much of which she was afterwards able to sing from memory. No one in the opera world took American voices seriously, and Norton might easily have been ignored had not a famous bandmaster "discovered" her and taken her to Europe on tour. Norton began studying voice in Milan with Antonio Sangiovanni, who soon persuaded her to change her name—which Italians had trouble pronouncing—to Nordica. The Italian public adored her, and a brilliant European career ensued for "La Nordica." After three years abroad she returned to what should have been a triumph in Boston. But the audience found her too "stiff," a stingy judgment of the artistic restraint that was to be one of her hallmarks as a singer.

Madame Nordica in full dress.

In 1887 she established herself in London, where she sang the immolation scene from Wagner's *Götterdämmerung* with Hans Richter conducting. In 1893 Wagner's widow invited Nordica to sing the role of Elsa in *Lohengrin* at the Bayreuth Festival—the first time a non-German had been offered a major role there—and much of the intensely nationalistic Wagnerian public was furious at this apparent "desecration." Nonetheless, Nordica proved a radiant and flawless performer, and was applauded by no less a critic and Wagner fan than George Bernard Shaw. The decade that followed was marked by one triumph after another, especially in the roles of Isolde and Brünnhilde at New York's Metropolitan Opera. Her personal life was less happy—she endured three disastrous marriages, which may have encouraged her to become active in the women's suffrage movement. Never forgetting her own penniless childhood in Boston, she also gave concerts at no charge for the poor. She continued to tour into her 50s, and in 1914 died of a tropical fever while in Java.

The Nordica Homestead, which looks like any other old Maine farmhouse, will win you over by its sheer unlikeliness: you step inside and suddenly confront Brünnhilde's feathered helmet and scarlet cloak. Scattered about the house are the trinkets of a major European operatic career, from an age when great sopranos had the celebrity of modern rock stars.

Another Farmington notable is Chester Greenwood, whose day is celebrated in town each year on the first Saturday of December. He had more than 100 patents and was named by the Smithsonian Institution as one of the fifteen outstanding American inventors— winning immortality for the invention of earmuffs.

■ NORLANDS LIVING HISTORY CENTER *map page 191, C-4*

"We're off the beaten path; you really have to want to find us," says Billie Gammon, who slips easily in and out of the present century. Each year, thousands of people show that determination: some of them come on school tours that may last an hour or two, some come for the day, and some of them stay for three days and three nights as "live-in" participants in one of the most extraordinary museum experiences in the country. "Most museums tell you what to look at," explains Mrs. Gammon, who typically wears the clothing of a Maine farm woman of the 1870s. "Here we tell you to shovel the manure!"

In her most recent incarnation, Mrs. Gammon is a scholarly former school teacher who a few decades ago became enchanted by the Washburn family of 19th-century **Livermore,** Maine, a small community in the Androscoggin Valley about 20 miles south of Farmington, or 28 miles north of Lewiston. She is the founder of the Norlands Living History Center, a 445-acre site that includes a one-room school, a granite-walled library, a farmer's cottage, a church, a large barn, the Washburn family mansion, and an assortment of personable livestock that would

Lunch at the Norlands Living History Museum re-creates a 19th-century atmosphere.

have delighted E. B. White in his *Stuart Little* days. Year-round she and the staff of Norlands greet visitors curious about Maine history or pre-industrial farm life, or people who simply want to escape the stresses of modernity. In her 19th-century incarnation, Mrs. Gammon is quick to disabuse anyone of the notion that life in the past was a scene from Currier and Ives. She is Miz Lovejoy, the village pauper, widowed and heavily burdened. She tells you stories about her youth in Livermore, many of them about death and misfortune, yet the kindness shown her by the residents of Norlands is also a lesson of sorts, about how people survived in times past.

If you come there to stay a few days, you are greeted by name—not your name in the outside world, but the name of a villager of the 1870s, whose persona you are to occupy for the next 72 hours. Back in the house at nightfall, the lanterns are lit, you eat from blue willow ware a huge meal of chicken and dumplings, with pitchers of milk and fresh butter from the farm, and you visit with neighbors. Over the next two days you learn how to do farm chores—from ploughing to cutting ice—or how to manage in a 19th-century kitchen. You also learn how a family in rural Maine thought and behaved and interacted with each other.

The adult "live in" programs at Norlands are so popular that they're often booked a year or more in advance. But there are numerous other ways to experience the place. Some 20,000 school children each year come for day visits, sometimes just to see the kitchen and barn, sometimes to "role play" in the one-room school or on the farm. The center takes its show on the road through outreach programs on such subjects as 19th-century childbirth, pre-modern medicine and health, funeral customs, and rural poverty.

For many visitors, discovering the Washburn family itself is a revelation. Of the seven sons of Israel and Patty Washburn, four became members of Congress, two state governors, one a secretary of state, one a senator, one minister to France, one the commander of a Union ship during the Civil War, one a Union general, one minister to Paraguay, several serving as bankers and manufacturers. Like so many of their contemporaries, they mostly had to leave Maine in pursuit of a career. They took their New England ways and values with them into other parts of the United States—but something of their ethos survives at Norlands. Some of the wisest lessons are implicit in the way the place operates, where everything is recycled, mended, reused. The frugality of old New England lives on in responsible stewardship: "Use it up, wear it out, make it do, or do without."

In the short but sweet summer on the lakes of central Maine, the fish are biting and the mosquitoes swarm.

FISHING IN MAINE

Maine offers something for fishermen of every skill level and preference. If you're a fly-fishing purist you can match the hatch on remote fly-in lakes, where you stalk the native squaretail trout in its only natural habitat. At a pond moments away, you may find a boy and his dad equipped with nothing but cane poles, bobbers, and some hand-dug worms can relax and fish like characters in a Mark Twain story. You can get up before sunrise, fish some of the streams for trout, the rivers for salmon, hit the lakes for small and largemouth bass, then break for lunch and drive to the coast. There you might stand on a slab of pink granite and cast into the ocean for flounder the size of doormats or trophy bluefish and stripers strong enough to sap any arm strength you've got left.

Of course, there's more to a great fishing day than catching a net full of trout or snagging a massive salmon—achievements which you'll forget in a month or two. What you'll remember is the moment when, while casting into a quiet stream, you see a deer peeking through the brush. After pausing to make sure you mean no harm, it pushes aside some pine seedlings and lowers its head to take a drink. Or while sitting in a canoe on a calm pond, you spot a bald eagle cruising over the treetops, riding currents of air. Such captivating encounters make you forget what you originally came to do. And so much of Maine preserves its natural splendor, that getting to an isolated lake or stream doesn't have to take long.

Once you reach your fishing destination, take some time to roam or paddle around. Look around to find your ideal fishing spot—for many of us the hours spent tramping about can amount to a fantastic vacation. If, however, time is at a premium and your sole objective is to catch your quarry, hiring a competent guide may be your best bet. These folks know the area and can tailor a trip to fit your own needs; if you're a beginning angler you can get a lesson or two, ensuring an enjoyable *and* productive trip. Many of these guides are listed in such publications as *Maine Sportsman*, as well as in magazines devoted to your favorite type of fishing. You can also inquire at local tackle shops. You'll end up with the equipment you need, and every now and then the knowledgeable shopkeeper himself may take you to one of his secret spots—at no charge.

The true aficionado of angling may enjoy one of the many camps devoted exclusively to the sport. Some of the packages these fishing camps offer include meals, lodging, guides, boats, and even equipment. The people who run the camps are anxious to please even the most finicky sportsman, and will go to great lengths to ensure the success of your trip. Before booking a trip, make sure the camp provides exactly what you're looking for; for example, some camps lead only catch-and-release trips, while others conduct only fly-fishing tours.

Grant's Kennebago Camps. Fly fishing only for brook trout, brown trout, and land-locked salmon up to six pounds. Box 786, Rangeley 04970; 207-864-3608. In winter, Edgewater Acres, Saco 04072; 207-282-5264.

Libby Camps. Fish a different remote pond or wild river every day for trophy squaretails or land-locked salmon. 34 Main St., Box V.R., Ashland 04732; 207-435-8274 or 207-435-2462.

Weatherby's. Bait casting, spin casting, trolling. Guides; boat and motor rentals. Box 69, Grand Lake Stream 04637; 207-796-5558. In winter, Village West #3, 5019 Woody Creek Lane, Carrabassett Valley 04947; 207-237-2911.

If you prefer fishing the wide-open sea to catch your dinner, experienced crews man Coast Guard–inspected charter and head boats, which are equipped with communications and safety devices. "Charter" boats take up to six people on day trips for a fixed price per boat, per day. "Head" boats charge by the head, can take around 30, and may be chartered for private groups.

Balmy Days Cruises. 2-hour mackerel-fishing trips on *Miss Boothbay.* Pier 8, Boothbay Harbor, 207-633-2284; www.balmydayscruises.com.

Bay Island Yacht Charters. Charters by day, week, and month. 120 Tillson St., Rockport; 207-596-7550; www.sailme.com.

Blackjack Sport Fishing. Half- and full-day charter trips for stripers and blues and the rest. Pier 7, Boothbay Harbor; 207-633-6445.

Bunny Clark Deep Sea Fishing. Various charter packages. Perkins Cove, Ogunquit; 207-646-2214; www.bunnyclark.com.

Maine Fishing and Diving Charters. Half- and full-day charters. South Portland. 207-799-9826 or 866-799-9826; www.fishinganddiving.com.

Olde Port Mariner. Operates half- and full-day fishing charter boats out of Portland Harbor, at 170 Commercial St.; 207-775-0727.

For more information, contact the **Maine Inland Fisheries & Wildlife** in Augusta; 207-287-8000; www.mefishwildlife.com.

–John Fuhrman

GREAT NORTH WOODS

For the first 300 years or so that Europeans knew the land we now call Maine, it was in their eyes hardly more than a thin line of fishing settlements scattered along the Atlantic. The backcountry was a howling wilderness, inhabited by largely hostile tribes and the occasional French Jesuit or trapper. On the eve of the Revolution, English-speaking settlers began to travel up the major rivers, seeking good farmland in the rich intervales and slowly hacking away and burning the forest. But it was really not until the lumber boom of the 1830s that much of the interior was explored and surveyed. The woodsmen saw trees as a bounteous, ever-replenished commodity that, given enough manpower and waterways, could be converted into cash. They led the way into the Great North Woods. The American essayist Henry David Thoreau (1817–62) was not an explorer of "virgin" lands, for everywhere he went in northern Maine he saw the evidence—the dams, the camps, the stumps—of a generation of logging. Yet for most people visiting the state, especially when seaside rustication became so fashionable after the Civil War, the upper half of Maine (an area larger than Vermont and New Hampshire combined) was as much terra incognita as it had been to the 16th-century mapmakers. It remains so today, unless you've come to hunt or fish or hike the Appalachian Trail. Route 1 and I-95 channel tourists through southern Maine; from the viewpoint of Houlton, Bangor looks like a coastal town. This is unfortunate in the sense that Maine has become too identified with its towns "Down East." Try to build a McDonald's on Mount Desert Island and you will face an explosion of protest. Destroy an entire ecosystem north of Katahdin and only a handful of environmentalists will even notice.

Most visitors do not have the time or curiosity to explore the north country, much of which, especially when seen from the highway, is a monotonous industrial forest. It smells good—year-round the lumber trucks perfume the air with their massive bundles of freshly cut hemlock and pine—but it fails to entrance the eye. There is little feeling of being in unspoiled nature, for only in some very inaccessible places has the mature forest been untouched by loggers. Nineteenth-century loggers went after the big trees, leaving the rest; modern ones go after the whole forest, the clear-cutting of acres and acres being considered more profitable (if only in the short run) than selective forest management. At the same time, there is even less a feeling in much of northern Maine of being on soil enriched by generation

Spotting moose near Sugarloaf Mountain.

after generation of human experience. There is something provisional, frontier-like about many northern Maine towns, as though they might not be there the next time you drive through.

Why travel north of Bangor? Because the place is full of surprises. There are small Victorian towns, and lakeside vistas that are among the most striking in New England. And at the very top of the state is the biggest surprise: the broad St. John Valley, whose rolling hills look more like the English Midlands than rocky Maine, but where many of the people speak French. And there is Mount Katahdin itself, that giant granite paperweight holding the rest of the state on the map.

■ NORTH TO THE WOODS *map page 209, B/C-5*

Even if you don't have a lot of time, you can still get a good glimpse of this region by driving about an hour north on I–95 to the Newport exit (which is roughly halfway between Waterville and Bangor). The first town you encounter, **Corinna,** was the birthplace of Gilbert Patten, who under the name of Bert L. Stadish wrote the Frank Merriwell series, an enormously popular group of some 1,000 adventure

THE FAR NORTH COUNTRY

Speaking relatively, I live in the far north—in the top, left-hand corner of Maine, just below the Canadian border—and there seems to be something about that country that fascinates people, even people who have never been there and never intend to go. Perhaps it's an inheritance passed down through the centuries from the time when for those who ventured away from the known coasts, the familiar landmarks, there was only one fixed point to steer by, the Pole Star, only one sure thing to guide them, the trembling needle pointing North. Or perhaps the North represents an idea, a state of mind, cold, detached, lonely and austere, sanctuary from the heat and confusion and indulgence of the modern world.... So I try to tell [these people] what the North is like.

In the first place, it is very, very beautiful. It's a country of lakes and forested mountains and tumbling rivers. It's beautiful all the time. In the spring the new leaves of the birches and the blossoms of the maples look like wisps of green and red smoke blowing across the staid dark background of the fir and spruce, and the forest floor is carpeted with flowers—huge purple violets and tiny white ones, and the fragile wood sorrel, and the pink twin-sisters. The leafless rhodora blazes in the swamps. Then the thrushes sing high on the ridges in the arrowy light from the setting sun, and the red deer come down the slopes, stepping daintily, into the dusk of the valleys to drink.

–Louise Dickinson Rich, *My Neck of the Woods,* 1950

stories for boys. **Dexter,** on Lake Wassookeag, is a famous shoe-manufacturing town. **Dover-Foxcroft,** another manufacturing town where Moosehead furniture is made, is typical of much of Maine in the way its two communities straddle a river (the Piscataquis), but unusual in that in 1922 they joined as one municipality.

Nearby **Sangerville** has the distinction of being the only New England town—probably the only American town—to produce two British knights, Sir Hiram Maxim and Sir Harry Oakes. Sir Hiram was knighted in 1901 by Queen Victoria for his inventions, among them the "Maxim gun," the first workable automatic machine gun. He began his career in a lathe shop in Dexter and later became a British subject. Sir Harry Oakes, the swashbuckling mining tycoon, was knighted by George VI in 1939 for his charitable donations in England. His gold mines made him the richest man in Canada. His brutal 1943 murder in Nassau—never solved—was one of the more sensational stories of the war years. (The suspects

ranged from the Mafia to the Nazis to members of his own family.) Sir Harry rests, with a suitable degree of pomp, in the Sangerville cemetery.

Maxim considered himself something of an art connoisseur, but a local resident with a much surer foothold in the 20th-century art world lived until her recent death up the road at **Monson** (and earlier in the woods near Lake Hebron at nearby Blanchard). Berenice Abbott, who in the 1920s had photographed Joyce and Cocteau in Paris, and who in the 1930s shot some of the most famous images of New York City, chose in 1966 to live with her friend Margaret Bennett in this remote part of Maine. Her tribute to her adopted state was *A Portrait of Maine* (1968), a photo essay that—despite its many views of men working—captures the essential stillness of life here just on the verge of all the changes the 1970s would bring.

■ MOOSEHEAD LAKE *map page 209, A/B-4*

From Monson it is a fairly short drive to **Greenville,** at the southern tip of Moosehead Lake, the state's largest body of fresh water. An attractive town that manages to be both a corporate center for the lumber industry and the gateway to all sorts of outdoor adventures on the lake, Greenville is the logical point (and from a hotel-and-restaurant point of view, almost the only point) from which to explore the region. Wrapping itself around two coves, the town was a much livelier place a century ago, when the train brought fashionable vacationers, including the rich anglers who built many of the massive stone lodges or Adirondack-style "camps" around the lake. Two railroads served Greenville by 1888, and at the peak of the season some 50 steamers crossed and recrossed the lake. One survivor of that era is the 1914 steamboat **S/S *Katahdin,*** relaunched in 1985 and maintained by the **Moosehead Marine Museum,** which offers three- and five-hour cruises from late June through Columbus Day. Since Moosehead and its ring of mountains can only really be appreciated from the water or the air, the boat ride is an important part of the local experience.

Another major place to recapture the past is the **Greenville Inn,** a hotel with a well-regarded restaurant, built in a lumber baron's large house overlooking the lake. Like the town's other hostelries, the inn is open most of the year, since the Moosehead region now offers winter sports.

On the dock at the Birches Resort.

■ ROCKWOOD AND MOUNT KINEO *map page 209, A/B-4*

If you've traveled as far as Greenville, you ought to drive the extra quarter hour north to Rockwood, which is linked by road to Jackman and by the highway to Quebec. The drive will give you a sample of Moosehead's 350 miles of shoreline (though most vacation homes and camps are at the ends of long, wooded drives). You're likely, also, to spot a moose; after all, up here they outnumber the people three to one. Across the narrowest part of the lake from **Mount Kineo,** Rockwood has dramatic views of the mountain's sheer, 760-foot cliff face, and has a public landing for launching canoes, which can be rented at many places along the shore. This part of Maine is renowned for its fishing; Moosehead is well supplied with landlocked salmon, brook trout, and lake trout (togue). In summer the Kineo Peninsula is accessible for swimming, hiking, and mountain biking; a passenger ferry leaves on the hour from Rockwood. After being neglected for decades, Rockwood once again offers lodging, dining, primitive camping, and golf. Thoreau stopped to climb Mount Kineo on his trip across Moosehead Lake; there are three trails that enable you to do the same for a spectacular view, from the top of the fire tower, of the northern lakes and distant Katahdin.

■ THE COUNTY

Aroostook County—at 6,453 square miles, Maine's largest, and indeed the largest county east of the Mississippi—is not what in the tourist trade is known as a "point of destination." You go there to do business or to see someone you know; very few travelers visit "The County" for its own sake. Its major point of contact with at least a cross section of the rest of the American population has been shut down: Loring Air Force Base, near Limestone.

Yet northeastern Aroostook County, particularly the **St. John Valley,** is a unique piece of the American puzzle; it's worth visiting if you really want to know the United States in all its variety. Unlike the wilderness areas in Aroostook's western interior, the valley is a series of softly folding hills, with the low, broad, often gray horizon of a Dutch landscape painting—an expanse of almost unbroken white after the first snowfall, and again in July when its famous potato fields are in bloom. The region shares its economy with the Canadians across the river, a border that has been peaceful since a brief flare-up in the 1830s. The people are a blend of Anglo-Saxon, Scandinavian, and Acadian French.

Fertile farmland produces the bulk of Maine's potato crop in the northeastern corner of the state.

Wilderness areas make up 90 percent of "The County's" landmass. The more populated northeastern edge falls into three regions: southern Aroostook, with its center in the county seat of Houlton; central Aroostook, the center of the potato industry and the area most deserving of a claim to be "the garden of Maine"; and the St. John Valley itself, linked at its western end to the famed Allagash Wilderness Waterway.

■ HOULTON *map page 209, D-3*

At one end of the 19th-century military road that linked the border and Bangor, Houlton is a pleasant Victorian town that has long been the commercial center of "The County." It enjoyed moments of considerable excitement in 1839–40 during the more or less bloodless "Aroostook War" between Maine and New Brunswick over their disputed boundary. Before the troubles were settled by the Webster-Ashburton Treaty in 1842, the young town was abuzz with militiamen. The arrival of the Bangor and Aroostook Railroad in the 1890s led to a short-lived business boom, but Houlton is a quieter place today.

THOREAU IN THE MAINE WOODS

"Two or three miles up the river, one beautiful country."

—*An Indian, pointing to the Penobscot, speaking to Thoreau
on his first visit to Maine, 1838*

That first trip of his was quick and businesslike. Unhappy with his job as a public schoolmaster in Concord, Massachusetts, he looked into other teaching posts as far away as Kentucky. Having no luck, he decided in the spring of 1838 to continue the search in person in Maine. The trip began inauspiciously: he got seasick. Never comfortable on saltwater—one of several ways he differed from many of his fellow New Englanders—Thoreau nonetheless knew that the overnight steamer from Boston to Portland was the most efficient way of reaching Maine. He made a quick tour through Brunswick, Bath, Gardiner, Hallowell, Augusta, China, Bangor, Old Town, Belfast, Castine, and Thomaston. It is interesting to consider what might have become of him had some district school teacher on that itinerary suddenly fallen ill or quit. But there were no jobs—it was a year of economic panic—and he returned, at age 21, to open a private academy of his own in Concord, a venture that attracted five students. He had caught a glimpse, however, of the wilderness that lay beyond Bangor, and it gave him some standard against which to judge Walden Pond.

Walden has become such a central text in the American perception of nature that it comes as a bit of a surprise that Thoreau did not think of the woods and pond he immortalized as being particularly wild. Symbolically, life at Walden Pond may have stood for everything that the materialistic "civilization" of Concord lacked. But in the back of his mind was what the Indian at Old Town had told him about the Penobscot.

In 1846, after a year at Walden and in the midst of his involvement in the antislavery movement, Thoreau left Concord to spend two weeks in the Maine Woods. He traveled by train to Portland, then took the overnight boat to Bangor. With his cousin George Thatcher and two other lumbermen, he traveled by stage to the end of the road at Mattawamkeag, where they continued in a batteau up the West Branch of the Penobscot to North Twin Lake, arriving by moonlight. Along Abol Stream they proceeded on foot to the south flank of Mount Katahdin. Thoreau twice climbed almost all the way to the top. The second time he was so lost in the mist, he was no longer sure of his direction. "It was like sitting in a chimney and waiting for the smoke to blow away," he wrote of the ridge between Baxter and South peaks. "It was, in fact, a cloud-factory."

The ascent of the mountain proved to be one of the shaping events of his imaginative life. Accustomed to the tameness of Concord's woods, with their dappled sunlight and many traces of human habitation, he was suddenly confronted on Katahdin with an experience of nature as, in the words of his biographer Robert Richardson Jr., "vast, drear, and indifferent to humankind." Writing up his notes of the trip back at home, he reflected on this new perception of "nature primitive—powerful gigantic aweful and beautiful, untamed forever." The Romantic writers saw man as a heroic actor, able to subdue the natural world even while claiming to live in harmony with it. But in Maine Thoreau had witnessed a drama in which humans merely played bit parts. He felt exposed, at the mercy of the elements—but not fatalistic. That fall he wrote not only the nature essay "Ktaadn" (this eccentric spelling alone suggesting the "primitive" quality of the mountain) but began work on one of his most radical political statements, "Resistance to Civil Government." It is as if the trip had cleared his mind and concentrated the power of his thought

In 1853 he returned to Maine. Landing again at Bangor, he traveled by open wagon with his cousin and a Penobscot Indian guide, Joe Aitteon, to Greenville and Moosehead Lake; they then canoed to Chesuncook Lake, west of Katahdin, and back to Moosehead. This time it was the Indians who fascinated him. In camp at night he would lie awake listening to them talk: "a purely wild and primitive American sound . . . I could not understand a syllable of it." In the essay "Chesuncook," based on this trip, Thoreau tried to balance in his own mind the conflict of the wild and the civilized (the killing and skinning of a moose played the role here that climbing the mountain had played in "Ktaadn"). As Richardson concludes, "Chesuncook" is "one of the founding statements of the conservation movement," a call for national wilderness preserves inspired not "by a distaste for human society or by a desire to escape it, but by a sense that true civilization will always require infusions of the spirit of wildness from time to time." In Thoreau's own words:

> Not only for strength, but for beauty, the poet must, from time to time, travel the logger's path and the Indian's trail, to drink at some new and more bracing fountain of the Muses, far in the recesses of the wilderness.

In 1857 he made his fourth and longest visit, which took him again to Chesuncook and then to the Allagash Lakes north of Katahdin, down the East Branch of the Penobscot, and back to Bangor. Traveling with a friend from Concord and a Penobscot Indian chief, Joe Polis, they covered 325 miles by canoe in just over ten days, in what was by far the most strenuous of his wilderness trips. (As the Thoreau scholar J. Parker Huber has written, "After repeating his Maine trips, I have a greater respect for his physical strength. This was no effete soul who in his thirties paddled the length of Moosehead Lake, carried a sixty-pound pack for five miles between Umbazooksus and Chamberlain lakes, and led the ascent of Katahdin through trailless woods by compass.") On this final trip it was Polis, age 48, who captured Thoreau's imagination: a Native American who, though a devout Christian and a representative in Washington for his people, never lost his ability to be at home in the woods.

The two essays, published ten years apart, were combined with an unpublished third essay, "The Allagash and East Branch," to form in 1864 the posthumous volume titled *The Maine Woods*. Although Thoreau spent a total of only nine weeks in the state, these experiences made an extraordinary impression on him (his last words were said to have been "moose" and "Indians.") In return, he left his distinctive mark on Maine: he constructed for his readers an image of Maine and the healing powers of its deep forests.

One sign of spring in Houlton is the annual **Meduxnekeag River Race;** while watching the boats race down the river, you can imagine the importance of those spring days in Maine's riverfront towns, when the ice broke. Another is the appearance of **fiddleheads,** the delicious green cinnamon fern shoots that Mainers eat with fresh fish. Like most of "The County," this is a place untouched by tourism, but it's a good jumping-off point for visiting Baxter State Park or the extensive **Lumberman's Museum** at Patten. If there is a souvenir to be taken home from this part of Maine, perhaps it would be a traditional potato basket of woven splints of ash.

■ CENTRAL AROOSTOOK *map page 209, D-2/3*

Say goodbye to I–95 at Houlton and rejoin U.S. 1 for its final stretch. About 40 miles north of Houlton the triangle made by the towns of Presque Isle, Caribou, and Fort Fairfield defines potato-growing central Aroostook. Best known today for its branch of the University of Maine, **Presque Isle** is an important agricultural and industrial hub for the mid-county, notable also for its **Crown of Maine Balloon Festival** (second weekend in July). The inland town got its name because Presque Isle Stream and the Aroostook River make it "almost an island."

Named for a variety of reindeer plentiful in Maine in pre-European times (and the subject in recent years of unsuccessful reintroduction attempts), **Caribou** is a major potato-shipping center. Its **Nylander Museum** is a collection formed earlier in this century by a Swedish-born geologist whose interests seem to have included the cultures of such prehistoric Maine inhabitants as the Red Paint People. Caribou is only 20 miles from the Canadian border, and closer to Quebec City (as the crow flies, 218 miles to the west) than to Portland (304 miles to the south).

On the Fort Fairfield road you'll find **Goughan's Berry Farm,** sort of a farm theme park that allows visitors to participate comfortably in local agriculture. You can pick your own strawberries, watch maple syrup or balsam wreaths being made, and show your kids the cows and pigs. A more austere site is **Fort Fairfield** itself, where there's a reconstructed blockhouse erected in 1840 to discourage an invasion by British troops from New Brunswick. The **Fort Fairfield Railroad Museum**, on the former Bangor and Aroostook railroad yard, displays a locomotive, caboose and other cars, and a restored station. Fort Fairfield's renovated **Friends' Meeting House**, on the National Register of Historic Places, was a stop on the Underground Railroad.

■ ST. JOHN VALLEY *map page 209, D-1*

Van Buren describes itself as "the gateway" to the St. John Valley. As you continue north and west, it is the first of a series of communities that were settled by French-speaking Acadians. Samuel de Champlain founded Acadia on an island in the St. Croix River in 1604, but the colony was relocated to Nova Scotia in 1605, becoming the center of the Acadian community. In 1713 the Treaty of Utrecht granted the island to Great Britain, and in the early 1750s, realizing the imminence of war with

(following pages) Mount Katahdin in Baxter State Park is Maine's highest peak at 5,267 feet.

France, the British demanded that the French farmers pledge allegiance to the Crown and the Church of England. The Catholic Acadians refused, and most were expelled. The Acadians who moved to Louisiana and became "Cajuns" are far better known than those who sought refuge in what was then an ill-defined northern extremity of Massachusetts. But the St. John Valley families prospered, in a modest way, on this rich soil. They managed to preserve much of their culture, centered on the Catholic Church; its steeples continue to dominate the local landscape. Acadian French is a different dialect from the varieties of Quebecois French spoken in southern Maine. Similarly, the Acadians remained a predominantly agricultural people, while most of the state's other Franco-Americans arrived originally to work in textile mills.

The best place to learn the story of northern Maine's Francophones is the **Acadian Village,** a collection of typical early farmhouses, near Keegan, a few miles upriver from Van Buren, or at the **Acadian Festival,** held each year in late June in the paper-mill town of Madawaska. Nineteen miles upriver lies another town preserving its Aroostook War blockhouse. Home to another branch campus of the University of Maine, **Fort Kent** welcomes visitors with a sign reminding them that "This Marks the Beginning of U.S. Rt. 1, Ending in Key West, Florida, 2209 mi. South."

The **Allagash Wilderness Waterway,** stretching from the town of Allagash in the north to Baxter State Park, is a 92-mile-long preserve filled with rivers, lakes, and streams. The waterway is a favorite destination for campers and canoeists.

■ BAXTER STATE PARK *map page 209, C-3/4*

This survey of Maine that began with one powerful symbol of the state—the placid Colonial Revival landscape of the lower Piscataqua Valley—ends with the awesome bulk of **Mount Katahdin** in Baxter State Park. Between the two places are many versions of Maine, some of them saltwater, some fresh; some tradition-loving, some experimental. Some envision the state as a distillation of Old New England, a time-less refuge where work is hard and life is simple. Others see in Maine raw nature: unspoiled ocean, miles of rugged coastline, and acres of woods where lovers of the great outdoors can test their muscle and mettle. These two views are not mutually contradictory—many people are sympathetic to both—but they help explain why the state sometimes can't decide whether it's a museum or a wilderness preserve. (Many Mainers, of course, don't want it to be either, but that's another story.)

But back to the mountain. From miles around, its silhouette is unavoidable; on a clear day you can see it from much of north-central Maine. But it's not a place for the casual visitor. For one thing, you have to find a place to spend the night, probably in the mill town of **Millinocket** (more or less totally built by the Great Northern Paper Company to house its workers in 1901) or at a campsite in the park. Climbing and descending Katahdin, unlike the mountains of Acadia National Park (none of which is too far from a paved road or too steep for a moderately active person to climb), requires a day or more and perhaps a 16-mile hike, much of it in a semi-lunar landscape above the treeline. Like Thoreau, you may get swallowed up in the clouds. You may find—especially in July and August—that several hundred other climbers are sharing your epiphanies. (There are, however, numerous other good climbs in Baxter State Park where you can be alone.) If you're serious about the climb, you need Stephen Clark's *Katahdin: A Guide to Baxter Park & Katahdin,* with its good maps and minutely detailed trail descriptions. And don't forget to check in with the park rangers.

Climb Katahdin if you can. It's a rite of passage unlike any other physical challenge New England can offer. And when you reach the summit, think fondly for a moment of Gov. Percival C. Baxter. Between 1930 and 1967 he bought up the park's 314 square miles of forests, mountains, streams, and lakes and donated them to the people of Maine—to be kept "forever wild."

One of the estimated 25,000 moose that wander through Maine.

SIGHTING A MOOSE

Surely the first sight of *Alces alces americana,* the North Woods' unmistakeable moose, will be one of the most memorable events you experience in Maine. Keep in mind that a close encounter with a 900-pound cow moose—or an even heftier bull with his 60-pound rack of antlers—can only happen by chance. But the chances are getting better. Today an estimated 25,000 moose wander through the state, most of them in the heavily wooded northern half of Maine, but with enough straying into more populated areas to justify those yellow MOOSE X-ING warnings that appear with increasing frequency on the state's highways. A collision at full speed with a deer is bad enough; with a creature the size of an adult moose it can be fatal for you both. The only factor working against such accidents is that moose, unlike easily frightened deer, rarely leap out into the road.

You can increase your chances of seeing a moose on your own terms if you follow a few suggestions. First, choose one of their well-known habitats, many of which involve weedy freshwater and densely wooded shores. Bill Silliker Jr.'s helpful paperback *Maine Moose Watcher's Guide* lists more than 30 such "haunts and hangouts," most of them accessible by road and most in the northerly counties. You can also ask locally. There's hardly a town north of Portland without its occasional visiting moose, and local residents can suggest some likely waterways. The best times to spot one are early morning, noon, and late afternoon (moose seem to like to eat three meals a day); the best season, late spring to summer near the water, and late summer in the woods. Be patient, spray yourself to ward off black flies and other pests, and look for such signs of your prey as tracks, moose scat (which is larger than deer droppings), and places where seven-foot-high animals have browsed on leaves and twigs. Finally, enjoy the outing whether you spot a moose or not. Sooner or later, you will.

In general, moose are gentle, placid vegetarians with such poor eyesight (not beyond 25 feet) that if you stand still they may not even see you against a wooded background (though if the wind is blowing toward them, they will quickly smell you). There are two times, however, when you should make sure to keep your distance: during rutting season (mid-September to mid-October), when the bulls become very aggressive and unpredictable in behavior; and during nursing periods, when mother moose can become belligerent if they feel their calves are in danger. As awkward and lumbering as moose may seem, they can in fact run as fast as 35 miles per hour and can swim at about the rate most people can paddle a canoe.

Perhaps the human fascination with moose arises from the way they seem so oddly constructed—those immense bodies on such delicate legs—yet so obviously well adapted to their native woods and streams. They made Thoreau "think of great frightened rabbits, with their long ears and half-inquisitive, half-frightened looks." He understood why it was necessary for men to hunt moose, although the sight of a freshly killed cow being stripped of her hide ruined his day. He did try moose meat —"It tasted like tender beef, with perhaps more flavor—sometimes like veal."

Plentiful in colonial times, moose had already begun to grow scarce in Maine by Thoreau's visit to the Chesuncook region in 1853; in 1830 the state legislature had already restricted the hunting season (though, as Thoreau noted, game wardens ignored the rules if the hunter gave them a shoulder of the meat). By the early 20th century, a combination of over-hunting, disease, logging, and increased competition with white deer populations reduced the state's moose population to a few thousand animals. Beginning in 1935, hunting was prohibited outright. But increased herd sizes led in 1980 to introduction of a one-week moose season each October, with 1,000 permits being sold, many to out-of-staters. A referendum in the 1980s to ban moose hunting got much publicity but not enough votes, in a state where hunting is still regarded less as a sport than as a way of life. Thoreau himself thought that shooting moose was "too much like going out by night to some wood-side pasture and shooting your neighbor's horses." He once noted that if you encountered one face on, the moose would turn sideways as if to give you a better shot. "These are God's own horses, poor, timid creatures, that will run fast enough as soon as they smell you, though they *are* nine feet high."

Perhaps the best news for today's Maine moose is that they've become a tourist attraction, each one a symbol of pure and enticing wildness to visitors wielding cameras rather than rifles. At Greenville, for example, biologists lead the curious to likely watering holes at dawn, and the local chamber of commerce has begun to market the town as a moose-watching center—including a month-long Moosemania festival in early summer.

Thoreau would have approved. Amid his detailed observations of Maine's flora and fauna, he allowed himself an occasional philosophical reflection. What did it mean to use nature for our own purposes, he asked—to cut down the pine tree as if its highest value was in providing us with lumber, or to think that discovering the value of whalebone and whale oil was "the true use of the whale"? He answered the question in these words: "These are petty and accidental uses; just as if a stronger race were to kill us in order to make buttons and ageolets of our bones; for everything may serve a lower as well as a higher use. Every creature is better alive than dead, men and moose and pine-trees, and he who understands it aright will rather preserve its life than destroy it."

PRACTICAL INFORMATION

NOTE: Compass American Guides makes every effort to ensure the accuracy of its information; however, as conditions and prices change frequently, we recommend that readers also contact the regional chambers of commerce for the most up-to-date information—*see* "Tourist Information," p. 302.

■ AREA CODE

The area code for all of Maine is 207.

■ TRANSPORTATION

■ BY AIRPLANE

Maine's major airports are **Portland International Jetport** and **Bangor International Airport**; each has daily flights by major U.S. carriers.

Hancock County/Bar Harbor Airport, in Trenton, eight miles northwest of Bar Harbor; **Knox County Regional Airport,** in Owls Head, three miles south of Rockland; **Augusta Airport;** and **Northern Maine Regional Airport** in Presque Isle are all served by **Colgan Air** from Boston. Book through **USAirways,** 800-428-4322; www.usairways.com.

Regional flying services, operating from regional and municipal airports, provide access to remote wilderness as well as the Penobscot Bay islands.

■ BY AUTOMOBILE

The **Maine Turnpike** and **Interstate 95** are the fastest routes to and through the state from coastal New Hampshire and points south. **U.S. 1** (also called **Route 1**), more leisurely and historic, is the principal coastal highway from New Hampshire to Canada. Vast areas of northwest Maine are accessible only by logging and other privately owned roads, some of which are gated and can be used only after paying a fee. Note that in 2004 the Maine DOT and the Turnpike Authority redesignated the numbers of the interstates and almost all the exits, to clear up the former confusion and install a mileage-based system. You can pick up a redesignation chart at any visitors center as soon as you get to Maine. Although residents welcome the change, they may still refer to the old numbers for a while.

In many areas a car is the only practical means of travel; in winter a four-wheel drive vehicle is a good idea. The *Official Maine Highway Map* is useful for driving throughout the state; it has directories, mileage charts, and enlarged maps of city areas. It is available free from offices of the **Maine Tourism Association.** Call 888-624-6345.

If you plan to go any distance off the interstate, the turnpike, or Route 1, the *Maine Atlas and Gazetteer* published by DeLorme is invaluable for its level of detail. It's available at most gas stations in the more traveled areas of the state, as well as directly from DeLorme, 800-452-5931; www.delorme.com.

■ BY TRAIN

Amtrak (800-872-7245; www.amtrack.com) has service between Boston and **Portland**, with stops in **Wells, Saco**, and **Old Orchard Beach** (seasonal), and a connecting bus service that runs as far north as **Belfast** and **Bangor**.

Seaplanes on Moosehead Lake near Greenville gather for the International Seaplane Fly-In.

■ By Bus

Vermont Transit (207-772-6587 or 800-231-2222), a subsidiary of Greyhound, connects towns in Maine with cities in New England and throughout the United States. **Concord Trailways** (800-639-3317) has daily service between Boston and Bangor (via Portland), with a coastal route (along Route 1) connecting towns between Brunswick and Searsport.

■ By Ferry

Marine Atlantic, 207-288-3395 or 800-341-7981, operates a car-ferry service year-round between Yarmouth (Nova Scotia) and Bar Harbor; **Prince of Fundy Cruises,** 800-341-7540 or 800-482-0955, operates a car ferry between Yarmouth and Portland (May-October.).

Within Maine: **Casco Bay Lines,** 207-774-7871, provides ferry service from Portland to the islands of Casco Bay; **Maine State Ferry Service,** 207-596-2202, provides ferry service from Rockland, Camden (Lincolnville), and Bass Harbor to islands in Penobscot and Blue Hill bays. Monhegan Island is served by the **Monhegan-Thomaston Boat Line,** 207-372-8547, from Port Clyde; by **Balmy Days Cruises**, 207-633-2284 or 800-298–2284, from Boothbay Harbor; and by **Hardy Boat Cruises**, 207-677-2026 or 800-278-3346, from New Harbor.

For local ferries from Acadia (Bass Harbor) to Swans Island call 207-526-4273; to Frenchboro call 207-244-3254. For ferries from Camden (Lincolnville) to Islesboro call 207-789-5611. For ferries from Rockland to Vinalhaven call 207-863-4421; to North Haven call 207-867-4441; to Matinicus call 207-596-2203.

■ CLIMATE

Maine's weather is a topic of much discussion among its residents—"Nice day if it don't rain" being a not uncommon refrain. The widely held perception of Maine as a cold, snowy place with eternal winters is by and large correct. However, brief glorious springs, short but intense summers, and a month (usually October) of spectacular fall colors are the exceptions to "winter rules."

In addition to being the largest state in New England, Maine offers you the chance to see all kinds of landscapes—rocky coasts, pine forests, lakes, and streams—transformed by the rich reds, golden yellows, and brilliant oranges of fall foliage. In general, peak fall color for the northern sections of Aroostook County and the Katahdin/Moosehead regions is during the last week of September; peak

CITY	FAHRENHEIT TEMPERATURE						ANNUAL PRECIPITATION	
	AVG. JAN.		AVG. JULY		RECORD		AVERAGE	AVERAGE
	HIGH	LOW	HIGH	LOW	HIGH	LOW	RAIN	SNOW
Portland	31	12	79	57	103	-39	42.05"	72"
Bar Harbor	32	15	76	56	98	-21	50.68"	58"
Eastport	30	14	68	52	93	-23	35.56"	66"
Caribou	20	1	76	54	96	-41	37.87"	112"
Bangor	30	10	82	60	104	-28	39.52"	103"
Millinocket	25	4	80	56	106	-41	41.60"	90"

color in the Western Lakes and Mountains, Kennebec Valley, and southern portions of the Katahdin/Moosehead regions is during the first week of October; and peak color along coastal Maine is during the second week of October.

Climate does vary within the state. In the far north, temperatures average 8 degrees F in January, while in Portland a balmy 22 degrees F is the average for the same month. In winter along the coast, northeasters frequently blow mild Atlantic air off the ocean and turn snowstorms into rain—a rare occurrence in the inland and northern regions. In summer, onshore breezes bring fog and cool temperatures to the coast, while the inland areas warm up and frequently experience real summer heat. The chart above indicates the climate for various regions of the state: Portland, Bar Harbor, and Eastport representing the coast; Caribou the far north; Bangor the "inland" region; and Millinocket, central Maine.

■ LODGING & RESTAURANTS

■ ABOUT MAINE LODGING

Maine has every type of accommodation, from inexpensive, old-fashioned roadside cabins to fancy seaside resorts. The listings below are merely a sample of what is available in the towns most visited by tourists. The number of bed-and-breakfasts, offering a more personal (though rarely inexpensive) alternative to standard motels, seems to increase each year. But be aware that in Maine motels can be wonderful—anything but the standard roadside bore. You'll find oceanfront rooms, country cabins with fabulous views, and family-friendly amenities and activities. Another option, if you want to stay in one place for a week or longer, is to rent a house or cottage, which, depending on size and location, can range in high season (July 4th to Labor Day) from about $600 to $2,000 a week or more for luxury properties. Write to local chambers of commerce for rental listings or look at the back pages of *Down East* magazine. Although Maine law prohibits excluding children from lodgings (except owner-occupied ones with five or fewer rooms), some inns will tell you they don't accept children, so be prepared.

Price codes are approximate for one room, one night, in summer, and are subject to change. Reservations are highly recommended in July and August. Most year-round establishments offer considerably reduced off-season rates. (If they don't, go elsewhere; innkeepers are desperate for winter and spring business.) Breakfast is included in many rates; other meals are sometimes included as well. State taxes and service charges are not included.

■ ABOUT MAINE RESTAURANTS

Most of Maine missed the all-around upgrade that swept through American dining in the 1980s, but by the 1990s the ski industry and coastal tourism had made restaurant-going a genuine pleasure. It's true that many of Maine's most popular restaurants are steak houses that also serve lobster, but even those hidebound relics might surprise you with a fresh mesclun salad before the meal and a creditable tiramisu after. The following listings include both the popular restaurants representative of the Maine tradition (which, after all, does arise from rural English and Irish roots) and some of the more sophisticated delights. Keep in mind that price codes are approximate and subject to rapid change.

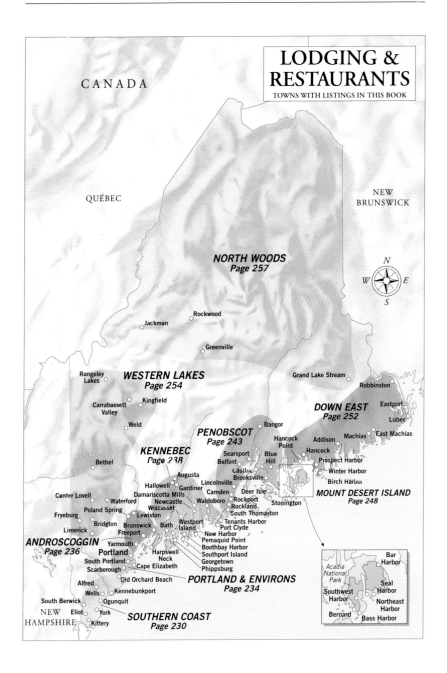

LODGING & RESTAURANTS
TOWNS WITH LISTINGS IN THIS BOOK

CANADA

QUÉBEC

NEW BRUNSWICK

NORTH WOODS
Page 257

Rockwood

Jackman

Greenville

Rangeley Lakes

WESTERN LAKES
Page 254

Grand Lake Stream

Robbinston

Carrabassett Valley

Kingfield

DOWN EAST
Page 252

Eastport

Lubec

Weld

Bangor

PENOBSCOT
Page 243

Hancock Point

Addison

Machias

East Machias

KENNEBEC
Page 238

Searsport

Belfast

Blue Hill

Hancock

Prospect Harbor

Bethel

Augusta

Castine

Brooksville

Winter Harbor

Birch Harbor

Center Lovell

Hallowell

Gardiner

Lincolnville

Camden

Deer Isle

MOUNT DESERT ISLAND
Page 248

Waterford

Damariscotta Mills

Newcastle

Waldoboro

Rockport

Stonington

Poland Spring

Wiscasset

Rockland

Fryeburg

Lewiston

South Thomaston

Bridgton

Brunswick

Bath

Westport Island

Tenants Harbor

Limerick

Freeport

Port Clyde

ANDROSCOGGIN
Page 236

Yarmouth

New Harbor

Pemaquid Point

Boothbay Harbor

Portland

Harpswell Neck

Southport Island

South Portland

Cape Elizabeth

Georgetown

Phippsburg

Scarborough

Old Orchard Beach

PORTLAND & ENVIRONS
Page 234

Alfred

Wells

Kennebunkport

South Berwick

Ogunquit

NEW HAMPSHIRE

Eliot

York

SOUTHERN COAST
Page 230

Kittery

Acadia National Park

Bar Harbor

Seal Harbor

Southwest Harbor

Northeast Harbor

Bernard

Bass Harbor

ROOM RATES
Per room, per night, in high season

$ = under $100	$$ = $100–$150	$$$ = over $150

RESTAURANT PRICES
Dinner for one, not including tax, tip, or drinks

$ = under $25	$$ = $25–$40	$$$ = over $40

SOUTHERN COAST & YORK COUNTY

◆ **ALFRED**

⚏ **Central House.** *11 Saco Rd.; 207-324-0180 or 877-541-6721.* This antiques-filled B&B on the green was an inn from 1850 to 1925. 2 rooms. $

◆ **ELIOT**

⚏ **Farmstead.** *379 Goodwin Rd.; 207-748-3145 or 207-439-5033; www.farmstead.qpg.com.* Built in 1704, this family-friendly B&B has mini-fridges and microwaves. 6 rooms. $

◆ **KENNEBUNKPORT**

⚏ **Cape Arundel Inn.** *208 Ocean Ave.; 207-967-2125; www.capearundelinn.com.* This old (1895) oceanfront inn has a good restaurant with Continental cuisine and lots of seafood. Breakfasts are especially good. Room 8 faces both Walker's Point and the luscious garden. 14 rooms. $$$

⚏ **Captain Lord Mansion.** *6 Pleasant St.; 207-967-3141; www.captainlord.com.* Splendidly opulent, antiques-filled, and frilled and furbelowed, this Federal house in town is said to be one of the country's most romantic inns. 20 rooms (inn and carriage house). $$$

⚏ **Colony Hotel.** *Ocean Ave. and Kings Hwy.; 207-967-3331; www.thecolonyhotel. com/maine.* This 1914 Georgian National Trust property is the sort of landmark where guests ask for the same room their grandparents used to take every summer. The expansive property overlooks the ocean, and there's a large pool. 124 rooms. $$$

⚏ **Franciscan Guesthouse.** *28 Beach Ave.; 207-967-4865; www.franciscanguesthouse. com.* Spartan accommodations (and breakfast) are in five buildings on the luxurious grounds Olmsted-designed riverside of a 1902 Tudor mansion (the monastery). They also have a saltwater pool. 57 rooms. $–$$

✠ **Green Heron Inn.** *Ocean Ave.; 207-967-3315; www.greenheroninn.com.* Two major appeals are the rocking-chair porch and the wonderful breakfasts. 10 rooms, 1 cottage. $$–$$$

✠ **Kennebunkport Inn.** *One Dock Square; 207-967-2621 or 800-248-2621; www.kennebunkportinn.com.* The pleasant, old-fashioned inn built around an 1890s in-town mansion and in two renovated buildings on the wharf has a steakhouse restaurant and a pool. 48 rooms. $$–$$$

✠ **Seaside Motor Inn and Cottages.** *80 Beach Ave.; 207-967-4461 or 866-300-6750; www.kennebunkbeach.com.* The motel units have private patios or decks, and the 11 heated cottages (rented by the week) look across to the harbor or the ocean—all this on 20 acres with a private beach. You also get a buffet breakfast. 22 rooms. $$$

✠ **White Barn Inn.** *37 Beach Ave.; 207-967-2321; www.whitebarninn.com.* Choose from antiques-furnished bedrooms in the farmhouse or capacious modern suites with fireplaces and whirlpool baths on the grounds of this luxurious Relais & Chateau property. The dining room, in the converted barn (open to the public), is perhaps the best in the state. (Sister properties equally luxurious are the newly renovated **Breakwater Inn & Hotel**, **The Yachtsman Lodge & Marina** on Ocean Ave., and **The Beach House** at Kennebunk Beach.) Pool; 16 rooms, 9 suites, 3 cottages. $$$

✗ **Grissini Italian Bistro.** *27 Western Ave.; 207-967-2211; www.restaurantgrissini.com.* At this classy, casual place you'll get delicious northern Italian food cooked in wood-fired ovens. $$$

✗ **Mabel's Lobster Claw.** *Ocean Ave.; 207-967-2562.* For lunch, nothing beats Mabel's lobster rolls, unless it's her clams or mussels. $

◆ **KITTERY/KITTERY POINT**

✗ **Cap'n Simeon's Galley.** *Route 103, Pepperell Cove; 207-439-3655.* A seafood restaurant built onto the original Frisbee's Store (1828) has great views of Portsmouth Harbor. $–$$

✗ **Warren's Lobster House.** *Just east of Route 1, on the Piscataqua River; 207-439-1630.* Built on pilings over the river, this 65-year-old institution has 150 feet of free dockage for boaters. They serve all kinds of seafood (and meat), and maintain a wonderful salad bar. $–$$

◆ LIMERICK

⊡ **Jeremiah Mason House.** *40 Main St.; 207-793-4858; www.jeremiahmasonhouse. com.* This redbrick 19th-century B&B has lots of fireplaces and good reading lights. Note the gorgeous gold mirror in the parlor. 10 rooms. $

✕ **Peppermill.** *25 Main St.; 207-793-2500.* This homey place has a full bar. Try the wonderful liver and onions. $

◆ OGUNQUIT

⊡ **The Anchorage.** *125 Shore Rd.; 207-646-9384; www.anchoragebythesea.com.* A pretty, new, year-round ocean-view resort has a poolside café and an indoor pool. 240 rooms. $$$

⊡ **Aspinquid Motel.** *57 Beach St.; 207-646-7072; www.aspinquid.com.* An old-fashioned shingle motel complex, with a pool, is just across the Ogunquit River from the main beach. 62 rooms. $$–$$$

⊡ **Hartwell House.** *312 Shore Rd.; 207-646-7210 or 800-235-8883; www.hartwellhouseinn.com.* Many antiques add to the loveliness of this in-town inn, as do the balconies and terraces overlooking the garden. 16 rooms. $$$

⊡ **Rockmere Lodge.** *150 Stearns Rd.; 207-646-2985; www.rockmere.com.* A shingle cottage just above the Marginal Way with over-the-top tchotchkes and three genial hosts. It's worth a stay just to see how the pristine baths have been shoehorned into the delightful rooms; breakfast on the porch is a bonus. 8 room. $$$

⊡ **Sparhawk Resort Motel.** *85 Shore Rd.; 207-646-5562.* This resort-like motor inn has gardens overlooking the river and beach. Heated pool. 87 rooms. $$$

✕ **Arrows.** *Berwick Rd.; 207-361-1100; www.arrowsrestaurant.com.* At this 1765 farmhouse with both kitchen gardens and beautifully illuminated ornamental gardens you'll get imaginatively prepared meals with classic and Asian accents, and a choice of designer butters. (It's expensive, however, for Maine.) $$$

✕ **Barnacle Billy's.** *Perkins Cove; 207-646-5575; www.barnbilly.com.* A popular, informal waterfront place with indoor, deck, or garden dining; take a number at its lobster pound next door, pick your table, and wait for your meal. $$

✕ **Hurricane.** *Perkins Cove; 207-646-6348; www.hurricanerestaurant.com.* Get the great grilled fish or the legendary lobster cioppino—but unless you have reservations or score a last-minute opening, you can forget it in July and August. $$–$$$

✕ **Jackie's Too.** *Perkins Cove; 207-646-4444; www.jackiestoo.com.* A casual year-round institution with plenty of outdoor seating right over the water. $

◆ Old Orchard Beach

▦ **Edgewater**. *57 West Grand Ave.; 207-934-2221 or 800-203-2034; www.janelle. com.* This spotless motel is right on the beach in the last of Maine's honky-tonk resort towns. 36 rooms. $$–$$$

◆ South Berwick

▦ **Academy Street Inn**. *15 Academy St.; 207-384-5633.* The solid, four-square house was once the headmaster's residence for Berwick Academy. 5 rooms. $$

◆ Wells

▦ **Beach Farm Inn**. *97 Eldredge Rd.; 207-646-8493; www.beachfarminn.com.* At this comfortably furnished farmhouse with a pool, friendly hosts, and two house-keeping cottages (by the week) you'll get an excellent breakfast. 8 rooms. $–$$

◆ The Yorks

▦ **Anchorage Inn**. *Route 1A, York Harbor; 207-363-5112; www.anchorageinn. com.* This large, family-friendly motel convenient to the interstate overlooks the beach. 200 rooms. $$–$$$

▦ **Cliff House**. *Off Shore Rd. at Bald Head Cliff; 207-361-1000; www. cliffhousemaine.com.* Play or unwind at this 70-acre resort with tennis, indoor and outdoor heated pools, and a sauna. 194 rooms in 4 buildings. $$$

▦ **Katahdin Inn**. *11 Ocean Ave. Ext., York Beach; 207-363-1824; www. thekatahdin.com.* An 1890s guest house overlooking Short Sands Beach. 11 rooms. $–$$

▦ **Stage Neck Inn**. *8 Stage Neck Rd., York Harbor; 207-363-3850 or 800-340-1130; www.stageneck.com.* This modern waterfront complex occupies a peninsula of its own, the site of the 19th-century Marshall House Hotel, which burned in 1916. They have two pools, and the formal restaurant and bar & grill are open to the public. 60 rooms. $$$

▦ **Ye Old Perkins Place**. *749 Shore Rd.; 207-361-1119.* A B&B in an 18th-century house on Cape Neddick with ocean views. 5 rooms. $

▦ **York Harbor Inn**. *Route 1A, York Harbor; 207-363-5119 or 800-343-3869; www.yorkharborinn.com.* In addition to its Colonial Revival vibe you'll get views across the famous harbor, a huge year-round hot tub, and two restaurants and a pub. 47 rooms. $$–$$$

✕ **Fazio's**. *38 Woodbridge Rd., York Village; 207-363-7019; www.fazios.com.* This traditional trattoria serves fresh pasta, steaks, and seafood. The sports bar upstairs has a TV in every booth. $$; Sports bar, $

✕ **The Goldenrod.** *York Beach; 207-363-2621; www.thegoldenrod.com.* A famous family restaurant since 1896, which makes saltwater taffy kisses on the spot and ships them anywhere you like. They have 135 flavors of homemade ice cream and the lunch menu is served through dinnertime. **$**

PORTLAND & ENVIRONS

◆ CAPE ELIZABETH

⊡ **Inn-by-the-Sea.** *40 Bowery Beach Rd.; 207-799-3134 or 800-888-4287; www.innbythesea.com.* This luxurious complex of cottages and other buildings is right on Crescent Beach, overlooking Kettle Cove. Notify the inn in advance, and you can bring your dog—who will get no less than royal treatment. The **Audubon Restaurant** serves excellent seafood and regional cuisine. 43 suites. **$$$**; restaurant **$$–$$$**

✕ **Two Lights Lobster Shack.** *Two Lights Rd.; 207-799-1677.* Not really a shack, this eatery has sit-down service—but it's best to order fried clams or chowder, then sit outside at a picnic table, from which you'll have a great view of craggy shore. It's just 15 minutes from downtown Portland. **$$**

◆ PORTLAND

⊡ **Andrews on Auburn.** *417 Auburn St.; 207-797-9157; www.andrewsonauburn. com.* Breathe easy in a residential part of town, but bring a car. 5 rooms. **$$-$$$**

⊡ **Eastland Park Hotel.** *157 High St.; 207-775-5411 or 888-671-8008; www. eastlandparkhotel.com.* This landmark in-town hotel has a rooftop cocktail lounge and a lobby restaurant that serves upscale pub food. It's near museums and shopping. 202 rooms. **$$$**

⊡ **Inn at Park Spring.** *135 Spring St.; 207-774-1059 or 800-437-8511; www. innatparkspring.com.* A lovely town house at the edge of the Old Port is within walking distance to everything downtown. Rates include parking. 6 rooms. **$$**

⊡ **Inn on Carleton Street.** *46 Carleton St.; 207-775-1910 or 800-639-1779; www.innoncarleton.com.* This is a Western Prom–area town house. 6 rooms. **$$$**

⊡ **Percy Inn.** *15 Pine St.; 207-871-7638 or 888-417-3729; www.percyinn.com* Your host, a former travel writer and critic, has thought of everything, from all-day snacks and hot drinks to the video, book, and CD library and the beach bags and coolers to borrow. In the West End historic district, it's close to everything. Beautifully appointed rooms in an 1830 brick row house with side yard and sun deck; long-term lodgings in 19th-century satellite buildings nearby. 7 rooms. $$–$$$

☵ **Pomegranate Inn.** *49 Neal St.; 207-772-1006 or 800-356-0408; www. pomegranateinn.com.* The best B&B in Portland (possibly in Maine) has a reservations book to match; plan ahead if you'd like a room. It's in the Western Prom area. 8 rooms. $$$

☵ **Regency.** *20 Milk St.; 207-774-4200 or 800-727-3436; www.theregency.com.* This restored redbrick armory has a great Old Port location, but watch out for the somewhat odd rooms built into the eaves—adaptive renovations of old buildings can sometimes be problematic. The restaurant serves typical Continental/ American food. 95 rooms. $$$.

✕ **Back Bay Grill.** *65 Portland St.; 207-772-8833; www.backbaygrill.com.* Restaurants come and go in Portland, but this one consistently offers some of the best regional American food around, and it has an impressive wine list. $$$

✕ **Becky's Diner.** *390 Commercial St.; 207-773-7070; www.beckysdiner.com.* Everyone eats breakfast here because it's cheap and good—you're likely to be seated between a lawyer and fisherman. $

✕ **Cinque Terre Ristorante.** *36 Wharf St.; 207-347-6154; www.cinqueterrremaine. com.* Traditional northern Italian food is served in an elegant modern setting. $$–$$$

✕ **Fore Street.** *288 Fore St.; 207-775-2717.* This American bistro with its wood-fired grill is considered one of Maine's best restaurants. The bar in front is a cozy place for oysters and a cocktail, and the main dining room is dramatic without being stuffy. $$$

✕ **Gritty McDuff's.** *396 Fore St.; 207-772-2739; www.grittys.com.* This is Portland's first brewpub. $–$$

✕ **Hugo's Restaurant.** *88 Middle St.; 207-774-8538; www.hugos.net.* Named one of *Food & Wine* magazine's Best New Chefs of 2004, Rob Evans continues to please with his imaginative prix-fixe and tasting menus. There are 30 wines by the glass. $$–$$$

✕ **Katahdin.** *106 High St.; 207-774-1740.* Sophisticated home cooking amid funky thrift-shop accents attracts the city's upper Bohemia. There are delicious potpies and cornbread, and desserts are huge. $$

✕ **Pepperclub.** *78–80 Middle St.; 207-772-0531.* This place has an excellent organic and mostly vegetarian menu. $-$$

✕ **The Porthole.** *Customhouse Wharf; 207-780-6533.* This salty, authentic seamen's place is open 365 days a year for three meals a day; they serve mostly seafood, and have famous homemade sausage and seafood chowder. $

✕ **Ruby's Choice.** *127 Commercial St.; 207-773-9099.* Expect burgers plus. $

✕ **Street & Company.** *33 Wharf St.; 207-775-0887.* Fresh, fresh fish—from simply grilled salmon to lobster diavolo—is served on copper-topped tables at this homey eatery. The pasta's good, too. $$

✕ **Uffa! Restaurant.** *190 State St.; 207-775-3380; www.uffarestaurant.com.* Traditional French country cuisine is served here; with a notable bouillabaisse and a popular Sunday brunch. $$

✕ **Walter's Cafe.** *15 Exchange St.; 207-871-9258.* This trendy bistro is in the heart of Old Port. $$

◆ SCARBOROUGH

🏠 **Black Point Inn.** *Black Point Rd. (Rte. 207); 207-883-2500 or 800-258-0003; www.blackpointinn.com.* Imagine a place as luxurious as a prewar ocean liner, sailing in this case through Winslow Homer's seas. A real London taxi will pick you up, by request, and can be at your disposal for a drive to Portland or elsewhere. Guests may use the Prouts Neck summer colony's yacht club, beach, pools, tennis courts, and golf course. The dining room is formal and serves a varied Continental-American menu. 80 guest rooms. $$$; restaurant $$$

◆ SOUTH PORTLAND

✕ **Joe's Boathouse.** *1 Spring Point Dr., at the Spring Point Marina; 207-741-2780; www.joesboathouse.com.* Locals come to this dockside restaurant off the tourist track to sit outside on the patio or the porch, or inside with a view of the bay. The place is informal, but the food's first-rate. $$

ANDROSCOGGIN RIVER

◆ BRUNSWICK

🏠 **Brunswick Bed & Breakfast.** *165 Park Row; 207-729-4914 or 800-299-4914; www.brunswickbnb.com.* Spacious, clean, and comfortable rooms in a Greek Revival house, carriage house, and garden cottage, on the town green, close to the Bowdoin campus. Great breakfast too, at your own table. 15 rooms. $$–$$$

⊡ **Captain Daniel Stone Inn.** *10 Water St.; 207-725-9898 or 877-573-5151; www.someplacesdifferent.com.* A newish hotel and restaurant built onto a Federal-period house is convenient to Route 1. 34 rooms. $$$; restaurant $$

⊡ **Pelletier Bed & Breakfast.** *40 Pleasant St.; 207-725-6538.* This 1930s B&B, which was once a convent, is within walking distance of downtown and the Bowdoin Campus. 3 rooms. $

✕ **Fat Boy's.** *111 Bath Rd.; 207-729-9431.* At this classic 1950s drive-in, where car-hops bring your lunch, you can munch on a Canadian BLT and watch the PC-Orions take off and land at Brunswick Naval Air Station. $

✕ **Great Impasta.** *42 Maine St.; 207-729-5858.* Northern Italian cuisine is served here; the seafood lasagna is great. $$

✕ **Henry & Marty's.** *61 Maine St.; 207-721-9141.* It's the in place for locals, and Brunswick's best-kept secret; seafood and more are served, with locally supplied organic produce and house-made desserts. $$–$$$

✕ **Richard's.** *115 Maine St.; 207-729-9673.* One of Maine's few German restaurants has, as you'd expect, a good beer list. $$

✕ **Starfish Grill.** *160 Pleasant St. (Rte.1); 207-725-7828; www.starfishgrill.com.* They have imaginative seafood and many wines by the glass. $$

◆ FREEPORT

⊡ **Harraseeket Inn.** *162 Main St.; 207-865-9377 or 800-342-6423; www.harraseeketinn.com.* This luxury hotel has the feeling of a cozy, unhurried country inn. The afternoon tea is delightful, the dining room excellent, and the pub's buffet lunch a good value. Breakfast and tea are included in the rate, and there's an indoor pool. 84 rooms. $$$

✕ **Crickets.** *175 Lower Main St.; 207-865-4005.* A popular family restaurant, it's also a good place to recover after shopping. $

✕ **Harraseeket Lunch & Lobster.** *Main St., on the dock; 207-865-4888 (lunch) and 207-865-3535 (lobster).* For 30-odd years this place next to Brewer's in South Freeport has served fresh-every-day lobsters plus a fried seafood lunch. Order at the window of your choice and sit indoors or out. $–$$

✕ **Jameson Tavern.** *115 Main St.; 207-865-4196.* This 1779 building was run as a tavern in 1801, and it's rumored that the documents separating Maine from Massachusetts were signed here in 1820. Lunch and dinner are served in the dining room and the tap room, and there's a patio for summer meals. $$

◆ Harpswell Neck

▦ **Harpswell Inn.** *108 Lookout Pt.; 207-833-5509 or 800-843-5509;
www.harpswellinn.com.* A ship captain's house in a gorgeous setting, and
everything is ship-shape. The hostess is friendly and knowledgeable. 9 rooms,
3 suites, 1 cottage. $–$$$

✕ **Dolphin Chowder House.** *End of Basin Point Rd.; 207-833-6000.* Here you
can expect excellent chowder, great fruit pies, an attractive Casco Bay setting, and a
lively view of the boats coming and going. $

✕ **Morse Lobster.** *Allen Point Rd.; 207-833-2399.* Eat your lobsters and home-
made desserts on the deck. BYOB. $–$$

◆ Lewiston

▦ **Ware Street Inn.** *52 Ware St.; 207-783-8171 or 877-783-8171;
www.warestreetinn.com.* Rest your head at a spacious white-shingled country house
B&B right around the corner from Bates College. 6 rooms. $–$$$

◆ Yarmouth

✕ **Muddy Rudder.** *Rte. 1; 207-846-3082; www.muddyrudder.com.* This lively,
well-run restaurant convenient to I–95 has a view of the Cousins River out back
and a varied menu. $–$$

✕ **Royal River Grill House.** *Lower Falls Landing; 207-846-1226.* The spacious
deck looks out over the harbor, and the restaurant serves steaks and seafood grilled
over an applewood fire. $$

Kennebec Valley & Midcoast

◆ Augusta

▦ **America's Best Inn.** *65 Whitten Rd.; 207-622-3776 or 800-237-8466;
www.bestinnmaine.com.* This prime member of a good chain, though just off I–95,
filters out the noise, and its "Evergreen" rooms filter the air and water to remove
allergens, chlorine, and hard minerals. They have a fitness room. 58 rooms. $–$$

▦ **Senator Inn & Spa** (Best Western). *284 Western Ave. near I–95; 207-622-
5804 or 877-772-2224; www.senatorinn.com.* Family owned and run since 1961,
this spic-and-span place has an extraordinary dining room and renowned
brunches. They have heated pools indoors and out. 125 rooms. $–$$$

◆ **Bath**

⊞ **Fairhaven Inn.** *118 North Bath Rd.; 207-443-4391 or 888-443-4391; www. mainecoast.com/fairhaveninn.* This 1790s house is on the Kennebec. 8 rooms. $–$$

⊞ **Inn at Bath.** *969 Washington St.; 207-443-4294; www.innatbath.com.* A historic house, it's on the town's "best" street; 8 rooms. $$–$$$

✕ **Mae's.** *160 Centre St., at High St.; 207-442-8577.* Locally famous for its baked goods, this place is especially good for brunch on the shady deck (they serve dinner, too). $$

✕ **Starlight Café.** *Corner of Front and Lambard Sts.; 207-443-3005.* For seven years they have been serving breakfast and lunch swiftly and with imagination. $

◆ **Boothbay Harbor**

⊞ **Fiddler's Green Inn.** *15 Atlantic Ave.; 207-633-9965 or 888-633-9965; www. thefiddlersgreeninn.com.* At this small B&B in a wonderful location, the two suites have kitchens and outdoor sitting areas. 7 rooms. $–$$$

⊞ **Linekin Bay Resort.** *92 Wall Point Rd.; 207-633-2494 or 866-847-2103; www.linekinbayresort.com.* A large shorefront resort on the quiet side of the Boothbay Peninsula has boating (19-foot Rhodes sailboats and a 30-foot Pearson), tennis, and a heated saltwater pool. 72 rooms in 5 lodges and 37 cabins. $–$$ (including 3 meals daily)

⊞ **Spruce Point Inn.** *88 Grandview Ave.; 207-633-4152 or 800-553-0289; www. sprucepointinn.com.* This resort complex on the eastern side of the harbor has tennis, two swimming pools, a spa, a restaurant, and a pub—and 15 acres to roam. 73 rooms. $$$

✕ **Boathouse Bistro.** *12 The By-Way; 207-633-7300.* An Austria-trained chef turns out Continental and American cooking; dine upstairs or down, or best of all under the stars on the roof deck. $–$$

✕ **Daily Catch.** *93 Townsend Ave.; 207-633-0777; www.realmainelobster.com.* Maine's "Lobster Chef of the Year" cooks great seafood; try his prizewinner: lobster risotto with herbs and vegetables. $–$$

✕ **Ebb Tide.** *43 Commercial St.; 207-633-5692.* This old-fashioned year-rounders' café has wood booths and famously scrumptious cinnamon rolls. $

◆ **Damariscotta Mills**

⊞ **Mill Pond Inn.** *50 Main St. (Rte. 215); 207-563-8014; www.millpondinn.com.* Swim in the pond, canoe for miles on Damariscotta Lake, and relax in the cozy rooms of a 1780 shingle house. It's a little bit of heaven. 6 rooms. $$

◆ **GARDINER**

✕ **A1 Diner**. *3 Bridge St.; 207-582-4804.* The Depression-era interior of this diner has been left virtually untouched. The food is eclectic, international, and cheap. (Next door there's A1 To Go , where you can get frozen A1 dinners and other goodies.) **$**

◆ **GEORGETOWN**

▦ **Grey Havens**. *96 Seguinland Rd.; 207-371-2616 or 800-431-2316; www. greyhavens.com.* The attractive old hotel, built in 1904, has panoramic ocean views. It's the kind of cottage you wish you'd inherited from your grandmother. 13 rooms. **$$–$$$**

✕ **Mama D's Lobster and Grill**. *90 Moore's Turnpike Rd.; 207-371-2722.* Get lunch or dinner or food to go for your boat (a PB&J sandwich with coleslaw costs $1). **$**

✕ **Osprey**. *Robinhood Rd. at the marina; 207-371-2530.* There's good food here in an outstanding setting overlooking a manicured marina and lovely cove in an osprey nesting area. **$$**

✕ **Robinhood Free Meetinghouse**. *210 Robinhood Rd.; 207-371-2188; www. robinhood-meetinghouse.com.* Delicious, creative dishes are served with high style in the starkly beautiful old 1855 meetinghouse. **$$$**

◆ **HALLOWELL**

▦ **Maple Hill Farm B&B Inn**. *11 Inn Rd.; 207-622-2708 or 800-622-2708; www.maplebb.com.* The old house on 130 acres (with a menagerie) has whirlpool tubs, gas fireplaces, and private decks; the new conference facility blends right in, and it still has the easygoing air of your grandmother's farm. The owner, a state legislator, is helpful and knowledgeable. 8 rooms. **$$–$$$**.

✕ **Café de Bangkok**. *272 Water St.; 207-622-2638.* Sit right over the water, looking down a bend in the river, and choose from a wide menu of reasonably priced Thai food (and sushi). **$**

✕ **Slate's**. *167 Water St.; 207-622-9575.* A stylish place with a bistro ambiance and art on the walls serves imaginative food astutely prepared. It bakes, and sells, its own bread down the street at **Slate's Bakery** (207-622-4104), in a restored former gas station. **$**

◆ NEWCASTLE

🏨 **Newcastle Inn.** *60 River Rd.; 207-563-5685 or 800-832-8669; www. newcastleinn.com.* A popular, upscale inn and truly excellent dining room (open to the public) overlooks the Damariscotta River. 15 rooms. **$$$**

✕ **Lathrop Restaurant.** *52 Main St.; 207-563-3102.* In this lovely old former ship chandlery (now on the National Register of Historic Places), the Cordon bleu–trained chef-owner serves imaginative European cuisine in the main dining room (extensive wine list) and lesser fare in the Grill Room (many beers on tap). **$$–$$$**

◆ NEW HARBOR

🏨 **Gosnold Arms.** *146 State Rte. 32; 207-677-3727; www.gosnold.com.* You'll find this rambling 1850 farmhouse and 1925 cottage colony in a picturesque village on the Pemaquid Peninsula. A buffet breakfast is served. 10 rooms, 17 cottages. **$–$$$**

✕ **Shaw's Fish & Lobster Wharf Restaurant.** *Rte. 32; 207-677-2200.* If you were scouting for a movie location, you couldn't do better than picnic-style Shaw's with its view of the working harbor and the menu of fin and shell fish. **$$**

◆ PEMAQUID POINT

🏨 **Hotel Pemaquid.** *3098 Bristol Rd.; 207-677-2312; www.hotelpemaquid.com.* A 19th-century farmhouse 200 yards from Pemaquid Light; converted in 1888 to a country inn, has a rocking-chair porch and antique furnishings. (Note that they serve only coffee in the mornings and don't take credit cards.) 30 rooms, 2 cottages. **$–$$**

◆ PHIPPSBURG

🏨 **1774 Inn.** *44 Parker Head Rd.; 207-389-1774; www.1774inn.com.* A pre-Revolutionary mansion on the National Register of Historic Places, this house on the Kennebec is a noted example of good detailing and fine proportions. 7 rooms. **$$–$$$**

◆ PORT CLYDE

🏨 **Ocean House Hotel.** *870 Port Clyde St. (Rte. 131); 207-372-6691 or 800-269-6691; www.oceanhousehotel.com.* Built in 1820 for ocean travelers, the hotel is a few minutes' walk from everything in town. You'll meet the locals at breakfast—on Sunday they come from miles around and the dining room fills up fast. Dinner is served Monday and sometimes Friday. 9 rooms. **$–$$**; restaurant **$**

◆ Southport Island

⊡ **Newagen Seaside Inn.** *P.O. Box 29, Newagen; 207-633-5242 or 800-654-5242; www.newagenseasideinn.com.* An attractive, secluded resort complex with a public dining room and pool sits at the tip of Southport Island, six miles from Boothbay Harbor. 30 rooms, 3 cabins. $$–$$$

◆ South Thomaston

⊡ **Weskeag Bed and Breakfast Inn and House.** *14 and 18 Elm St.; 207-596-6676 or 800-596-5576; www.weskeag.com.* A pretty, white, Carpenter Gothic inn (1830) and neighboring house (1854) are at the head of the harbor. 12 rooms in both buildings. $–$$

◆ Tenants Harbor

⊡ **East Wind Inn.** *21 Mechanic St.; 207-372-6366 or 800-241-8439; www. eastwindinn.com.* This welcoming, upscale village inn has an excellent dining room and casual lunches in the Chandlery on the wharf. It's in the country Sarah Orne Jewett made famous as "Dunnet Landing." 25 rooms, suites and apartments in three buildings. $$–$$$

✕ **Farmer's Restaurant.** *48 Main St.; 207-372-6111.* Breakfast, lunch, dinner, and take-out. The dining room's on the left, but on the right is the counter where everybody meets to schmooze, peel the potatoes, and settle the affairs of the world. $

◆ Waldoboro

✕ **Moody's Diner.** *Rte. 1; 207-832-7468.* It's over-sentimentalized by its admirers, but this venerable Route 1 landmark still packs the crowds in. $

◆ Westport Island

⊡ **Squire Tarbox Inn.** *1181 Main Rd.; 207-882-7693 or 800-818-0626; www. squiretarboxinn.com.* The atmospheric 1763 farmhouse has a good restaurant (open to the public), where you can taste the Swiss chef-owner's European/American food. 11 rooms. $$–$$$; restaurant $$.

◆ Wiscasset

✕ **Le Garage.** *Water St.; 207-882-5409.* This pleasant, popular restaurant overlooks the Sheepscot River. $$$

Penobscot River & Bay

◆ Bangor

⊟ **Charles Inn.** *20 Broad St.; 207-947-0411; www.thecharlesinn.com.* This downtown hotel is in a renovated 1873 building on West Market Square. 32 rooms. $–$$

⊟ **Country Inn at the Mall.** *936 Stillwater Ave.; 207-941-0200 or 207/244-3961; www.maineguide.com/bangor/countryinn.* This pleasant enough chainlike motel is convenient to the airport. 96 rooms. $

⊟ **Riverside Inn.** *495 State St.; 207-973-4100 or 800-252-4044; www.riversidebangor.org.* The Eastern Maine Medical Center's hotel is the best deal in town—some of the pleasant rooms have views of the Penobscot River, and Continental breakfast (included) is served in the adjacent hospital's cafeteria. 56 rooms. $–$$

✕ **Sea Dog Brewing Company.** *26 Front St.; 207-947-8004.* On the bank of the Penobscot River, with outdoor seating, this place has a good pub menu and a good selection of brews. $$

✕ **Thistles.** *175 Exchange St.; 207-945-5480.* This small downtown family-run restaurant has a good classic international menu and live music. $$

◆ Belfast

⊟ **Alden House.** *63 Church St.; 207-338-2151 or 877-337-8151; www.thealdenhouse.com.* Original details are intact in this sparkling 1840 Greek Revival. Guest rooms are sumptuously renovated. 7 rooms. $–$$

⊟ **Harbor View House of 1807.** *213 High Street; 207-338-3811 or 877-393-3811; www.harborviewhouse.com.* At breakfast on the deck of this beautiful Federal house, you can gaze out at the harbor and watch the world go by. 6 rooms. $–$$$

⊟ **White House.** *One Church St.; 207-338-1901 or 888-290-1901; www.mainebb.com.* The stylishly renovated classic Greek Revival house (on the National Register) with lavishly done rooms has reasonable rates. Its gorgeous copper beech tree is the oldest in Maine. 6 rooms. $$–$$$

✕ **Bay River Bistro & Restaurant.** *39 Main St.; 207-338-5888; www.bayrivermarket.com.* An elegant new place on the water downtown, it has a deli, bakery, and espresso bar as well. $$

✕ **Chase's Daily.** *96 Main St.; 207-338-0555.* This vegetarian restaurant serves three meals a day (dinner only on Friday) in an old Woolworth's building with high tin ceilings. $

✕ **Darby's.** *155 High St.; 207-338-2339.* This cozy pub and café is in an 1865 wood building, with tin walls, a tin ceiling, and an antique bar. The menu, a step above the standard fare, includes an Atkins diet special. $–$$

◆ BLUE HILL

☲ **Blue Hill Farm Country Inn.** *578 Pleasant St. (Rte. 15); 207-374-5126; www.bluehillfarminn.com.* A converted farmhouse commands 48 acres with nature trails. 14 rooms. $$

☲ **Blue Hill Inn.** *40 Union St.; 207-374-2844 or 800-826-7415; www.bluehillinn.com.* This cozy and comfortable inn (since 1840) is in the center of town. 11 rooms, 1 suite. $$$

✕ **Arborvine.** *33 Main St. at Tenney Hill; 207-374-2119; www.arborvine.com.* This restaurant serves creative contemporary food in an elegant setting. $$–$$$ Its adjoining piano bar, **The Vinery** (207-374-2441) has more casual fare. $

✕ **Pain de Famille.** *Main St.; 207-374-3839.* This wonderful bakery, which specializes in artisanal breads, also has vegetarian take-out. $

◆ BROOKSVILLE/SOUTH BROOKSVILLE

☲ **Eggemoggin Reach B&B.** *92 Winneganek Way; 207-359-5073 or 888-625-8866; www.eggreachbb.com.* A spacious newish house on the water, with six stylishly comfortable studios, and four adjacent cottages (each with one studio). All have kitchenettes, covered porches, and stunning water views. Breakfast is served only on the first morning of your stay. 10 studios. $$$

☲ **Oakland House and Shore Seaside Inn.** *435 Herrick Rd.; 207-359-8521 or 800-359-7352; www.oaklandhouse.com.* This classic rambling inn and cottage resort has been doing things right for more than a century. (The 50-acre compound at the edge of Eggemoggin Reach was shown in "A Place Apart" on Maine PBS.) It has rowboats, beaches, hiking trails, and lake swimming. The dining room is open to the public for dinner. 15 cottages, most with fireplaces and kitchens; 10 rooms in the inn. $$$ (including breakfast and dinner)

◆ CAMDEN

☲ **Hartstone Inn.** *41 Elm St; 207-236-4259 or 800-788-4823; www.hartstoneinn.com.* An elegant in-town 1835 Victorian inn, with Jacuzzis in some rooms and fireplaces in most. It has a notable kitchen where you can take cooking classes, and the restaurant is open to the public. 6 rooms, 6 suites. $$–$$$; restaurant $$$

⊡ **Maine Stay.** *22 High St.; 207-236-9636; www.camdenmainestay.com.* Camden's best B&B has lovely, big rooms, a walk-to-town location, and an exquisite garden. The owners are enthusiastic innkeepers and it shows. 8 rooms. $$–$$$

⊡ **Whitehall Inn.** *52 High St.; 207-236-3391 or 800-789-6565; www.whitehall-inn.com.* The grande dame of Camden's traditional summer inns has simple rooms, and those at the front may be a bit noisy due to Route 1 traffic, but the overall charm more than compensates. The dining room is open to the public. 50 rooms. $$–$$$; restaurant $$

✕ **Cappy's.** *1 Main St.; 207-236-2254.* This bustling pub in the center of town serves chowder and other light fare. $$

✕ **Frogwater Cafe.** *31 Elm St.; 207-236-8998; www.frogwatercafe.com.* A tiny eatery with an ambitious menu that includes such dishes as sweet-potato cakes, crab and artichoke tart, and vegetarian shepherd's pie. $$

✕ **Waterfront.** *Bayview St.; 207-236-3747; www.waterfrontcamden.com.* This place has a great location and a deck on the inner harbor. The kitchen serves an updated seafood menu. $$

◆ CASTINE

⊡ **Castine Harbor Lodge.** *147 Perkins St.; 207-326-4335 or 866-566-1550; www.castinemaine.com.* The only waterfront lodging in Castine has moorings and a dock for boats. In the 1893 Edwardian shingled mansion all rooms (even the bathrooms) have water views. The restaurant and oyster bar are open to the public. 16 rooms. $–$$$

⊡ **Castine Inn.** *33 Main St.; 207-326-4365; www.castineinn.com.* This impressively well-run inn with an outstanding dining room (open to the public) has been going since 1898. The owner-chef, who trained in France and New York, serves exclusively tasting menus now, from five to twelve courses. Most rooms are simple, but spacious, though Rooms 8, 9, 11 (a favorite), 17, and 19 have been re-done in high style. 19 rooms. $–$$$; restaurant $$$

⊡ **Manor Inn.** *15 Manor Dr., off Battle Ave.; 207-326-4861 or 800-464-7559; www.manor-inn.com.* This is a grand mansion on a hill, and at the edge of a conservation trust's cool forest. 14 rooms. $$–$$$

⊡ **Pentagoet Inn.** *26 Main St.; 207-326-8616 or 800-845-1701; www.pentagoet. com.* This turreted Victorian in the heart of the village has sweet rooms and a restaurant (open to the public) that serves classic home cooking in the apricot dining room or on the porch. The appealing **Passports Pub** has an oak bar, vintage photographs, and memorabilia of trips abroad. 16 rooms. $–$$$; restaurant $$

✕ **Dennett's Wharf.** *15 Sea St.; 207-326-9045; www.dennettswharf.com.* One of the few places in the area with dockside dining, Dennett's has a nicely rounded pub and seafood menu. It's worth the dollar contribution to see how Gary got all those bills up on the ceiling. After 9/11/01 he peeled off the dollars that had accumulated since 1990, and donated all $12,313 to the widow of a World Trade Center employee. And now he's sticking them up again. There's also a sideline business here—sea kayaking tours and bike rentals. $–$$

◆ **DEER ISLE/LITTLE DEER ISLE**

⊡ **Eggemoggin Landing.** *204 Little Deer Isle Rd. (Rte. 15), on the island end of the Deer Isle Bridge; 207-348-6115; www.acadia.net/eggland.* The clean, comfortable motel rooms have knockout views of Eggemoggin Reach. **The Sisters Restaurant,** across the marina, serves a homey menu, skillfully prepared. 20 rooms. $; restaurant $–$$

⊡ **Goose Cove Lodge.** *300 Goose Cove Rd. (Rte. 15A) in Sunset; 207-348-2508 or 800-728-1963; www.goosecovelodge.com.* With woods behind and the sea in front, this meticulously maintained resort takes full advantage of its natural surroundings—there's sailing, hiking, kayaking, swimming, and birdwatching. The restaurant is open to the public for dinner. 25 rooms in cabins and lodge. $$$

⊡ **Pilgrim's Inn.** *20 Main St., Deer Isle Village; 207-348-6615 or 888-778-7505; www.pilgrimsinn.com.* At the edge of town, overlooking Northwest Harbor, this terrific place seamlessly combines its antique structure (it's on the National Register) and furnishings with all the comforts of an upscale inn. The food in the dining room, which is open to the public, is superb. 12 rooms, 3 cottages. $$–$$$; restaurant $$-$$$

✕ **Eaton's.** *18 Lobster Pool Ln., Blastow Cove on Little Deer Isle; 207-348-2383; www.eatonslobsterpool.com.* It's not easy to find, but worth the search: a true classic for lobster in a priceless setting looking west over Penobscot Bay. Call ahead to order a baked stuffed lobster. $$

◆ LINCOLNVILLE/LINCOLNVILLE BEACH

▼ **Inn at Ocean's Edge.** *1 Broutin Ln., off Rte. 1; 207-236-0945; www.innatoceansedge.com.* A polished, upscale inn on seven acres has rooms in two buildings, plus a pool, fireplaces, and in-room Jacuzzis. Plans for expansion next door will add a restaurant and pier for private boat and water-taxi access. 32 rooms. $$$

✕ **Lobster Pound Restaurant.** *Rte. 1; 207-789-5550; www.lobsterpoundmaine. com.* This huge place is at the edge of Ducktrap Harbor near the Islesboro Ferry Terminal. $$

◆ ROCKLAND

▼ **Captain Lindsey House.** *5 Lindsey St.; 207-596-7950 or 800-523-2145; www.rocklandmaine.com.* Stylish comfort describes this 1835 hotel with a down-town location convenient to the Farnsworth Museum. 9 rooms. $$–$$$

▼ **LimeRock Inn.** *96 Limerock St.; 207-594-2257 or 800-546-3762; www.limerockinn.com.* This B&B in an 1890 turreted Victorian House is on the National Register. 5 rooms. $$ $$$

✕ **Primo.** *2 South Main St. (Rte. 73); 207-596-0770; www.primorestaurant.com.* Owner-chef Melissa Kelly runs a classy enterprise on two floors of a Victorian house near the Owls Head line; she serves Mediterranean cuisine to well-heeled foodies. $$$

◆ ROCKPORT

▼ **Samoset Resort.** *At Rockland Breakwater off Rte. 1; 207-594-2511 or 800-341-1650; www.samoset.com.* This full-service resort on the ocean has a health club, golf, tennis, swimming, and a children's day camp. 178 rooms. $$$

◆ SEARSPORT

▼ **Carriage House Inn.** *120 E. Main St. (Rte. 1); 207-548-2167 or 800-578-2167; www.carriagehouseinmaine.com.* A spacious Victorian, on the National Register, it's set well back from the road in a shady garden. 3 rooms. $–$$

▼ **Yardarm Motel.** *172 E. Main St. (Rte. 1); 207-548-2404; www.searsportmaine. com.* This spotless motel with pillow-top beds and eiderdown quilts is a find. It's set well back from Route 1. Not all the rooms are identical—ask for No. 19, which has a State of Maine mural and cathedral ceiling and a separate living room with a sofabed. 18 rooms. $

✕ **Anglers.** *215 E. Main St. (Rte.1); 207-548-2405.* If you like fried or broiled seafood, you'll find it first-rate here. It's a popular family place that's hopping all day. $

✕ **Rhumb Line Restaurant.** *200 East Main St. (Rte. 1); 207-548-2600; www.therhumblinerestaurant.com.* This eatery in an 1846 ship captain's house is run by Martha's Vineyard émigrés who brought their considerable culinary abilities to the Maine coast. On the menu are a horseradish-crusted salmon served with remoulade sauce, grilled rack of lamb with fig-infused mint vinegar sauce, and pan-seared peppered swordfish with Vidalia-onion piccalilly. $$–$$$

◆ STONINGTON

▣ **Inn on the Harbor.** *45 Main St.; 207-367-2420 or 800-942-2420; www.innontheharbor.com.* Don't be misled by the plain facade of the inn's four buildings—on the water side there's a wonderful deck, and the newly renovated, crisply decorated rooms have up-close views of the harbor. 12 rooms, 1 suite, 1 apartment. $$–$$$

✕ **Cockatoo Takeout and Carter's Seafood.** *24 Carter Ln., off Oceanville Rd.; 207-367-0900.* For tasty Portuguese food, try this alfresco place for lunch or early dinner. You choose it and they'll cook it, or you can take it home. Kayakers paddle in, and others boats can dock nearby. BYOB. $

✕ **Fishermen's Friend Restaurant.** *40 School St.; 207-367-2442.* Did we say local? It's not fancy, but the lobster stew is wonderfully meaty and the lobster and crab rolls are a deal and a half. $

✕ **Maritime Café.** *Main St.; 207-367-2600; www.maritimecafe.com.* A small, brand-new restaurant with a clean design, right on the water, has a large deck for lunch and a light, eclectic, mainly seafood menu. The seafood pastas and crepes are a hit. BYOB. $$

MOUNT DESERT ISLAND

◆ BAR HARBOR

▣ **Balance Rock Inn.** *21 Albert Meadow; 207-288-2610 or 800-753-0494; www.barharborvacations.com.* The rooms are wonderful in this exquisite little waterfront hotel with great views, a pool, and elegant common areas. 27 rooms. $$$

▣ **Bar Harbor Hotel–Bluenose Inn.** *Rte. 3; 207-288-3348 or 800-445-4077; www.bluenoseinn.com.* High above Frenchman Bay on the approach to town, this sparkling resort with comfortable, large rooms has an excellent restaurant open to the public. 97 rooms. $$$

⊡ **Bar Harbor Inn.** *Newport Dr.; 207-288-3351 or 800-248-3351; www.barharborinn.com.* This latest incarnation of a historic 8-acre property overlooking the town pier has the famous Reading Room as its dining room, plus a pool. 153 rooms. $$$. (The new **Bar Harbor Grand,** a sister hotel on Main St., 888-766-2529, has 70 less expensive rooms.)

⊡ **Harborside Hotel & Marina.** *55 West St.; 207-288-5033 or 800-328-5033; www.theharborsidehotel.com.* You'll find this huge, new, mock-Tudor hotel on the harbor, with a marina and a pool, downtown. 187 rooms. $$$

⊡ **Holbrook House.** *74 Mount Desert St.; 207-288-4970 or 800-860-7430; www.holbrookhouse.com.* This homey, comfortable B&B with a friendly owner is right in the center of town. 10 rooms, 2 two-bedroom cottages. $$–$$$

⊡ **Inn at Bay Ledge.** *Rte. 3, Sand Point Rd.; 207-288-4204; www.innatbayledge.com.* Overlooking scenic Frenchman Bay, this inn clings to the cliffs of Mount Desert Island above a private stone beach. 8 rooms. $$$

⊡ **Ivy Manor Inn.** *194 Main St.; 207-288-2138 or 888-670-1997; www.ivymanor.com.* This upscale French country inn, in an old Tudor mansion with antiques and fireplaces, is in the middle of town. The dining room, **Michele's Fine Dining Bistro,** is as plush as the inn and is open to the public for dinner. 8 rooms. $$$; restaurant $$$

⊡ **Manor House Inn.** *106 West St.; 207-288-3759 or 800-437-0088; www.barharbormanorhouse.com.* This finely done Victorian has antique furnishings and is on the National Register. 18 rooms. $$–$$$

⊡ **The Tides.** *119 West St.; 207-288-4968; www.barharbortides.com.* This Georgian Revival mansion (on the National Register) boasts a fireplace on the verandah that overlooks the parterre and Frenchman Bay. 1 room, 3 suites. $$$

✕ **Cafe Bluefish.** *122 Cottage St.; 207-288-3696.* One of the smaller and quieter restaurants in Bar Harbor is charmingly eccentric, with dark wood booths, plants and books everywhere, and mismatched napkins and china. A noteworthy lobster strudel and pecan-crusted catch-of-the-day with Creole brown butter sauce are among its creative seafood dishes. $$–$$$

✕ **Café This Way.** *14 Mt. Desert St.; 207-288-4483; www.cafethisway.com.* Look sharp to find this place, down a little alley, where you can get good, light food at breakfast and dinner in a cozy room with a wood stove and bookshelves or on the pleasant open porch. Try the sesame-crusted tuna with salmon sausage. $$

✕ **George's.** *7 Stephen's Ln.; 207-288-4505; www.georgesbarharbor.com.* This lively seasonal restaurant has been going for 25 years. It's just off Main Street behind the bank. There's a piano player on weekends, and the food is mostly imaginative seafood dishes, but you might like the Australian lamb tenderloin too. **$$**

✕ **Havana Restaurant.** *318 Main St.; 207-288-2822.* People flock here to devour American food with a Latin flair; it's one of the best places in town. **$$**

✕ **McKay's Public House.** *231 Main St.; 207-288-2002.* The happy staff here adds to the pleasure of eating both the imaginative pub fare and the excellent main dishes. Dine indoors in peace or people-watch out front. **$$**

✕ **Thrumcap.** *123 Cottage St.; 207-288-3884.* This stylish, low-key restaurant—a cozy bar with sofas and a fireplace—has a sophisticated four-course prix-fixe menu and excellent wines. **$$**

◆ **BERNARD/BASS HARBOR**

▣ **Bass Harbor Cottages and Country Inn.** *Rte. 102A; 207-244-3460; www.bassharborcottages.com.* A tree-shaded country inn that has 1- to 3-bedroom housekeeping cottages with fireplaces and skylights. 3 rooms, 3 cottages. **$–$$$**

✕ **Thurston's.** *Steamboat Wharf Rd.; 207-244-7600.* This great out-of-the-way lobster pound has a gorgeous view and roll-down curtains around the deck for windy days. **$$**

◆ **NORTHEAST HARBOR**

▣ **Asticou Inn.** *15 Peabody Dr. (Rte. 3); 207-276-3344 or 800-258-3373; www.asticou.com.* An old-line classic, this inn has rooms that are kept wonderfully fresh (constant attention is paid to detail). The harbor views are spectacular, especially when dozens of picturesque yachts are at the moorings. 48 rooms. **$$$**; restaurant **$$–$$$**

▣ **Grey Rock Inn.** *Route 198; 207-276-9360; www.greyrockinn.com.* In a mansion on a hill overlooking the harbor, this inn has large, elegantly—even grandly—appointed rooms. 8 rooms. **$$$**

▣ **Maison Suisse Inn.** *Main St.; 207-276-5223 or 800-624-7668; www.maisonsuisse.com.* A Fred Savage–designed 19th-century house set back from the road has comfortable and large, if not fancy, rooms. The rates, for the center-of-town location, are quite reasonable. **$$**

✕ **151 Main Street.** *207-276-9898.* This popular, small-but-bright spot serves a casual bistro menu; some of its plates of comfort food would feed two. **$$**

◆ SEAL HARBOR

✕ **Jordan Pond House.** *Park Loop Rd.; 207-276-3316; www.jordanpond.com.*
It's best known for its afternoon tea popovers, but this place also has a unique
setting for dinner. $–$$

◆ SOUTHWEST HARBOR

▥ **The Birches.** *Fernald Point Rd.; 207-244-5182; www.birches.com.* It's the sort
of place that feels like your grandmother's summer house, with large, airy rooms
and a tree-shaded path to the water. 3 rooms. $$

▥ **The Claremont.** *22 Claremont Rd.; 207-244-5036 or 800-244-5036;
www.theclaremonthotel.com.* Expect spectacular views, croquet on the lawn, and an
air of turn-of-the-century leisure. The restaurant and boathouse are open to the
public. 32 rooms in 3 buildings, 14 cottages. $$$

▥ **Inn at Southwest.** *371 Main St.; 207-244-3835; www.innatsouthwest.com.*
This crisply updated Victorian is in the center of town. 5 rooms, 2 suites. $$-$$$

▥ **Kingsleigh Inn.** *373 Main St.; 207-244-5302; www.kingsleighinn.com.*
Some of the fresh and pretty rooms here have water views. 8 rooms. $$ $$$

▥ **Lindenwood Inn.** *118 Clark Point Rd.; 207-244-5335 or 800-307-5335;
www.lindenwoodinn.com.* This beautifully renovated sea captain's house is replete
with exotic art and artifacts from the owner's Asian travels. No. 9 on the top floor
has its own blissful hot tub on the roof. 9 rooms. $$–$$$

▥ **Penury Hall.** *374 Main St.; 207-244-7102 or 866-473-6425; www.penuryhall.
com.* Stay here if you prefer being in a comfortable private house with friendly,
knowledgeable hosts. 3 rooms. $$

✕ **Deck House.** *11 Apple Ln., at Great Harbor Marina; 207-244-5044.*
Traditional American food is accompanied by accomplished performances, with
piano, of Broadway songs. $$

✕ **Quiet Side Café and Ice Cream Shop.** *360 Main St.; 207-244-9444.*
Soups, subs, and crab rolls are typical, along with homemade desserts. $

✕ **Red Sky.** *14 Clark Point Rd.; 207-244-0476.* Sunset-yellow minimalist
furnishings complement the fine American nouvelle cuisine here. $$-$$$

✕ **Seaweed Café.** *146 Seawall Rd.; 207-244-0572.* This café serves really first-rate
Asian-French seafood and other dishes (some vegetarian), plus sushi, from local
organic sources. $–$$$

✕ **XYZ.** *End of Bennett Ln., off 102A; 207-244-5221.* Authentic (really) Mexican
cuisine and delicious fresh-lime margaritas are served here. $–$$

DOWN EAST

◆ ADDISON

▦ **Pleasant Bay Bed & Breakfast Llama Keep.** *386 West Side Rd.; 207-483-4490; www.nemaine.com/pleasantbay.* On a working llama and red deer farm, in a spacious, newish house on a hill at the edge of the Pleasant River, this B&B would be a find anywhere—it has oriental rugs, comfy beds, reasonable rates, and friendly hosts—but the llamas dotting the hill make it really grand. 3 rooms, 1 housekeeping suite. $–$$

◆ BIRCH HARBOR

✕ **Bunkers Wharf.** *260 East Schoodic Dr.; 207-963-2244; www.bunkerswharf.com.* An American menu is served at lunch, dinner, and Sunday brunch in Schoodic's newest restaurant. Whether you choose to eat outside, in the pub, or by the fire, you can still see the working harbor and beyond to the ocean. $$

◆ EAST MACHIAS

▦ **Riverside Inn & Fine Dining.** *Rte. 1; 207-255-4134 or 888-255-4344; www.riversideinn-maine.com.* A beautifully restored Victorian perched at the edge of the East Machias River has a restaurant—on a glassed-in porch—that's open to the public for dinner. 4 rooms. $–$$; restaurant $

◆ EASTPORT

▦ **Milliken House.** *29 Washington St.; 207-853-2955 or 888-507-9370; www.eastport-inn.com.* An 1846 Victorian has huge, ornate antiques left by the original owner—you'd have to take the house apart to move them. Here you'll get the kind of solid comfort not usually found in B&Bs. 6 rooms. $

▦ **Motel East.** *23A Water St.; 207-853-4747; www.eastportme.info/moteleast.html.* This good motel has large, well-furnished and balconied rooms, some with kitchenettes, and all overlooking the harbor. 14 rooms and a cottage. $–$$$

▦ **Todd House Bed & Breakfast.** *1 Capen Ave.; 207-853-2328.* This wonderful 1775 Cape Cod on the National Register is filled with antiques of the period. Pets and children are welcome. 4 rooms. $

▦ **Weston House.** *26 Boynton St.; 207-853-2907 or 800-853-2907; www.westonhouse-maine.com.* This 1810 Federal house on the National Register sits on a quiet Eastport side street in a gorgeous, large garden with a gazebo. The baths are shared but the rooms, especially those in front, are terrific, and a good value. Meals in the dining room are available on request with advance notice. 3 rooms. $

✕ **Eastport Chowder House**. *169 Water St.; 207-853-4700.* Serving mainly seafood, this place is right on the lobster pound wharf. **$**

✕ **La Sardina Loca**. *28 Water St.; 207-853-2739.* This Mexican café imaginatively and wildly decorated with tons of tchotchkes—signs, pennants, papier-maché animal heads, flags—is incongruously charming. **$**

✕ **Waco Diner**. *47 Water St.; 207-853-4046.* The popular local diner with a deck on the harbor specializes in lobster and other seafood dishes. **$**

◆ HANCOCK/HANCOCK POINT

⌷ **Crocker House**. *967 Hancock Point Rd.; 207-422-6806; www.crockerhouse.com.* A quietly tasteful inn in a peaceful summer community with a restaurant, popular with summer residents, that's open to the public for dinner. 11 rooms. **$$**

⌷ **La Domaine**. *Rte. 1; 207-422-3395.* Since the 1940s this has been a Down East gastronomic landmark with an emphasis on classic French country cooking. Now you can stay here in one of the five luxurious bedrooms. **$$$**; restaurant **$$$**

◆ LUBEC

⌷ **Lighthouse Inn and Chowder House**. *7 Water St.; 207-733-4300; www.lighthouseinnmaine.com.* The simple rooms with spectacular vistas (No. 9 has an 180-degree view) are above the restaurant, which serves light food (no alcohol) and presents live acoustic music on weekends. 9 rooms, 1 suite, 1 apartment. **$–$$**

◆ MACHIAS

✕ **Helen's**. *28 East Main St.; 207-255-8423.* A Washington County landmark famous for its seafood and high-rise pies (piled high with meringue or a tall crust over a filling). **$–$$**

◆ PROSPECT HARBOR

⌷ **Oceanside Meadows Inn**. *Rte. 195 at Sand Cove; 207-963-5557; www.oceaninn.com.* If you're looking for a real respite, stay at this old sea captain's house and adjacent farmhouse with lovely rooms—in some the windows open to the ocean, and in others to the meadows and woods. There are 200 acres to roam, so you can work up an appetite for the delicious breakfasts. Concerts and lectures are held in the renovated barn in summer. 14 rooms. **$$–$$$**

◆ ROBBINSTON

⌷ **Brewer House**. *Rte. 1; 207-454-2385.* This elegant, splendidly restored 1828 Greek Revival house—once a stop on the underground railroad—is perched on a hill overlooking Passamaquoddy Bay. Inside are antiques-furnished rooms and bathrooms you could live in. The owners run an art and antiques gallery on-site, and summer concerts are held in the garden. (The owners are, respectively, an artist and a musician—he's on the faculty of the Pierre Monteux School of Music in Hancock.) 4 rooms, 1 apartment (pets allowed). $–$$$

☷ **Redclyffe Shore Motor Inn.** *Rte. 1; 207-454-3270.* The especially pleasant rooms here also have great views, and the dining room is open to the public. 16 rooms. $

◆ WINTER HARBOR

✕ **Mama's Boy Bistro.** *10 Newman St.; 207-963-2365; www.mamasboybistro.com.* This popular, good-looking place with oriental rugs, polished floors, and a high, beamed barn ceiling with skylights serves stylish European/Provençal food that comes from local purveyors. $$$

WESTERN LAKES & MOUNTAINS

◆ BETHEL

☷ **Bethel Inn and Country Club.** *Broad St., on the Common; 207-824-2175 or 800-654-0125; www.bethelinn.com.* This full-service resort (built around a 1913 inn) in Sunday River country provides a wide range of lodging, an 18-hole golf course, a tennis court, an outdoor heated pool (open year-round), nordic skiing, and lake swimming, canoeing, and kayaking. The dining room is open to the public. 58 rooms, 40 two-bedroom townhouses. $$$ (including breakfast and dinner)

☷ **L'Auberge** and **Bistro l'Auberge.** *24 Mill Hill Rd.; 207-824-2774 or 800-760-2774; www.laubergecountryinn.com.* A renovated old carriage house on a relaxed four acres of lawns and gardens, cozy rooms furnished with European antiques, and a popular French country bistro. It's a popular place for weddings. The management is friendly, and they'll arrange to walk your dog. 7 rooms. $–$$$; restaurant $$–$$$

☷ **Sudbury Inn** and **Restaurant.** *151 Main St.; 207-824-2174 or 800-395-7837; www.thesudburyinn.com.* This long-established and recently refurbished inn, on the Mountain Explorer shuttle line to the slopes, has several suites and a large apartment. Stylish food is served in the dining room, pub grub in the popular **Suds Pub.** 11 rooms, 6 suites, 1 apartment. $$–$$$; restaurant $$

☷ **The Victoria.** *32 Main St.; 207-824-8060 or 888-774-1235; www.victoria-inn.com.* At this old mansion you can stay in lavishly decorated rooms and enjoy a full breakfast. 15 rooms. $–$$$

✕ **Sunday River Brewing Co.** *1 Sunday River Rd.; 207-824-4253.* A slopeside brewer with good pub fare is at the base of the access road. Beers range from light ales to the aptly named Brass Balls Barleywine. **$$**

◆ BRIDGTON
⌑ **Noble House.** *81 Highland Rd.; 207-647-3733 or 888-237-4880; www.noblehousebb.com.* This fine turn-of-the-century country B&B, in an antiques-filled town, has glimpses of the lake. 9 rooms. **$$–$$$**

◆ CARRABASSETT VALLEY
✕ **Sugarloaf Brewing Co.** *Access Rd., Sugarloaf; 207-237-2211.* This brewpub near the slopes makes crisp ales light on hops. **$$**

◆ CENTER LOVELL
⌑ **Center Lovell Inn & Restaurant.** *Rte. 5; 207-925-1575 or 800-777-2698; www.centerlovellinn.com.* It's in-town rather than lakeside, but it's a well-kept, rambling 200-year-old house with large rooms. The dining room (open to the public) serves mini beef Wellingtons, crab wontons, calamari, and sashimi tuna. 10 rooms. **$**
⌑ **Pleasant Point Inn.** *Pleasant Pt.; 207-925-3008; www.pleasantpoint.com.* In the midst of a summer cottage colony, the lodge offers spacious rooms, many with views of Lake Kezar. Some of the cottages are also available for rent through the inn. 8 rooms, 2 suites. **$$–$$$**
⌑ **Quisisana.** *Pleasant Pt.; 207-925-3500; www.quisisanaresort.com.* An air of purposeful pleasure permeates this impeccably maintained cottage colony at the edge of Lake Kezar, from the winding drive to the sandy beach. The cottages and lodge rooms are stylishly furnished and gracefully informal. Founded years ago as a summer music camp, Quisisana blends its student-musician staff's talents (they perform each evening after dinner) with a well-orchestrated, full-service resort. 40 cottages, 15 lodge rooms. **$$$** (including all meals)

◆ FRYEBURG
⌑ **Oxford House Inn.** *548 Main St.; 207-935-3442 or 800-261-7206; www. oxfordhouseinn.com.* It's on the main drag, but it has wonderful views of the White Mountains from the back and pleasant rooms throughout. The popular dining room serves stylish country food to the public. 4 rooms. **$$–$$$**; restaurant, **$$**

◆ KINGFIELD

⌑ **Herbert Grand Hotel.** *246 Main St.; 207-265-2000 or 888-656-9922;*
www.herbertgrandhotel.com. An upcountry outpost of luxury in 1918, the Herbert
maintains a craggy sort of character, rather like grandpa in a frayed smoking
jacket—the perfect antidote to the base-lodge slickness found at Sugarloaf. The
restaurant opened in 2004, with a new chef who has his own following. 27 rooms.
$-$$$; restaurant $$-$$$

⌑ **Inn on Winter's Hill.** *33 Winter Hill St.; 207-265-5421 or 800-233-9687;*
www.wintershill.com. In a palatial manor overlooking town, with an indoor pool
and hot tub and a feeling that's just right after a day on the slopes. Try to get one of
the four grand rooms in the main house; these are decorated in luxurious fabrics
and rich, dark colors. The motelish rooms in the annex aren't bad, however. The
restaurant, open to the public, is outstanding. 20 rooms. $-$$$

⌑ **One Stanley Avenue** and **Three Stanley Avenue.** *1 and 3 Stanley Ave.;*
207-265-5541. The restaurant's casual elegance, friendly service, and unbelievably
good food will send your post-ski aching body to bed with a smile. And you can
hop next door to do just that, in a Victorian house with individually furnished
rooms. $; restaurant $-$$$

◆ POLAND SPRING

⌑ **Inns at Poland Spring**. *41 Ricker Rd.; 207-998-4351; www.49weekend.com.*
Golf, tennis, swimming, bingo, tai chi, fishing, croquet, hiking, and more are only
some of the possibilities on 800 acres of the old Poland Spring Inn property. You
can opt for weekends, long weekends, or five-night midweek stays only, in various
buildings. It's rather like summer camp—no elevator, no room phone. You bring
your own soap and towels and carry your own bags. All this costs less than you'd
believe. 181 rooms. $ (including breakfast and dinner)

◆ RANGELEY LAKES

⌑ **Bald Mountain Camps.** *125 Bald Mountain Rd., Oquossoc; 207-864-3671 or*
207-864-3788; www.baldmountaincamps.com. In 1897 it was strictly a fishing
camp on Mooselookmeguntic Lake, but now there's boating and water-skiing,
sailing, canoeing, tennis, hiking, a little beach, and a playground for kids. 15
cabins sleep 2–8 each. $$ (including breakfast and dinner)

⌑ **Rangeley Inn.** *51 Main St., Rangeley; 207-864-3341 or 800-666-3687; www.*
rangeleyinn.com. This big old-fashioned inn next to the Haley Pond bird sanctuary

has verandahs and lawns and a lakeside motor lodge. It also has a formal dining room and a tavern, and the whole place was recently restored. 50 rooms. $–$$

◆ WATERFORD

☷ **Lake House.** *Corner of Routes 35 & 37; 207-583-4182 or 800-223-4182; www.lakehousemaine.com.* The owner-chef is attentive to both aspects of the inn, but it's the dining room that shines, and you can attend cooking school there. The rooms are attractive in an understated sort of way (and what a treat to be able to retire immediately upon finishing dinner). 7 rooms. $$–$$$

◆ WELD

☷ **Kawanhee Inn.** *12 Anne's Way (Rte. 142); 207-585-2000; www.maineinn.net.* This priceless old lodge is up on a hill across the lake from Mount Blue State Park. It has rooms upstairs and cabins down along the shore. The cabins, which are quite basic and vary in size, have fireplaces and screened porches. The dining room (open to the public) serves nouvelle/New World cuisine, and the setting is right out of *On Golden Pond.* 10 rooms, 10 cabins. $–$$

GREAT NORTH WOODS

◆ GRAND LAKE STREAM

☷ **Canal Side Cabins.** *207-796-2796; www.canalsidecabins.com.* Six rustic year-round housekeeping cabins stand by the canal that floated hemlock bark to the tannery. Rates are by the week or day (two person minimum), and your pet comes too. Sports include fishing, hunting, and snowmobiling. 13 rooms. $ (no meals)

☷ **Leen's Lodge.** *207-796-2929 or 800-995-3367; www.leenslodge.com.* On 23 acres right on West Grand Lake, this small, well maintained lakeside resort has facilities and programs for families and fishermen. 9 cabins. $$ (including breakfast and dinner). BYOB

☷ **Weatherby's.** *207-796-5558; www.weatherbys.com.* An Orvis endorsed fishermen's resort, with upland game shooting and a fly-fishing school, is the sort of place where the fish descriptions take up more brochure space than the cabin descriptions. The cabins are grand (by fishing lodge standards), comfy as an old leather armchair, and clean. The food is down-home and hearty. 15 cottages. $$ (including 3 meals).

◆ **GREENVILLE**

▦ **Black Frog.** *17 Pritham Ave.; 207-695-1100; www.theblackfrog.com.*
This casual place on the water has outdoor seating on a barge (they also have cocktail cruises) and two large housekeeping suites upstairs $$–$$$; restaurant $

▦ **Blair Hill Inn.** *351 Lily Bay Rd.; 207-695-0224; www.blairhill.com.*
Perched on a hill with grand views of the lake, this inn has very fine, plush rooms—high four-posters with feather beds, some fireplaces, terrific old-new bathrooms, and a wonderful porch with wicker rockers. Best of all, in the dining room you can get lobster spring rolls with lemongrass and coconut. A summer concert series is held here. 8 rooms. $$$

▦ **Greenville Inn.** *40 Norris St.; 207-695-2206 or 888-695-6000; www. greenvilleinn.com.* These are comfortable rooms in an in-town 1895 Victorian. The restaurant is open to the public. 4 rooms, 3 suites, 6 cottages. $$$

▦ **Lodge at Moosehead.** *368 Lily Bay Rd.; 207-695-4400; www.lodgeatmooseheadlake.com.* An inn with stunning views luckily has an owner who takes genuine pleasure in providing robber-baron comfort and concierge service, to great results. The attention to detail is exacting. 8 rooms. $$$

✕ **Flatlander's.** *36 Pritham Ave.; 207-695-3373.* You get basic food at basic prices, but the place is usually packed. $

◆ **JACKMAN**

▦ **Attean Lake Lodge.** *Birch Island; 207-668-3792; www.atteanlodge.com.*
For a magical setting—on an island in a lake surrounded by mountains—you can't beat Attean, owned by the same family since 1900. The main lodge is open to the spectacular view and warmed by a stone fireplace; the cabins, all with fireplaces and porches and all right on the water, are nicely furnished and maintained (it's kerosene and gas lighting). It's a schlep to get here, but for a swimming, hiking, and boating vacation, it simply doesn't get any better. 15 cabins. $$$ (including 3 meals).

◆ **ROCKWOOD**

▦ **Maynard's in Maine.** *131 Maynard's Rd.; 207-534-7703 or 866-699-0857; www.maynardsinmaine.com.* Since 1919 this simple, rustic place has been lodging and feeding happy campers. They provide badminton, horseshoes, fishing, canoeing, and swimming. One house is open all year for hunting, snowmobiling, or ice fishing. The old-fashioned cabins have wainscoting and rustic furniture—and heat. 13 cabins. $ (including 3 meals).

■ FESTIVALS & EVENTS

The **Maine Tourism Association** maintains an extensive calendar of events: *327 Water St., Hallowell 04347-1341; 207-623-0363.* Following are some highlights:

■ JANUARY
Rangeley: Snow-de-o. Snowmobile displays, games, parade and fireworks. 207-864-5364.

■ FEBRUARY
Bridgton: Musher's Bowl. Sled-dog races, ski touring. 207-247-5167.
Camden: Annual U.S. National Toboggan Championships. Camden Snow Bowl. 207-236-3438.

■ MARCH
Fort Kent: CAN-AM **Crown International Sled Dog Races.** 60- and 250-mile races with awards and a Grand Musher's Ball. 207-834 5354.

Portland: Maine Boat Builder's Show. The latest craft and their makers. 207-774-1067; General festival information. 207-772-6828.

Statewide: Maine Maple Sunday. Maple-sugar houses open to the public. Contact Maine Department of Agriculture. 207-287-1132.

■ APRIL
Boothbay Harbor: Fisherman's Festival. Old-fashioned fish fry, fish chowder contest, lobster crate race, Miss Shrimp Princess pageant, boat parade, Blessing of the Fleet. 207-633-2353.

Rockport: Spring by the Sea Fine Arts and Crafts. Held at Samoset Resort the Saturday before Easter, with the Easter Bunny around to take your picture. 207-596-0376; www.therealmaine.com.

■ MAY
Lewiston and Auburn: Annual Maine State Parade. Participants from more than 60 communities. Attracts 25,000 spectators. 207-784-0599.

Moosehead Lake: MooseMainea. Established in 1992 when residents realized they were outnumbered by moose. Moose watching (about 5,000 sightings), canoe races, fly-casting championships, bike events, lake regatta. 207-695-2702.

■ JUNE

Bethel to Rockport: Trek Across Maine–Sunday River to the Sea. Three-day weekend bicycle ride (180 miles) to benefit Maine Lung Association. 207-622-6394.

Boothbay Harbor: Windjammer Days. Two-day celebration of town's maritime heritage: antique boat parade, street parade, concerts, shipyard open houses, fireworks. Highlight is arrival and departure of windjammers. 207-633-2353.

Madawaska: Acadian Festival. Parade, cultural displays, and entertainment. 207-728-7000.

New Sweden: Midsummer Celebration. The Swedish national holiday, celebrated on the summer solstice with a maypole and traditional Swedish foods. 207-896-5874.

Portland: Portland Book, Print, & Paper Show. The Maine Antiquarian Booksellers Assn. and the Maine Historical Society co-sponsor this annual expo of books, prints, maps, and manuscripts; held in the Portland Exposition Building. 413-528-2327; www.mainebooksellers.org.

Wiscasset: Annual Strawberry Festival & Auction. Old-fashioned fair at St. Phillip's Church, with strawberry shortcake, crafts, plants, and country auction. Since early 1950s. 207-882-7184.

■ JULY

Bangor State Fair. Since 1850, a premier Maine agricultural fair; giant midway, and live stage shows. 207-947-5555.

Bar Harbor: Native American Festival. Basketmaking demonstrations and sales, dancing, music, and storytelling. 207-288-3519.

Bath: Heritage Days. Commemorates Bath shipping and shipbuilding with historic walking tours, boatbuilding demos, fireworks. 207-442-7291.

Bethel: Annual Art Fair. Artists and artisans displaying and selling their work on the first Saturday. 207-824-2282; www.bethelmaine.com.

Bethel: Molly Ockett Day. Celebrating, on the third Saturday at the Artists' Covered Bridge, the life of a powerful Native American medicine woman whose influence in the area, it is said, continues to this day. Foot races, arts and crafts, fiddling contests, duck race, and fireworks. 207-824-3575.

Camden: Arts and Crafts Show. Juried show of artists and craftspeople in Camden Amphitheater. 207-236-4404; www.visitcamden.com.

Fort Fairfield: Maine Potato Blossom Festival. Aroostook County's major agricultural fair, with arts and crafts, crowning of Maine Potato Blossom Queen. Highlight is mashed-potato wrestling. 207-472-3802.

Jonesport: Moosabec World's Fastest Lobster Boat Race. Part of Jonesport's Fourth of July extravaganza, with parade and fireworks. 207-497-5926.

Lisbon Falls: Moxie Festival. Huge parade, crafts fair, firemens' auction, and barbershop quartet singing to celebrate Maine's unique beverage. 207-783-2249.

Milbridge: Milbridge Days. Parade, lobster feast, crafts, and a codfish relay race. 207-483-2131.

Rangeley: Logging Museum Festival Days. Woodsmen's competitions and carving, music, and a parade. 207-864-5595.

Rockland/North Haven: Annual Great Schooner Race. Over two dozen windjammers and other tall ships gather for an annual, all-day race in midsummer. 800-807-9463; www.sailmainecoast.com.

Rockland: North Atlantic Blues Festival. For two days over the second weekend; pub crawls at night and many bands playing all day. 207-596-6055; www.northatlanticbluesfestival.com.

Thomaston. 4th of July Parade and Celebration. Pancake breakfasts, pet shows, horseshoe tournament, baking contest, and crafts exhibits. 207-596-7478; www.thomaston4thofjuly.com.

Waterville: Maine International Film Festival. Ten days screening more than 100 international and indie films. 207-861-8138; www.miff.org.

■ AUGUST

Bangor: American Folk Festival. A city-wide annual three-day multi-stage festival held the last weekend, centered at the Bangor waterfront. Founded through the Smithsonian Institution to celebrate American folk culture; many groups of traditional performers. 207-992-2630; www.nationalfolkfestival.com.

Brooklin: Eggemoggin Reach Regatta. Windjammers and others in the harbor on the first Saturday. 207-374-3242 or 207-359-4651; www.woodenboat.com.

Brunswick: Maine Highland Games. Day of traditional Scottish events: piping, Celtic harp, highland dance competitions, Gaelic song workshops, sheepherding by border collies, and athletics (caber toss and stone put). 207-688-4515.

Cumberland: United Maine Craftsmen Annual Crafts Show. More than 350 Maine craftspeople working in stained glass, leather, furniture, basketry, wood, other mediums. 207-621-2818.

Greenville: Forest Heritage Days. On the second weekend, with wood-sawing contests and other woodsmen's events. Crafts displays. 207-695-2702; www.mooseheadlake.org.

Machias: Maine Wild Blueberry Festival. Celebrates Machias as shire town of blueberry county and site of first naval battle of Revolution. Many blueberry-eating opportunities and performances of the original local musical, *Red, White, and Blueberry.* 207-255-4402.

Owls Head: Transportation Rally and Aerobatic Show. Antique autos, high-wheel bicycles, and aircraft. Daily aerobatic shows. Owls Head Transportation Museum. 207-594-4418.

Rockland: Maine Boats & Harbors Show. Held the 2nd weekend, it's more than a boat show with music—coastal living: fine art, architecture, furniture making, and the hilarious Boatyard Dog Trials. 800-565-4951; www.maineboats.com.

Rockland: Maine Lobster Festival. Since 1947. More lobsters are landed at Rockland than in the rest of the state. Festival launches with King Neptune and his court stepping ashore Friday night; Saturday morning is the parade. Lobster dinners cooked continuously. 207-596-0376.

Skowhegan: State Fair. Oldest continuing agricultural fair in the country—since 1819. 207-474-2947.

Southwest Harbor: Claremont Croquet Classic. Nine-wicket singles and doubles. 207-244-5036.

Union: Union Fair/State of Maine Wild Blueberry Festival. Traditional week-long fair noted for Friday Blueberry Festival with a blueberry-pancake breakfast, pie-eating and baking contests, selection of Blueberry Queen, and all manner of blue food: jams, candy, ice cream, juice. 207-785-3281.

Winter Harbor: Lobster Festival. On the 2nd Saturday, with blueberry-pancake breakfast, lobster boat races, craft fair, lobster dinner, and a parade. 207-963-7658; www.acadia-schoodic.org.

■ **SEPTEMBER**

Bethel: 8th Annual Harvest Fest and Chowdah Cook-off. On the third Saturday, celebration of fall and all that goes with it. 207-824-2282; www.bethelmaine.com.

Blue Hill: Annual Fair. Traditional Labor Day country fair (of Charlotte and Wilbur fame) with agricultural exhibits, blueberry pie–eating contest, ox pulls, fireworks. 207-374-3701.

Brunswick: Bluegrass Festival. National and New England bluegrass artists. 207-725-6009.

Camden: Windjammer Weekend. Labor Day celebration of windjammer heritage with parade of sail, fireworks, nautical activities. 207-236-4404.

Cumberland County Fair. Longtime host to the International (U.S. and Canada) Horse and Ox Pull. Largest Holstein Futurity in the nation. 207-829-5531.

Greenville: International Seaplane Fly-In Weekend. Seaplane demonstrations and contests. 207-695-2702.

Oxford: County Fair. Traditional fair (159 years) the week after Labor Day, with horse and cattle shows, 4-H exhibits, harness racing, woodsmen's competition, four-wheel-drive and tractor pulls. 207-674-2694; www.oxfordcountyfair.com.

Rockland: Rockland HarborFest Jazz and Arts Festival. Live music, windjammers, crafts and food. 207-596-0376; www.therealmaine.com

Unity: Common Ground Country Fair. Sponsored by the Maine Organic Farmers & Gardeners Association, a fair celebrating sustainable rural living in all its harvest-time glory. 207-568-4142; www.mofga.org.

Wells: Laudholm Nature Crafts. Crafts, food, music and children's games. 207-646-4521.

■ **OCTOBER**

Fort Kent: Scarecrow Festival. Scarecrow contest, parade, barn dance, games. 207-834-5354.

Freeport: Chowdah Contest. Crafts, music, and of course the chowdah tastings. 207-865-1212.

Fryeburg: Maine's largest fair (a week long, about 300,000 people attend) has livestock; harness racing; horse, ox, and tractor pulls. 207-935-3268; www. fryeburgfair.com.

■ **NOVEMBER**

Rockport: Holiday Crafts Market. Annual show, held the Saturday after Thanksgiving at Samoset Resort, with Santa around for photographs. 207-596-0376; www.therealmaine.com.

■ **DECEMBER**

Camden: Christmas by the Sea. Horse-drawn wagon rides, Santa, and entertainment. 207-236-4404.

Portland: New Year's Portland. New Year's Eve celebration takes place in the downtown arts district. 207-772-6828; www.newyearsportland.com.

■ PERFORMING ARTS EVENTS

Try www.mainemusic.org *to find musical events of all kinds all over Maine.*

■ JUNE, JULY, AUGUST

Bangor: Bangor Band Concerts. The band dates from 1859. Tuesday evenings mid-June to mid-August in Paul Bunyan and other local parks. Many picnic on the lawn; others sit in their cars and honk after each piece. 207-992-4490.

Bar Harbor: Arcady Music Festival. Music from Renaissance rondos to ragtime, plus concerts by members of the New York Philharmonic, at venues throughout Maine. 207-288-2141; www.arcady.org.

Bar Harbor: Bar Harbor Music Festival. A variety of musical events from string orchestra to jazz and pops. Primarily at Bar Harbor Congregational Church. 207-667-5744 (July and August) or 212-222-1026 (year-round); www.barharbormusicfestival.com.

Berwick: Hackmatack Playhouse. Take your own or buy a picnic dinner for the series of plays, concerts, and various musical, comedy, or children's performances. 538 School St. 207-697-1807; www.hackmatack.org.

Blue Hill: Kneisel Hall Chamber Music and Festival. Live chamber concerts by world-renowned faculty, student concerts, events all summer. 207-374-2811; www.kneisel.org.

Brunswick: Bowdoin International Music Festival. Primarily chamber music and some full orchestral works performed at Brunswick High School or on Bowdoin's campus. 207-373-1400; www.bowdoinfestival.org.

Hancock: Pierre Monteux School for Conductors and Orchestra Musicians Symphony Concerts. Orchestra and chamber music works ranging from classical to modern on Sunday and Wednesday evenings. 207-422-3931.

Harrison: Sebago–Long Lake Region Chamber Music Festival. Chamber music programs at Deer Trees Theatre. 207-583-6747.

Lewiston: Bates Dance Festival. Three weeks of public performances, lecture-demonstrations, workshops, and forums highlight contemporary and ethnic dance; Bates College. 207-786-6381.

Ogunquit: Capriccio. Arts festival features folk, blues, and chamber music concerts; performances by local theater group. 207-646-6170 or 207-646-2939.

Ogunquit: Ogunquit Playhouse. Professional summer theater offers three musicals, two plays each summer season; Route 1. 207-646-2402 or 207-646-5511.

Portland: Portland Symphony Orchestra Summer Performances. "Independence Pops" concerts with fireworks displays are held in several locations over the Fourth of July weekend. 207-773-6128.

Rockport: Bay Chamber Concerts. Acclaimed local, national and international musical talent performs, with pre-concert lectures and post-concert receptions—all in the 1891 Rockport Opera House. 207-236-2823.

Steuben: Opera Maine. Opera, pops, and contemporary (for example, Cole and Coward) programs in venues from Blue Hill to Machias during July and August. 207-546-4495.

■ **THROUGHOUT THE YEAR**

Bangor Symphony Orchestra. Bangor; 207-942-5555 or 800-639-3221.

L/A Arts. Lewiston; 207-782-7228 or 800-639-2919.

Maine Center for the Arts. University of Maine, Orono; 207-581-1755 or 800-622-8499.

Maine State Music Theatre. Brunswick; 207-725-8769.

Penobscot Theatre Company. Bangor; 207-942-3333.

Portland Stage Company. Portland; 207-774-0465.

Portland Symphony Orchestra. Portland; 207-773-6128.

Schoolhouse Arts Center. Sebago Lake; 207-642-3743.

■ **MUSEUMS & HISTORIC HOUSES**

Maine is richly endowed with historic houses, museums, local historical societies, and other institutions devoted to the study and care of Maine's past—as well as with small galleries and sometimes large museums that reflect the state's key role as a refuge for urban artists seeking the open air. Many are on the National Register of Historic Places and many are owned by Historic New England, formerly the Society for the Preservation of New England Antiquities (617-227-3956; www. historicnewengland.org). In addition to the selection listed below, many public libraries also house a local historical society, with collections of old photographs, town archives, and genealogical records. Some institutions listed here are quite well known, with professional staffs and extensive outreach programs. Most, however, are small operations with minuscule budgets. Because this second group often depends on volunteers, many are open only in summer and for limited hours even then; call ahead to verify days and times.

SOUTHERN COAST & YORK COUNTY

◆ KENNEBUNK
Brick Store Museum (1825). *117 Main St.; 207-985-4802.* Three adjoining 19th-century commercial buildings house this regional history museum and its important collection of Federal decorative arts and Thomas Badger portraits.

◆ KENNEBUNKPORT
Nott House. ("White Columns") *8 Maine St.; 207-967-2751; www.kporthistory. org.* Greek Revival house, Victorian furnishings. Restored original gardens.
Seashore Trolley Museum. *195 Log Cabin Rd.; 207-967-2800 or 207-967-2712.* This is the oldest and largest trolley museum in the world, with more than 200 electric trolleys and other vehicles.

◆ KITTERY/KITTERY POINT
Kittery Historical and Naval Museum. *Rogers Rd. at Rte. 1; 207-439-3080.* Exhibits relate to local and maritime history.
Lady Pepperell Mansion. *Rte. 103 in Kittery Point.* Restored Georgian house, privately owned, with gardens and period furnishings. No phone.

◆ NEWFIELD
Willowbrook. *Off Rte. 11; 207-793-2784, mid-May–September.* A restored 19th-century village that's a living-history open-air museum. Many historic buildings and exhibits with authentic artifacts and equipment. Carriages and sleighs and a carousel.

◆ OGUNQUIT
Ogunquit Museum of American Art. *183 Shore Rd., south of town; 207-646-4909; www.ogunquit.org.* A stunning building, whose glass-walled sculpture court faces the ocean at beautiful Narrow Cove. Twentieth-century works.

◆ OLD ORCHARD BEACH
Old Orchard Beach Historical Society Museum. *Harmon Memorial, 4 Portland Ave.; 207-934-9319.* Early resort history; photos of transatlantic flights that landed on the beach.

◆ SACO
Saco Museum. *371 Main St.; 207-282-3031 or 207-283-0684; www.sacomuseum. org.* Important collections of 18th- and 19th-century decorative arts from northern York County and Brewster portraits.

◆ SOUTH BERWICK

Counting House–Old Berwick Historical Society (ca. 1830). *Rte. 4; 207-384-0000; www.obhs.net.* Greek Revival commercial building with collections on local shipbuilding.
Hamilton House (ca. 1785). *40 Vaughan's La., off Rte. 236; 207-436-2454; www.historicnewengland.org.* Handsome 18th-century house overlooking Salmon Falls River, with restored garden.
Sarah Orne Jewett House (1774). *5 Portland St.; 207-384-2454; www. historicnewengland.org.* Large in-town Georgian house with memorabilia of the famous writer.

◆ WELLS

Meetinghouse Museum. *Rte. 1; 207-646-4755.* Local historical and genealogical collection.
Wells Auto Museum. *Rte. 1; 207-646-9064.* More than 80 vehicles from 1900 to 1963.

◆ YORK

Old York Historical Society. *207-363-4974; www.oldyork.org.* Eight buildings are run by the Old York Historical Society in York, including **Elizabeth Perkins House** (ca. 1730) on South Side Road, a Colonial Revival restoration of an early house. On Lindsay Road are the **Emerson-Wilcox House** (1742) at York Street (Rte. 1A), a museum of local history and decorative arts; **Jefferds Tavern,** a mid-18th-century saltbox moved from Wells; **John Hancock Warehouse and George Marshall Store,** an 18th-century warehouse and adjoining store with exhibits on York River life; **The Ramsdell House** (1740), a two-room workingman's house; **Old Gaol Museum** (1719) at York Street, one of the oldest public buildings in North America; and the **Old Schoolhouse** (1745), a one-room schoolhouse.

◆ YORK HARBOR

Sayward-Wheeler House (1718). *9 Barrel La., Ext.; 207-384-2454.* Original furnishings of 18th-century merchant's family; a Historic New England property.

PORTLAND & ENVIRONS

◆ PORTLAND

Children's Museum of Maine. *142 Free St.; 207-828-1234.* Hands-on exhibits of arts and sciences. Excellent gift shop.
Maine Historical Society. *489 Congress St.; 207-774-1822; www.mainehistory.org.* Founded 1822. Important research library—books and documents relating to all

aspects of Maine history. Popular genealogical research facility. Also operates adjacent **Wadsworth-Longfellow House** (1785), the poet's boyhood home, which has a charming in-town garden.

Maine Narrow Gauge Railroad Company and Museum. *58 Fore St.; 207-828-0814.* Tells the story of the two-foot-wide railroads that ran through countryside inaccessible to standard-gauge railroads, with half-mile ride along the waterfront.

Neal Dow Memorial (1829). *714 Congress St.; 207-773-7773.* Federal town house of famous prohibitionist and Civil War general.

Portland Fire Museum (1836). *157 Spring St.; 207-767-3826.* Early fire-fighting equipment and collection of photographs of the devastating 1866 fire.

Portland Museum of Art. *7 Congress Sq.; 207-775-6148; www.portlandmuseum.org.* Major collection of American and European art. Notable State of Maine collection, including Winslow Homer.

Portland Observatory (1807). *138 Congress St.; 207-774-5561.* Landmark watchtower on Munjoy Hill.

Tate House (1755). *1270 Westbrook St.; 207-774-6177 or 207-774-9781; www.tatehouse.org.* Stroudwater house of Colonial agent for mast trade.

U.S. Customhouse (1872). *312 Fore St.* Dignified French Renaissance Revival building.

Victoria Mansion/Morse-Libby House (1858). *109 Danforth St.; 207-772-4841.* Italianate summer house for Portland–New Orleans family. Lavish interiors, Herter furniture.

◆ SCARBOROUGH

Hunnewell House (1673). *Rte. 207, Black Point Rd.; 207-883-8427.* Renovation of very early house.

◆ YARMOUTH

Old Ledge School (1738). *W. Main St.; 207-846-6259.* One-room Colonial-era schoolhouse with exhibits.

ANDROSCOGGIN RIVER

◆ BRUNSWICK

Bowdoin College Museum of Art, Walker Art Building (1894). *Bowdoin College; 207-725-3275; www.bowdoin.edu/artmuseum.* McKim, Mead & White building. Especially strong in Colonial and Federal portraits, Old Master drawings, antiquities.

First Parish Church (1846). *United Church of Christ, Maine St.; 207-729-7331.* Richard Upjohn's Carpenter Gothic church. Harriet Beecher Stowe had her "vision" of Uncle Tom's death here.

Joshua L. Chamberlain Museum (1825). *226 Maine St.; 207-729-6606.* Restored home of hero of Little Round Top at Gettysburg. Longfellow lived in house earlier.
Peary-MacMillan Arctic Museum. *Hubbard Hall, Bowdoin College; 207-725-3416.* Ethnographic exhibits on the Far North. Many relics of Admiral Peary's 1909 expedition.
Skolfield-Whittier House Museum (1858). *161 Park Row; 207-729-6606.* "Time capsule" house museum virtually unchanged since 1925.

◆ HARPSWELL
Adm. Robert E. Peary Home. *Casco Bay, Eagle Island; 207-693-6231.* Explorer's summer house, much as he left it.

KENNEBEC VALLEY & MIDCOAST

◆ ALNA/HEAD TIDE
Alna Center School House Museum, second-oldest one-room school surviving in Maine, and **Old Alna Meetinghouse** (1789), especially well preserved 18th-century building with original box pews. *Both, Alna Center, Route 218; visits by appointment.* **Head Tide Church** (1838), serene white church with trompe-l'oeil painting of window behind pulpit. Head Tide Road; *all three: 207-586-5313 or 207-586-5680.*
WW&F Railway Museum. *Sheepscot Station on Cross Road, just off Rte. 218 in Alna; 207-882-4193; www.wwfry.org.* Narrow-gauge railway rolling stock and steam locomotives of the Wiscasset, Waterville & Farmington Railway, which ran between Wiscasset and Albion in the first third of the 20th century.

◆ AUGUSTA
Blaine House (1833). *192 State St.; 207-287-2301.* Originally, home of James G. Blaine. Since 1919, official residence of Maine's governors. Olmsted grounds are being restored.
Children's Discovery Museum. *265 Water St.; 207-622-2209.* Lots of hands-on exhibits.
Maine Military Historical Society Museum. *Building 6, Camp Keyes, Upper Winthrop St.; 207-626-4483.* Former stable now housing military memorabilia 1763–2004.
Maine State Museum. *Capitol Complex, State St.; 207-287-2301; www.state.me.us/museum.* Encyclopedic collection of 12,000 years of Maine history.
Old Fort Western. *City Center Plaza; 207-626-2385; www.oldfortwestern.org.* Site of Pilgrims' 17th-century Cushnoc trading post and reconstructed block-

houses and palisade of 18th-century fort. Original barracks/store survives. Occasional demonstrations of Colonial arts and crafts.

State House (1829). *Capitol and State Sts.; 207-287-2301.* Portico of Hallowell granite remains from original Bulfinch building. Replicas of Civil War battle flags in rotunda (originals in Maine State Museum).

◆ BATH

Maine Maritime Museum and Shipyard. *243 Washington St.; 207-443-1316; www.mainemaritimemuseum.org.* Complex of buildings on Kennebec illustrating how boats were built, used, and salvaged, from Colonial to modern times.

◆ BOOTHBAY HARBOR

Boothbay Region Historical Society. *72 Oak St.; 207-633-0820.* Italianate house of 19th-century sea captain.

Boothbay Railway Village. *Rte. 27; 207-633-4727; www.railwayvillage.org.* Complex of some two dozen buildings. Rides on antique trains.

◆ DRESDEN

Pownalborough Court House (1761). *Rte. 128; 207-882-6817.* Oldest court building in Maine. John Adams practiced law here on circuit. Good exhibit on Kennebec ice industry.

◆ NEWCASTLE

St. Patrick's Roman Catholic Church (1808). *Academy Hill Rd.* Oldest surviving Catholic church in New England; it has a Paul Revere bell and is on the National Register of Historic Places.

◆ NEW HARBOR

Colonial Pemaquid (1600s) and **Fort William Henry**. *Off Rte. 130; 207-677-2423 or 207-624-6075.* Ongoing archaeological dig, with museum and graveyard, and replica of part of 1692 English fort.

◆ NORTH EDGECOMB

Fort Edgecomb (1808–09). *Old Fort Rd., Davis Island.* Original Sheepscot River blockhouse fort built to protect Wiscasset.

◆ OWLS HEAD

Owls Head Transportation Museum. *Rte. 73 just north of South Thomaston; 207-594-4418; www.ohtm.org.* Stupendous collection of cars, planes, motorcycles, bikes, and baby carriages. Engines, too.

◆ PEMAQUID/PEMAQUID POINT

Fisherman's Museum. *Terminus of Rte. 130; 207-677-2494.* In former lighthouse-keeper's house.

Harrington Meeting House & Museum of Old Bristol (1772). *Old Harrington Rd.* Restored 18th-century meeting house with local museum.

◆ PHIPPSBURG

Fort Popham (1861). *Terminus of Rte. 209.* Half-moon granite fort guarding mouth of Kennebec.

◆ PITTSTON

Arnold Expedition Historical Society. *Arnold Rd., off Rte. 27; 207-582-7080.* Major Reuben Colburn house (1765) is undergoing ongoing restoration. Contains relics of Benedict Arnold's ill-fated march to Quebec.

◆ SKOWHEGAN

History House (1839). *66 Elm St.; 207-474-6632.* Small brick cottage on the National Register; 19th-century furnishings, Civil War memorabilia, and vintage toys.

◆ THOMASTON

Montpelier, the General Henry Knox Museum. *Rte. 1 and State Rte. 131 South; 207-354-8062; www.generalknoxmuseum.org.* An outstanding replica of the 1795 house built by the hero of the Revolution, Secretary of War, founder of West Point and father of thirteen. Many original furnishings.

◆ WATERVILLE

Colby College Museum of Art. *5600 Mayflower Hill Dr.; 207-872-3228; www.colby.edu/museum.* Outstanding permanent collection of American art; Asian and Greek art; works of John Marin and Alex Katz.

◆ WISCASSET

Castle Tucker (1807). *Lee St. (at end of High St.); 207-882-7169; www. historicnewengland.org.* Regency-style house with a gorgeous view, virtually unchanged since the late 19th century. Owned by Historic New England.

Nickels-Sortwell House (1807). *121 Main St. (Rte. 1).* High-style Federal mansion rescued in Colonial Revival period, also owned by Historic New England.

PENOBSCOT RIVER & BAY

◆ **BANGOR**
Bangor Museum and Center for History *(www.bangormuseum.org). At 6 State Street (207-942-1900)*, changing exhibits on local history and culture; *at 159 Union Street (207-942-5766)*, tours of the **Thomas A. Hill House and Civil War Museum** (1836), a high-style Greek Revival house, headquarters of the Bangor Historical Society, which runs walking tours of Mount Hope Cemetery (1836), second oldest in the country.
Cole Land Transportation Museum. *405 Perry Rd.; 207-990-3600; www.colemuseum.org*. From roller skates to a diesel locomotive, via heavy machinery—two centuries of working wheels.

◆ **BLUE HILL**
Jonathan Fisher House (1814). *Main St.; 207-374-2459*. Built by polymath clergyman. Many of his paintings are on view.

◆ **BRADLEY**
Maine Forest and Logging Museum. *Leonard's Mills in Penobscot Experimental Forest, off Rte. 178; 207-581-2871*. Reconstruction of 1790s logging community.

◆ **CASTINE**
Fort George (1779). Earthworks constructed by British to defend Penobscot Valley against colonials.
Wilson Museum. *107 Perkins St.; 207-326-9247; www.wilsonmuseum.org*. Collections of prehistoric artifacts from the Americas, Europe, and Africa, as well as ship models, local historic and archival items, and historic buildings; a Blacksmith Shop, the Hearse House, and the **John Perkins House** (1763–1783), a pre-Revolutionary building, moved from Court Street, rebuilt and furnished in period style.

◆ **ISLESBORO**
Sailor's Memorial Museum and Lighthouse (1850). *Grindle Point (ferry dock); 207-734-2253*. Maritime relics.

◆ **MONHEGAN ISLAND**
Monhegan Museum (1824). *Lighthouse Hill; 207-596-7003*. An art gallery in a replica building, and historic and cultural exhibits housed in former lighthouse-keeper's dwelling.

◆ **OLD TOWN**
Penobscot Nation Museum. *5 Down St., Indian Island; 207-827-4153; www.old-town.org*. Small collection of Penobscot artifacts.

◆ Orono

Hudson Museum. *Maine Center for the Arts, University of Maine; 207-581-1901; www.umaine.edu/hudsonmuseum.* World-wide ethnographic collections, particularly strong in pre-Columbian art. Interesting gift shop.

University of Maine Museum of Art. *5712 Carnegie Hall; 207-581-3255; www.ohwy.com/me/u/umma.htm.* Mostly 20th-century artists, with many of the works on revolving exhibit throughout the campus.

◆ Rockland

Farnsworth Art Museum and Wyeth Center. *19 Elm St.; 207-596-6457; www.farnsworthmuseum.org.* This complex is a must-visit for art lovers. The impressive collection of paintings is especially strong in depictions of Maine.

Shore Village Museum (Maine's Lighthouse Museum). *104 Limerock St.; 207-594-0311; www.lighthouse.cc/shorevillage.* Largest collection of lenses and other lighthouse artifacts in country; moving in 2005 to Rockland's waterfront.

William A. Farnsworth Homestead (1850s). *21 Elm St.;* and **Olson House** (1871). *Cushing; 207-596-6457.* Well-preserved house typical of prosperous mid-Victorian coastal families; and rural home of Hathorns and Olsons, now open for tours and painting classes.

◆ Searsport

Penobscot Marine Museum. *Church St., 207-548-2529; www.penobscotmarinemuseum.org.* Complex of historic buildings illustrating maritime history, especially in Penobscot region. Important collection of Buttersworth marine paintings, and changing special exhibits each year, including hands-on exhibits for children.

Mount Desert Island

◆ Acadia National Park

Abbe Museum. *Sieur de Monts Spring, Acadia National Park; 207-288-3519; www.abbemuseum.org.* Small but important trailside museum with exhibits about Maine's Native American history. Open from Memorial Day to mid-October, but a Bar Harbor branch is open year-round.

Nature Center. *Sieur de Monts Spring, off Rte.3; 207-288-3003 or 207-288-3338.* Small seasonal museum with exhibits on flora and fauna of the park. Adjoins wild gardens of Acadia.

◆ **BAR HARBOR**
Abbe Museum. *26 Mount Desert St.; 207-288-3519; www.abbemuseum.org.*
The Abbe's downtown Bar Harbor location has a permanent exhibit about the
Wabanaki people, along with changing exhibitions, workshops, and demonstrations
by and about Maine's Native Americans. Open year-round.
Bar Harbor Historical Society Museum. *33 Ledgelawn Ave.; 207-288-0000.*
Memorabilia of the town's Gilded Age in a former convent, now on the National
Register of Historic Places.
George B. Dorr Natural History Museum. *College of the Atlantic, 105 Eden St.;
207-288-5395 or 207-288-5015; www.coa.edu/nhm.* Small science museum on
large "summer cottage" campus on Frenchman Bay, with displays of plant and
animal life indigenous to the area.

◆ **SOUTHWEST HARBOR**
Wendell Gilley Museum of Bird Carving (1981) *Main St. and Herrick Rd.;
207-244-7555; www.wendellgilleymuseum.org.* More than 200 birds carved by a
local craftsman, with lessons and demonstrations, in an innovative building that
uses a Finnish fireplace and solar panels to augment the heat.

DOWN EAST

◆ **COLUMBIA FALLS**
Ruggles House (1818). *One quarter mile off US 1; 207-483-4637;
www.ruggleshouse.org.* Exceptional small Federal house with intricate woodwork
and magnificent double "flying staircase."

◆ **EASTPORT**
Tides Institute and Museum of Art. *43 Water St.; 207-853-4047;
www.tidesinstitute.org.* New works of photography and printmaking; collections of
art and architecture; a reference library; workshops and changing exhibitions. In
restored 1890 Eastport Savings Bank.

◆ **ELLSWORTH**
Colonel Black Mansion "Woodlawn" (1827). *19 Black House Dr. (off Rte. 172),
207-667-8671; www.woodlawnmuseum.com.* Stately home, attractive grounds,
beautiful mid-19th-century furnishings.
Stanwood Homestead Museum (1850). *Rte. 3; 207-667-3595.* Memorial to
pioneer ornithologist Cordelia Stanwood, with family furnishings. And **Birdsacre**,
a 185-acre woodland bird sanctuary.

◆ **Lubec**
Rier's Old Sardine Museum. *Rte. 189; 207-733-2822.* History of local canning industry from 1830s through its peak in 1930s.
Roosevelt's Campobello International Park. *Campobello Island; 506-752-2922; www.campobello.com.* FDR's summer home.

◆ **Machias/Machiasport**
Burnham Tavern Museum (1770). *Main and Free Sts. (Rte. 192), Machias; 207-255-4432; www.burnhamtavern.com.* Oldest surviving building in eastern Maine; one of 21 in the country named as significant to the Revolution. Period furnishings and Revolutionary War artifacts.
Gates House (1807). *Rte. 92; 207-255-8461.* A Federal-style house at the edge of the river in Machiasport, with several furnished restored rooms, historic ship models, and a genealogical library. On the National Register of Historic Places.

Western Lakes & Mountains

◆ **Bethel**
Dr. Moses Mason House Museum (1813). *14 Broad St.; 207-824-2908; www.bethelhistorical.org.* Beautifully restored Federal house of U.S. Congressman. Rufus Porter murals. Important research library for western Maine history and genealogy.

◆ **Bridgton**
Bridgton Historical Society Museum. *Gibbs Ave.; 207-647-3699.* Local history in 1902 fire station.

◆ **Bryant Pond**
Woodstock Historical Society Museum (1873–74). *Rte. 26; 207-665-2450.* Barn converted into local history museum.

◆ **Casco**
Friends Schoolhouse (1841). Raymond-Casco Historical Society. One-room school.

◆ **Farmington**
Nordica Homestead Museum (ca. 1840). *Holley Rd.; 207-778-2042.* Birthplace of Lillian Norton, first American to sing at Bayreuth. Much opera memorabilia. On the National Register.

◆ **Kingfield**
Stanley Museum. *40 School St.; 207-265-2729; www.stanleymuseum.org.* Devoted to inventors of Stanley Steamer (and much else), and their gifted sister, photographer Chansonetta Stanley Emmons.

◆ **LIVERMORE**
Norlands Living History Center. *290 Norlands Rd.; 207-897-4366; www. norlands.org.* 19th-century farm complex. Washburn family homestead and library.

◆ **NAPLES**
Naples Historical Society Museum. *The Village Green, Rte. 302; 207-693-6790.* Local history, including canal and Sebago Lake steamboat lore.

◆ **NEW GLOUCESTER**
Sabbathday Lake Shaker Museum. *707 Shaker Rd. (Rte. 26); 207-926-4597; www.shaker.lib.me.us.* Farming and religious buildings of Maine's only surviving Shaker community, including 1794 meeting house.

◆ **PARIS HILL**
Hamlin Memorial Library and Museum (Old Stone Jail). *Off Rte. 26; 207-743-2980; www.hamlin.lib.me.us.* Mementos of Lincoln's first vice president. Famous view of White Mountains.

◆ **PHILLIPS**
Sandy River & Rangeley Lakes Railroad. *128 Bridge St.; 207-778-3621; www. srrl-rr.org.* Restored narrow-gauge train offers one-mile rides.

◆ **POLAND SPRING**
State of Maine Building (1893). *Rte. 26; 207-998-4142.* Relic of Chicago 1893 Columbian Exposition. On the grounds of the former Poland Spring resort, now the Inns at Poland Spring. On the National Register of Historic Places.

◆ **RANGELEY**
Wilhelm Reich Museum. *Dodge Pond Rd.; 207-864-3443.* Home, studio, and laboratory of controversial émigré psychiatrist.

◆ **READFIELD**
Union Meeting House (1827). *Church Rd.; 207-685-3831.* Extensive trompe-l'oeil interior by Charles Schumacher.

◆ **STANDISH**
Daniel Marrett House (1789). *Rte. 25; 207-642-3032; www.historicnewengland. org.* Furnishings reveal family's history through two centuries. Attractive garden. A Historic New England property.

◆ **WELD VILLAGE**
Weld Historical Society. *207-585-2542.* Complex of 19th-century buildings illustrating life in small mountain village.

◆ **WINDHAM**
Windham Historical Society Museum (1833). *234 Windham Center Rd.; 207-892-1433.* History of the town and the families who settled the area.

GREAT NORTH WOODS

◆ **ALLAGASH**
Allagash Historical Society. *Rte. 161; 207-398-3335.* Log house with local artifacts.

◆ **CARIBOU**
Nylander Museum. *657 Main St.; 207-493-4209; www.nylandermuseum.org.* Extensive natural history collections.

◆ **FORT KENT**
Fort Kent Blockhouse (1840). *Block House St. off Rte. 1; 207-834-3866.* Relic of "Aroostook War" with Canada.

◆ **GREENVILLE**
S/S *Katahdin* (1914). *Moosehead Marine Museum, 12 Lily Bay Rd., 207-695-2716; www.katahdincruises.com.* Artifacts and photographs of marine history of the region and cruises on the restored lake steamer.

◆ **LILLE-SUR-ST. JEAN**
Notre Dame du Mont-Carmel. *U.S. 1; 207-895-3339.* Restored Catholic church, now museum, Acadian cultural center.

◆ **PATTEN**
Patten Lumbermen's Museum. *25 Waters Rd. (Rte. 159); 207-528-2650; www.lumbermensmuseum.org.* Some 5,000 artifacts, 1,000 early logging photos, two log haulers, and an 1820 logging camp in 9 buildings.

◆ **ST. AGATHA**
Ste Agathe Historical Society (ca. 1850). *Main St.-Rte. 162; 207-543-6364.* Local and religious artifacts.

◆ Van Buren

Acadian Village. *859 Main St. (Rte. 1); 207-868-5042; www.themainelink.com/ acadianvillage.* Complex of 16 reconstructed and relocated buildings, 1785–1900s, illustrating Acadian culture in St. John River valley.

■ Sandy Beaches

Despite its reputation for a rocky coastline, Maine has some spectacular sand beaches, most of them along the southern coastal plain. Just don't expect warm water. And don't be surprised if you have trouble, in July and August, finding a parking place. The beaches listed below are public, but parking is often restricted to local residents with stickers. Call ahead to the town office to inquire about parking, and plan to arrive early. **Beaches are listed southwest to northeast.** *Refer also to map on page 27 for smaller beaches.*

Crescent Beach. *Kittery.* 625 yards long, on a narrow peninsula. On the other side is Seapoint Beach (550 yards).

Long Beach. *York.* Popular and often crowded crescent (2,180 yards). On the other, more protected side of Cape Neddick is Short Sands (410 yards).

Ogunquit Beach. *Ogunquit.* One of the two best barrier beaches in Maine (Popham being the other). Fine white sand (1,620 yards). Not crowded away from the motel end.

Moody Beach. *Wells.* Locus of a much-publicized lawsuit over public access below high tide mark in privately owned stretch (the public lost). Public part (2,750 yards) is accessible.

Wells Beach. *Wells.* Long (4,000 yards), very popular, good birdwatching along nearby salt marsh.

Drakes Island Beach. *Wells.* Dunes, nature area, swimming beach (940 yards). Adjoins (access on foot only) Laudholm Beach, near the nature preserve.

Crescent Surf Beach and **Parsons Beach.** *Kennebunk.* Fine white sand stretch of beach near salt marsh (totaling 1,700 yards).

Kennebunk Beach. *Kennebunk.* Popular surfing spot (820 yards). Nearby is Gooch's Beach (1,300 yards), with rocky point.

Goose Rocks Beach. *Kennebunkport.* Fourth longest stretch of sand in Maine (3,600 yards), about two miles north of Cape Porpoise.

Fortunes Rocks Beach. *Biddeford.* Second longest (3,740 yards), just south of the Biddeford Pool summer colony at East Point. On the north side of the point is Hills Beach (530 yards), another sand spit sheltering the Pool.

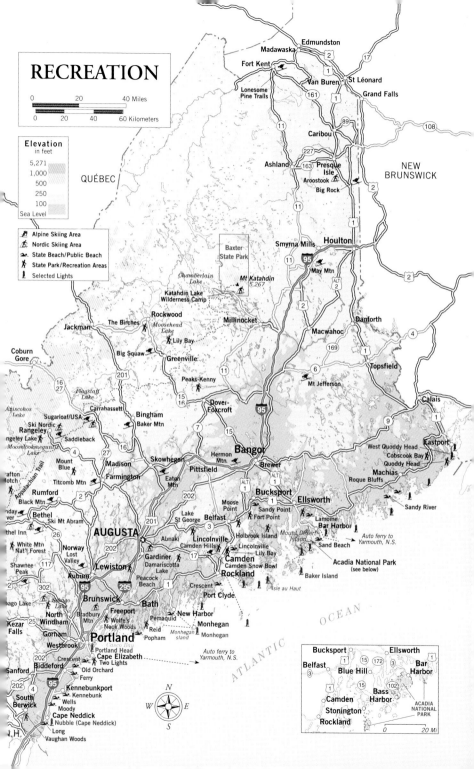

RECREATION

Scale
0   20   40 Miles
0   20   40   60 Kilometers

Elevation
in feet

5,271
1,000
500
250
100
Sea Level

- 🎿 Alpine Skiing Area
- 🎿 Nordic Skiing Area
- State Beach/Public Beach
- State Park/Recreation Areas
- Selected Lights

QUÉBEC

NEW BRUNSWICK

Edmundston
Madawaska
Fort Kent
Van Buren   St Léonard
Lonesome Pine Trails   Grand Falls
161
Caribou
Ashland   Presque Isle
227
163
Aroostook
Big Rock
Smyrna Mills   Houlton
95
Baxter State Park   May Mtn
ALT 2
Chamberlain Lake
Mt Katahdin 5,267
Katahdin Lake Wilderness Camp
Millinocket
Danforth
Rockwood   Macwahoc
The Birches   169
Jackman   Moosehead Lake   Topsfield
Lily Bay   6
Big Squaw   Mt Jefferson
Greenville   Calais
Peaks-Kenny
Dover-Foxcroft   9
Flagstaff Lake
15 16
Aziscohos Lake
Sugarloaf/USA   Carrabassett   Bingham   95
Ski Nordic   Baker Mtn
Rangeley   7
Rangeley Lake   Saddleback   15
Mooselookmeguntic Lake   Hermon Mtn.   West Quoddy Head
Mount Blue   Madison   Skowhegan   Bangor   Cobscook Bay   Eastport
Titcomb Mtn   Farmington   Pittsfield   Brewer   Quoddy Head
Grafton Notch   Eaton Mtn   ALT 1   Machias
Rumford   202   ALT 1   Roque Bluffs
Black Mtn   Bucksport
Sunday River   Lake St George   Moose Point   Sandy Point   Sandy River
Bethel   Belfast   Fort Point   Ellsworth
Bethel Inn   Ski Mt Abram   3   Holbrook Island   Lamoine   Sand Beach
AUGUSTA   Abnaki   Lincolnville   Bar Harbor   Auto ferry to Yarmouth, N.S.
White Mtn Nat'l Forest   26   Camden Hills   Mount Desert Island
Norway   Gardiner   Lincolnville   Acadia National Park (see below)
Shawnee Peak   Lost Valley   Damariscotta Lake   Lily Bay
117   Auburn   17   Camden   Baker Island
Lewiston   Camden Snow Bowl
302   Rockland
Sebago Lake   95   295   Peacock Beach   Crescent
Kezar Falls   North Windham   Brunswick   Port Clyde   Isle au Haut
25   Freeport   Bath   New Harbor
Gorham   Bradbury Mtn   Pemaquid   Monhegan
Sanford   Westbrook   Wolfe's Neck Woods   Reid   Monhegan Island   Monhegan
202   Crescent   Portland   Popham
South Berwick   4   95   Biddeford   Portland Head   Auto ferry to Yarmouth, N.S.
Cape Elizabeth   Two Lights
Kennebunkport   Old Orchard
Kennebunk   Ferry
Wells
Moody
Cape Neddick
Nubble (Cape Neddick)
Long
N.H.   Vaughan Woods

ATLANTIC OCEAN

N W E S

(inset map)
Bucksport   Ellsworth
Belfast   15   172   3   Bar Harbor
Blue Hill
Camden   15   102   Bass Harbor
Stonington   ACADIA NATIONAL PARK
Rockland
0   20 Mi

Ferry Beach. *Saco.* Longest of Maine's beaches (4,500 yards), just above the mouth of the Saco River. Part of Ferry Beach State Park. Ample parking, but there is a fee.

Old Orchard Beach. *Old Orchard Beach.* Very popular (3,320 yards, including adjacent Surfside). Fine white sand. Traditional "warm water port" for Quebecois.

◆ PORTLAND & ENVIRONS
Refer also to map on page 51 for smaller beaches.

Grand Beach, Pine Point Beach, Ferry Beach, and Western Beach. *Scarborough.* Group of beaches on both sides of the mouth of the Scarborough River, totaling 4,200 yards.

Scarborough Beach. *Scarborough.* Barrier beach (2,060 yards), freshwater marsh. Immediately north of Prouts Neck.

Higgins Beach. *Scarborough.* Mix of rocks and fine sand (910 yards) near summer colony.

Crescent Beach. *Cape Elizabeth.* Popular beach (1,560 yards) within a state park, 15 minutes from downtown Portland.

Willard Beach. *South Portland.* Small, urban crescent beach near Spring Point.

◆ MIDCOAST AND PENOBSCOT
Refer also to maps on pages 99 and 127 for smaller beaches.

Head Beach. *Phippsburg.* Crescent beach (360 yards) near the tip of the Phippsburg peninsula, 15 minutes from Bath.

Popham Beach. *Phippsburg (in state park).* Maine's best, thanks to fine sand (3,640 yards), natural dunes, good swimming and fishing. Sufficiently remote never to feel crowded, but not far from Bath and Brunswick. Ample parking (fee). Nearby is smaller Hunnewell Beach.

Half Mile Beach and Mile Beach. *Georgetown.* Part of Reid State Park. Half Mile Beach (650 yards) is a barrier spit protecting a salt marsh; Mile Beach (1,160 yards) includes rocky areas and dunes.

Lamoine Beach. *Lamoine.* Popular state park beach (2,740 yards) with great views across Frenchman Bay to Mount Desert Island.

Pemaquid Beach. *Bristol.* Beautiful crescent beach (575 yards) on the Johns River, just by Fort William Henry, about two miles north of Pemaquid Point.

Birch Point (Lucia) Beach. *Owls Head.* Small pocket beach (220 yards), near South Thomaston.

Crescent Beach. *Owls Head.* Popular beach (1,100 yards) near summer colony.

Lincolnville (Ducktrap) Beach. *Lincolnville.* Popular beach (850 yards) near summer colony.

Sandy Point Beach. *Stockton Springs.* Beach (1,370 yards) and nature preserve at the fork of the Penobscot River, below Bucksport.

◆ MOUNT DESERT ISLAND
See also map on page 149
Sand Beach. *Mount Desert Island.* Pocket beach (290 yards) made of finely ground shell fragments in Acadia National Park.

◆ DOWN EAST
See map on page 173
Sandy River Beach. *Jonesport.* Sand and cobbles (500 yards), just north of Jonesport.
Roque Bluffs Beach. *Roque Bluffs.* Steep pocket (910 yards) in Roque Bluffs State Park, a few minutes from Machias.

■ MAINE'S MOST FAMOUS ISLANDS

Less than one percent of Maine's population lives year-round on its coastal islands, but—thanks to several generations of artists, writers, and summer people—these once impoverished outposts today seem to represent "Maine" to much of the outside world. Perhaps because most of them are still hard to reach, they survive remarkably unchanged, at least visually (although many of them are having trouble maintaining viable year-round communities as fewer people want to stay). **Islands are listed southwest to northeast.**

Isles of Shoals. Five of them are in Maine, four in New Hampshire. Several can be visited by boat from Portsmouth, N.H.; the largest, Celia Thaxter's Appledore and nearby Star, can be easily seen from Rye Beach, N.H. (look for the former's World War II submarine watch tower). *See* "Southern Coast & York County."

Eagle Island. Several of the larger Casco Bay islands (Peaks, the Diamonds, Long, Great Chebeague, Cliff) can be visited on Casco Bay Lines' regular mail boats, but the most interesting of all—Eagle Island—requires joining a cruise out of Portland or renting a small boat in South Harpswell. The attraction is Admiral Peary's 1904 summer home, where he planned several Arctic expeditions and which looks as if he were about to return.

Monhegan Island. Probably the most famous Maine island in American art, thanks to Rockwell Kent, George Bellows, Jamie Wyeth, Robert Henri, Edward Hopper, and others attracted by its dramatic cliffs and spectacular scenery. The year-round population of about 55 increases tenfold in summer, augmented by more than 100 day visitors in July and August. Reached by mail boat from Port Clyde, about an hour away, or by excursion boats out of Boothbay Harbor and New Harbor.

Matinicus Island. Most remote of the inhabited islands (23 miles from Rockland) and much less self-consciously "quaint" than Monhegan. The year-round population of fishing families (about 45 people) is linked to the mainland by the Maine State Ferry Service (Rockland) one day a month or by private boat and plane charters.

Vinalhaven. Less artsy than Monhegan (although Robert Indiana is its most famous resident), this is perhaps the island that best conveys to the casual visitor the feeling of off-shore life. Its 1,200 people, many of them descendants of granite quarrymen of the 1880s, rely on fishing and tourism. Reached by Maine State Ferry from Rockland.

North Haven. Rather private island known for its Old Guard summer cottages on the Fox Islands Thorofare (the short cut if you're sailing to and from the shores of Penobscot Bay). It has a small knit-wear business, using the local wool; art galleries; and a few places for visitors to eat and sleep. About an hour by car ferry from Rockland.

Isle au Haut. One of the most beautiful, unspoiled, and little visited of the major islands, about half of it part of Acadia National Park. Reached by mail boat from Stonington.

Islesboro. One of the most accessible (20 minutes by ferry from Lincolnville Beach), though a place without a great deal to do (other than bicycling or picnicking) unless you know somebody there. Dark Harbor is another very private Old Guard summer colony. There are good views west to the Camden Hills and east to Cape Rosier and the smaller Penobscot Bay islands, including Great Spruce Head (private), made famous by the nature photography of Eliot Porter and the paintings of Fairfield Porter.

The Cranberries and Swan. Off Mount Desert Island. At 14 square miles, Swan Island is popular for hiking and biking. Fine Sand Beach is good for swimming, but the water is very cold. Reached by Maine State Ferry from Bass Harbor. The five islands that are known collectively as the Cranberry Isles are small enough to explore on foot. Little Cranberry (Islesford) is an especially popular day trip, with a historical society and dock-side restaurant. The Cranberries are reached by mail boat from Northeast Harbor. *See* "Mount Desert Island."

Campobello. Well worth the drive all the way to Lubec and then across the bridge into New Brunswick, Canada, to see FDR's summer place. *See* "Down East."

■ STATE & NATIONAL PARKS & FORESTS

Maine's parks offer all sorts of activities, from ocean swimming to wilderness hiking to cross-country skiing and snowmobiling. Thirteen state parks, Acadia National Park, and the Allagash Wilderness Waterway also allows camping; a number of campsites are available by reservation (call 207-287-3824; in-state 800-332-1501; www.campwithme.com). Fees for camping and day use vary depending on the facilities provided. Season passes are available. For more information, contact: Maine Bureau of Parks and Lands, 22 State House Station, Augusta, ME 04333-0022; 207-287-3821. **Parks are listed by region, geographically from southwest to northeast.**

◆ SOUTHERN COAST AND YORK COUNTY

Ferry Beach State Park. A fine sand beach, woods and trails, picnic and play areas. Route 9 in Saco. 207-283-0067.

Vaughan Woods State Park. Forested park on the Salmon Falls River; picnic area. Off Vaughan's Lane, South Berwick. 207-384-5160.

◆ PORTLAND AREA

Crescent Beach State Park. One of Maine's finest beaches, picnic tables, hiking. 9 miles from Portland on Route 77 in Cape Elizabeth. 207-799-5871.

Two Lights State Park. Picnic areas overlooking rugged coastline. Hiking and surf fishing from rocks. Near Crescent Beach, off Route 77 in Cape Elizabeth. 207-799-5871.

◆ ANDROSCOGGIN RIVER

Bradbury Mountain State Park. Small (440 acres) camping area, playgrounds, hiking trails, and view of Casco Bay from 460-foot summit of Mount Bradbury. Cross-country ski and snowmobile trails. On Route 9, 6 miles from Freeport exit off I–95. 207-688-4712.

Wolfe's Neck State Park. Shoreline hiking trails, salt marshes, bird sanctuary. Some nature trails can accommodate wheelchairs. Off Route 1 south of Freeport on Wolfe's Neck Road. 207-865-4465; off-season, 207-624-6080.

◆ MIDCOAST

Damariscotta Lake State Park. 17-acre lakeside park with sandy beach; picnic tables and grills. Route 32 in Jefferson. 207-549-7600; off-season, 207-941-4014.

Lake St. George State Park. Spring-fed lake provides excellent fishing for bass, salmon, perch, and brown trout. Bathing beach with bathhouse; overnight camping. 278 Augusta Belfast Road, Liberty. 207-589-4255.

Peacock Beach State Park. Swimming at sandy beach; picnicking. Off U.S. 201 on Pleasant Pond in Richmond, 207-582-2813; off-season, 207-624-6080.

Reid State Park. Maine's largest oceanside park, with two long beaches. Surf casting for striped bass. 14 miles south of Woolwich on Route 127; 207-371-2303.

◆ PENOBSCOT BAY

Camden Hills State Park. 30 miles of hiking trails, camping on 5,474 acres. Drive or hike to summit of Mount Battie for views of Camden Harbor and Penobscot Bay. 207-236-3109; off-season, 207-236-0849.

Fort Point State Park. Small oceanside park on tip of a peninsula in Penobscot Bay. In Stockton Springs off U.S. 1. 207-941-4014.

Holbrook Island Sanctuary State Park. 1,600-acre preserve on Cape Rosier in Brooksville. Upland forests and rocky shores for hiking and cross-country skiing. 207-326-4012.

Moose Point State Park. Seaside picnic area on Penobscot Bay. On U.S. 1 between Belfast and Searsport. 207-548-2882; off-season, 207-941-4014.

Warren Island State Park. The state's most secluded state park, reachable only by boat. Campsites and hiking. Off mainland from Lincolnville, just south of Islesboro. 207-236-3109; off-season, 207-236-0849.

◆ MOUNT DESERT ISLAND

Acadia National Park. 44,000-acre preserve covering parts of Schoodic Peninsula and Isle au Haut, and about half of Mount Desert Island. Hiking, camping, swimming. Close to Bar Harbor; accessible by boat or from Route 3. 207-288-3338; www.nps.gov/acad/home.htm.

Lamoine State Park. Oceanside park with campsites and picnic areas; boat launching facilities on Frenchman Bay. 8 miles southeast of Ellsworth on Route 184. 207-667-4778; off-season, 207-941-4014.

◆ DOWN EAST

Cobscook Bay State Park. 888 acres with fishing, hiking, camping, and picnic areas. Close to Quoddy Head and Campobello International Park. 207-726-4412.

Quoddy Head State Park. Easternmost point of land in continental U.S. 400-acre oceanside park with rocky ledges along coast; West Quoddy Head Light. 4 miles off Route 189 at Lubec. 207-733-0911; off-season, 207-941-4014.

Roque Bluffs State Park. 300-acre seaside park with hiking trails and swimming at both an ocean beach and a freshwater pond. Off U.S. 1 south of Machias on an unnumbered road. 207-255-3475; off-season, 207-941-4014.

◆ **Western Lakes and Mountains**

Grafton Notch State Park. A series of natural attractions on 3,000 acres. Appalachian Trail cuts through park. Along both sides of Route 26 between Upton and Newry. 207-824-2912; off-season, 207-624-6080.

Mount Blue State Park. 5,000 acres on Webb Pond; bathhouses and showers, boat rentals, camping, cross-country skiing, snowmobiling. Fishing for bass, perch, and pickerel. Hiking trails on Mount Blue and Tumbledown Mountain. Follow signs from Weld in Franklin County. 207-585-2261.

Rangeley Lake State Park. 700-acre park with camping and swimming facilities along the lake. Major snowmobile trail. Take Route 17 from Rumford, or Route 4 from Farmington. 207-864-3858; off-season, 207-624-6080.

Sebago Lake State Park. Really a combination day-use park with swimming and boating facilities, off U.S. 302 in Casco. Overnight camping is available (14-day limit) at area off U.S. 302 in Naples. 207-693-6613 camping only; year-round, 207-693-6231.

White Mountain National Forest. 5 campgrounds within 42,000 acres. Hiking, climbing. Southwest of Bethel on U.S. 2 or Route 113. 207-824-2134.

◆ **North Woods**

Allagash Wilderness Waterway. 92-mile-long waterway between Baxter State Park's western edge and Twin Falls near the Canadian border is a canoe camper's paradise, and is used extensively in winter for ice fishing and snowmobiling. If you plan to canoe the Allagash, write: Northern Region, Bureau of Parks and Lands, 106 Hogan Rd., Bangor 04401. 207-941-4014; off-season 207-723-8518.

Aroostook State Park. Campsites, swimming, boating, trails, snowmobiling. Located on Echo Lake off U.S. 1, 5 miles south of Presque Isle. 207-768-8341.

Baxter State Park. 46 mountain peaks, including Mt. Katahdin, allow excellent mountain climbing. 130 miles of trails in a 200,000-acre preserve. Access to park from Greenville on the west, Millinocket on the south, and Patten on the east. Reservations are advised for the campsites. Write to Baxter State Park HQ, Reservations Clerk, 64 Balsam Dr., Millinocket 04462. 207-723-5140; www. baxterstateparkauthority.com.

Lily Bay State Park. Excellent fishing for brook trout, togue, and salmon; 2 camp-grounds. On Moosehead Lake north of Greenville on Lily Bay Road. 207-695-2700; off-season, 207-941-4014.

Peaks-Kenny State Park. Within a forested, hilly area along Sebec Lake; bathing beach in a quiet cove, nature trails, camping. Fishing for small-mouth bass and landlocked salmon. North of Dover-Foxcroft on U.S. 153. 207-564-2003; off-season, 207-941-4014.

■ NATURE CONSERVANCY PRESERVES

More than 100,000 acres of some of Maine's most scenic and most environmentally important land has been protected through the work of The Nature Conservancy (207-729-5181; www.nature.org). Listed below are sites that are open to the public in daylight hours or easily seen from roads or from the sea. Public use is limited to hiking, bird-watching, photography, and non-intrusive nature study. No fires, camping, pets, or collecting of specimens are allowed. Some islands with important bird colonies are off limits during nesting season (usually mid-April to mid-August); visitors should also avoid walking in fragile bog habitats, where it may take years for human footprints to disappear. Boaters visiting the Conservancy's islands should exercise caution because of strong currents and tricky tides.

Despite those restrictions, the Conservancy welcomes thoughtful visitors. A series of excursions to see most, or even all, of these sites would be a good way to organize a summer or fall in Maine. The listing below is by general region from southwest to northeast and alphabetically within regions.

◆ SOUTHERN COAST

Kennebunk Plains Preserve. *Kennebunk.* Sand-plain grassland provides habitat for endangered and threatened species, including grasshopper sparrows, upland sandpipers, and the world's largest population of northern blazing star. Visit in late August/early September when the purple blazing star burst into bloom.

Saco Heath Preserve. *Saco.* A parking lot on Route 112 is the starting point for a quarter-mile woods trail that leads to a half-mile boardwalk across this unusual heathland. It is the southernmost raised coalesced bog in North America, all the more remarkable for being in the heart of the state's most populous area.

Waterboro Barrens. *Waterboro.* The best example known in the world of a rare pitch pine/scrub oak barrens. This natural community about 10 miles northwest of Saco thrives on an otherwise inhospitable base of 50 or so feet of glacial outwash (sand and gravel). Excellent for hiking and cross-country skiing.

◆ KENNEBEC RIVER

Indian and Fowl Meadow Islands Preserve. *Embden.* Two small typical floodplain islands in the Kennebec north of Skowhegan. Accessible by canoe.

The Maine Loon

We had hoped to see a moose even by now, but none has yet appeared in lake, stream, or river. Meanwhile, the loon will do. He is out there cruising still, in the spiralling morning mist, looking for fish, trolling. He trolls with his eyes. Water streams across his forehead as he moves along, and he holds his eyes just below the surface, watching the interior of the lake. He is gone. He saw something, and he is no doubt eating it now. When he dives, he just disappears. As a diver, there is nothing like him. Not even mergansers can dive like the loon. His wings close tight around his body, condensing everything—feathers, flesh—and he goes down like a powered stone, his big feet driving. He is known as the great northern diver. He can go two hundred feet down. He can swim faster than most fish. What he catches he eats without delay. His bill is always empty when he returns to the surface, and fifteen fish might be in his stomach. Because loons eat trout and young salmon, sportsmen (so-called) have been wont to shoot them—a mistaken act in any respect, because loons eat as well the natural enemies (suckers, for example) of salmon and trout.

–John McPhee, *The Survival of the Bark Canoe*, 1975

◆ **Midcoast**

Bald Head Preserve. *Arrowsic.* An eagle nesting area between Phippsburg and Georgetown on the Kennebec, which includes 160-foot pine-covered cliffs above the Back River and salt marshes—relatively rare in Maine. An important wintering site for bald eagles. Best observed from the river. Access to Bald Head is by river; be cautious of strong currents there.

Brothers and Hay Ledge Preserve. *St. George.* A cluster of four small islands a mile off the tip of the peninsula. Very important seabird nesting site, especially for laughing gulls, Arctic terns, and eiders. Closed March 15 to August 15.

◆ **Penobscot Bay**

Appleton Bog Preserve. *Appleton.* Part of a 680-acre bog containing one of the northernmost stands of Atlantic white cedar in the country, 15 miles west of Camden. No trails; a guide and a compass are needed. A National Natural Landmark.

Big Garden and Big White Islands Preserve. *Vinalhaven.* Characteristic Penobscot Bay islands with granite shores, dark spruce and fir woods, nesting osprey. Accessible by private boat or easily seen from the ferry. Big Garden Island was donated in 1967 by Charles and Anne Morrow Lindbergh.

Crockett Cove Woods and Barred Island Preserves. *Stonington and Deer Isle.* "Fog forest" habitats on the Deer Isle Peninsula and just offshore. Access to parts of Barred Island may be restricted at times to protect a nesting eagle. Crockett Cove can be reached by car, Barred Island on foot at low tide after a one-mile walk from the parking lot; otherwise by boat.

Fernald's Neck Preserve. *Camden.* More than 1,800 feet of thickly forested shoreline on a large peninsula on Megunticook Lake. Especially impressive when seen from a canoe. Good trails. Accessible by car from Route 52.

Lane's Island Preserve. *Vinalhaven.* 45 acres of windswept fields and rugged coast, with spectacular surf on windy days, only a 10-minute walk across the Indian Creek Causeway from Main Street in Vinalhaven. Ancient site of Susquehanna and Red Paint People villages. No car is needed if you make a day-trip on the state ferry from Rockland.

◆ MOUNT DESERT ISLAND

Indian Point-Blagden Point Preserve. *Pretty Marsh.* A forested 110-acre preserve in a part of Mount Desert Island that escaped the 1947 fire. Some 1,000 feet of Western Bay frontage offers many good spots for watching harbor seals sun themselves on ledges. Good trails. Near Somesville on the "back" side of the island.

◆ DOWN EAST

Flint and Shipstern Island Preserves. *Harrington.* A pair of rugged islands with nesting eagles in Pleasant Bay, near Milbridge. Best viewed from the water. Closed February 15 to August 15.

Great Wass Island Preserve. *Beals.* One of the Conservancy's most interesting preserves, extending into the Gulf of Maine from the Jonesport-Addison Peninsula. The windswept shorefront includes sub-arctic species, twisted jack pines, osprey, eagles, herons. There are two trails. Accessible by car from Jonesport, but no access by car through the private road past the parking lot.

Mistake Island Preserve. *Jonesport.* A treeless outpost at the entrance of Eastern Bay, with "coastal headland shrub" and "shrub-slope peatland" habitats found in the United States only in this part of Washington County. Lovely boardwalk across the heath; lighthouse at point. Accessible by boat.

Preble Island and Dram Island Preserves. *Gouldsboro and Sorrento.* Spruce-covered Preble is one of the four Porcupines off Bar Harbor. Preble Island protects Sorrento Harbor. Both can easily be seen from shore.

Turtle Island Preserve. *Winter Harbor.* 136 acres of a 150-year-old spruce-fir forest, with a blue heron colony, cobble beaches, and tidal pools. Reached by boat from Winter Harbor. Closed March 15 to August 15.

◆ WESTERN LAKES AND MOUNTAINS
Step Falls Preserve. *Newry.* A dramatic stretch of Wight Brook with cataracts and pools, near Grafton Notch State Park and the New Hampshire state line.

◆ NORTH WOODS
Upper St. John River. This is the Conservancy's largest preserve in Maine. Starting at Baker Lake, it protects nearly 40 miles of the longest stretch of wild, undammed, undeveloped river left in the East. The river can only be canoed reliably in the spring, when melting snows feed the river and its many tributaries.

■ GARDENS

Maine's climate severely tests even the hardiest gardener—the growing season is short, the soil is rocky, the deer have voracious appetites, and the fogs are laden with salt. Most year-rounders confine their efforts to neat rows of hardy vegetables, perhaps because ambitious cutting gardens are still identified with the rich summer people of an earlier time, though once in a while you might spot a colorful kitchen garden in the dooryard of a weathered Cape at the edge of the road. Given the riches of the natural scenery, it's hard to find fault with favoring food over esthetics. The roadside itself bursts forth with the purples and pinks of lupine in spring, daisies in June and July, and muted goldenrod in August, signaling the approach of fall. By late September the blueberry fields turn a glorious red, covering the hills in blazing hues that rival the turning tree leaves for beauty. Nonetheless, interest is growing each year as nurseries expand their offerings to serve the growing summer population, and residents discover there is more to summer than a regimental array of marigolds. Tours of private gardens are becoming increasingly popular in many coastal towns; July brings annual fund-raising events in Kennebunk, Damariscotta, Camden-Rockport, Union, and Belfast. Meanwhile, here are a few public gardens that show what is possible.

◆ CAMDEN

Merryspring. *Conway Rd., off Rte. 1; 207-236-2239.* A 66-acre garden and nature preserve on the Goose River; frequent educational programs in summer.

◆ FREEPORT

Tidebrook Conservation Trust. *38 Bartol Rd.; 207-865-3856.* An idyllic 45-acre saltwater farm on the Harraseeket River with gardens and nature trails. Especially beautiful in late May when thousands of daffodils bloom in the orchard.

◆ MOUNT DESERT ISLAND

Abby Aldrich Rockefeller Garden. *Off Rte. 3, Seal Harbor.* This is one of the greatest gardens in North America, and it's open by reservation only on Thursday mornings in August. Beatrix Farrand, who was Edith Wharton's niece, collaborated with Mrs. John D. Rockefeller Jr. in the 1920s to create a garden about the size of a football field, surrounded by a wall topped with glazed tiles from the Imperial Palace in Peking. It's on a hilltop surrounded by scenic woods that feel both Chinese and Maine-like at once. This "orientalizing" effect has had a major influence on contemporary garden design in Maine.

Asticou Azalea Gardens. *Intersection of Rtes. 3 and 198, Northeast Harbor; 207-276-3727 or 207-276-3699.* Landscape designer Charles Savage designed this Japanese-influenced garden around a stream and pond. The azaleas (at their peak in late May and early June) and rhododendron include rarities brought from Beatrix Farrand's famous Reef Point garden in Bar Harbor (which she had uprooted in a fury upon learning in 1955 that the town had declined her offer of the landmark as a horticultural center).

Thuya Garden and Lodge. *Asticou Terraces, Rte. 3, Northeast Harbor; 207-276-3727 or 207-276-5130.* In 1912, rusticator Joseph Henry Curtis built a small house on the terraced side of Eliot Mountain; Charles Savage later carved out Gertrude Jekyll–style perennial borders in back (restored by Patrick Chassé). The result is the most beautiful garden in Maine. Curtis's Thuya Lodge, with its botanical library, oriental rugs, and cedar-log walls, embodies the semi-rustic, semi-luxurious style in which the old summer colony lived. The garden and cottage can be reached by a narrow drive off Route 3 or by a short hike up the hill's pink granite steps from Asticou Landing.

Wild Gardens of Acadia. *Sieur de Monts Spring, Rte. 3, Bar Harbor.* A small, well-labeled botanical collection near the Abbe Museum and the Tarn displaying more than 300 plants indigenous to Mount Desert Island.

◆ PORTLAND

Deering Oaks. *Forest Ave., Portland.* A 51-acre city park designed by Frederick Law Olmsted to incorporate the famous grove celebrated in Longfellow's poem "My Lost Youth." Of special horticultural interest is the Rose Circle, containing 600 varieties.

■ FOR THE GARDENER

Gardeners whose interests are more culinary than horticultural may want to make the pilgrimage to **Johnny's Selected Seeds** (184 Foss Hill Road; 207-861-3900) in Albion, a pioneer in the effort to preserve heirloom varieties of vegetables suitable for northern climates. For perennials for sale in a naturalized setting, the best display is at **Fieldstone Gardens** (55 Quaker Lane; 207-923-3836) in Vassalboro.

■ DAY SAILS & EXCURSIONS

There are so many ways to get out on the water, it's hard to imagine coming all this way and missing the opportunity. Whether it's getting a view of a grand old summer place from the deck of a windjammer as it screams up Somes Sound on a high Canadian wind, sighting a couple of whales from the deck of a whale-watcher as they cavort offshore by the long rays of the setting sun, or hearing the haunting call of loons echoing off the shore as you paddle a canoe on one of the western lakes, there's nothing like a little time on the water to make you forget the toll-booth lines and help you remember why you came. No matter whether your taste runs to the adventure of a white-water rafting trip, the delicious solitude of kayaking the coast or canoeing a lake, a week on a windjammer, or a simple hour-long tour around the harbor on a trim motor vessel, there's a boat available to meet the need.

A day sail may take the full day or just long enough to get out of the harbor, raise the sails and take a quick spin in the cool breezes of the bay. Similarly, an excursion boat may turn around several boatloads a day, spend the day offshore in search of whales to watch, or provide scheduled service throughout the day between the mainland and an island. Most of these boats offer private charters as well.

■ PORTLAND & ENVIRONS

◆ PORTLAND

Bagheera (1924). 72-foot schooner, 48 passengers, 2-hour harbor tours and charters. 207-766-2500 or 877-246-6637; www.portlandschooner.com.

Bay View Lady. 66-foot motor vessel, 117 passengers, 1- to 2-hour cruises (meals available). 207-761-0496; www.bayviewcruisesme.com.

Casco Bay Lines. Mail boat and commuter ferries take cargo and passengers on 1¾-hour to all-day cruises to bay islands, daytime and evening, and to Bailey Island. 207-774-7871; www.cascobaylines.com.

Eagle Island Tours. m/v *Fish Hawk* and **m/v** *Kristy K,* each 49 passengers, 4-hour cruise to see Admiral Peary's summer house on Eagle Island, 1½-hour lighthouse cruise, and 3-hour Land & Sea Tour on the Discovery trolley and around Casco Bay. 207-774-6498; www.eagleislandtours.com.

Lucky Catch. A regular Maine lobster boat, 37 feet, 1½ hour lobstering trips to learn how it's done. 207-761-0941; www.luckycatch.com.

Palawan. 58-foot racing sailboat, 24 passengers, 2- to 3-hour or longer sails. 207-773-2163; www.sailpalawan.us.

m/v *Scotia Prince.* 485-foot luxury ferry, 200 vehicles, 1,000 passengers, overnight cruise to Yarmouth, N.S.; newly refurbished, with hot tubs, gambling casino, duty-free shop, floor shows. 866-568-2040; www.scotiaprince.com.

■ KENNEBEC VALLEY & MIDCOAST

◆ BELGRADE

Belgrade Lakes Mail Boat. Pontoon boat, 3- to 4-hour tours. 207-495-2213.

◆ BOOTHBAY HARBOR

Balmy Days II. 65-foot motor vessel, 145 passengers, daily trips to and from Monhegan Island. In addition, *Novelty, Miss Boothbay,* and *Bay Lady* (31 foot Friendship sloop) provide 1-hour harbor tours, fishing trips, and sailing excursions, respectively. 207-633-2284; www.balmydayscruises.com.

Cap'n Fish's Cruises. *Pink Lady, Pink Lady II, Island Lady,* 80-foot motor vessels, 149 passengers each. 1- to 3- hour whalewatching and sightseeing trips, departing from Pier 1. 800-636-3244; www.mainewhales.com.

◆ Georgetown Island

From the tiny village of Five Islands the **Mid Maine Water Taxi's** 26-foot cruiser *Sea Wife* takes up to six passengers. (The captain can perform marriages too.) 207-371-2288; cell 207-837-2449.

◆ New Harbor

Hardy Boat. 60-foot motor vessel, 120 passengers, 1- to 2-hour cruises, plus a daily run to and from Monhegan Island. 207-677-2026 or 800-278-3346; www.hardyboat.com.

◆ Port Clyde

Laura B and *Elizabeth Ann.* Trips to and from Monhegan Island (an hour each way) on large motor vessels, plus nature and lighthouse cruises and private charters. 207-372-8848; www.monheganboat.com.

■ Penobscot Bay & River

◆ Camden

Betselma. 38-foot motorboat, 31 passengers, 1- to 2-hour trips. 207-236-4446; www.betselma.com.

Lively Lady Too. 38-foot lobster boat, 41 passengers, 2-hour lobster-fishing trips. 207-236-6672; www3.simpatico.ca/lively.lady.

Appledore. 65-foot schooner, 49 passengers, 2-hour sails. 207-236-8353; www.appledore2.com.

Lazy Jack. 48-foot schooner, 18 passengers, 2-hour sails, and private charters. 207-230-0602; www.schoonerlazyjack.com.

Olad. 50-foot schooner, 21 passengers, 2-hour sails. 207-236-2323; www.maineschooners.com.

Surprise. 44-foot schooner, 18 passengers, 2-hour sails. 207-236-4687; www.camdenmainesailing.com.

◆ Rockland

Morning in Maine. 55-foot ketch, 21 passengers, 2-hour sails. 207-691-7245; www.amorninginmaine.com.

◆ Rockport

Shantih II. Classic 40-foot wooden sloop, 6 passengers. Charters. 207-236-8605 or 800-599-8605; www.woodenboatco.com.

■ MOUNT DESERT ISLAND

◆ BAR HARBOR

Bar Harbor Whalewatch Co. 110-foot catamaran, the *Friendship V*, 350 passengers, 3- to 3½-hour cruises. 207-288-2386 or 800-942-5374; www.whalesrus.com.

Bay Ferries, Ltd. *The Cat.* High-speed 319-foot catamaran makes two daily crossings (3 hrs.) to Yarmouth, N.S. (one crossing off season), carrying cars and passengers. Movie, duty-free shop, casino. 207-288-3395 or 888-249-7245; www.catferry.com.

Margaret Todd. 151-foot four-masted schooner, 150 passengers, 1½- to 2-hour sails. 207-288-4585; www.downeastwindjammer.com.

Seal. 51-foot motorboat, 49 passengers (run by Dive-in Theater). On 3 trips a day Captain Ed dives in Frenchman Bay, and passengers watch him live on the big screen while he collects examples of underwater life for hands-on learning. Two trips a week accompanied by a naturalist/park ranger. 207-288-3483; www.divered.com.

◆ NORTHEAST HARBOR

Blackjack. 33-foot Friendship sloop, 6 passengers, four 1½-hour cruises a day off Mt. Desert Island. 207-288-3056.

Sea Princess. Park naturalists narrate in-shore, 1½ to 2¾- hour nature cruises to the Cranberry Islands and Somes Sound. 207-276-5352.

■ DOWN EAST

◆ EASTPORT

Sylvina W. Beal. 84-foot 1911 schooner, 50 passengers, 2-hour sunset and 3-hour whalewatching cruises. 207-853-2500 or 207-853-4303; www.eastportwindjammers.com.

■ GREAT NORTH WOODS

◆ ROCKWOOD

Moose Cruise Boat. 30-foot pontoon boat *Discovery,* 20 passengers, 3-hour cruises on Moosehead Lake to see (what else?) moose. 207-534-7305 or 800-825-9453; www. birches.com.

◆ GREENVILLE

The Katahdin (1914). Restored 110-foot lake steamer 3- to 6-hour cruises. 207-695-2716.

■ WHITEWATER RAFTING

Two of the three Maine rivers renowned for their white water, the **Kennebec** and the **Dead**, converge at **The Forks,** a wilderness village five hours north of Boston that serves as the base for most of Maine's rafting companies. The largest of the three rivers, the **Penobscot,** flows almost in the shadow of Mt. Katahdin, the state's highest mountain. All three rivers are dam-controlled and provide high-water rafting from late April through mid-October. Here's a selection of rafting outfitters that operate trips on these rivers. Many belong to a professional association, **Raft Maine,** P.O. Box 3, Bethel 04217; 207-824-3694 or 800-723-8633; www.raftmaine.com.

◆ BINGHAM

Maine Whitewater, *800-345-6246; www.mainewhitewater.com,* and **North Country Rivers,** *207-672-4814 or 800-348-8871; www.northcountryrivers.com,* both use the same base facility (site of Gadabout Gaddis Airport), with cabins, campground, and restaurant. Snowmobiling in winter. Trips: Kennebec, Dead, Penobscot rivers.

◆ BRUNSWICK

Three Rivers Whitewater. *800-864-2676; www.threeriversfun.com.* Base facility on Parlin Pond, with cabins, swimming, windsurfing, lake canoeing. Trips: Kennebec, Dead, Penobscot rivers.

◆ THE FORKS

Magic Falls Rafting. *800-207-7238; www.magicfalls.com.* Inflatable kayak trips on the lower Kennebec and Dead. Trips: Kennebec, Dead, Penobscot rivers.

Moxie Outdoor Adventures. *800-866-6943; www.wild-rivers.com.* Based at a classic Maine sporting camp on Lake Moxie. Trips: Kennebec, Dead, Penobscot rivers.

Northern Outdoors. *800-765-7238; www.northernoutdoors.com.* Oldest outfitter. Also offers ropes courses, rock-climbing, mountain biking, fishing, snowmobiling. Trips: Kennebec, Dead, Penobscot rivers.

◆ MILLINOCKET AND CARATUNK

New England Outdoor Center. *800-766-7238; www.neoc.com.* In two locations. Also kayak instruction, guide training course, guided fishing and hunting, moose safaris. Trips: Kennebec, Dead, Penobscot rivers.

◆ Moose River

Windfall Outdoor Center. *800-683-2009; www.raftwindfall.com.* Cabins, restaurant and B&B. Trips: Kennebec, Dead rivers.

◆ Rockwood

Wilderness Expeditions. *800-825-9453; www.birches.com.* Based at The Birches Resort on Moosehead Lake, year-round wilderness recreation. Trips: Penobscot River.

◆ West Forks

Professional River Runners. *800-325-3911; www.proriverrunners.com.* Overnight camping trips along the rivers. Trips: Kennebec, Dead, Penobscot rivers, and Hudson and Moose rivers in N.Y.

■ WINDJAMMER CRUISES

Maine's 5,500-plus miles of coastline make the state a recreational sailor's paradise. Hundreds of private yachts ply these cold waters during the summer, but non-yachting visitors tend to gravitate either to the day-sail excursion boats found in most major harbors or to the thrill of a few days or a week on one of the sailing ships of Maine's windjammer fleet. Most of these vessels are refitted coastal schooners that once hauled timber and stone from Maine as far south as the Carolinas. Because the windjammers are extremely popular, it's best to book an excursion several months ahead. Passengers may, if they wish, participate in all aspects of windjamming, including handling sails, taking a turn at the wheel, navigating, rowing, or helping out in the galley. Meals are hearty—homemade breads and desserts, roasts, chowders, and fresh seafood—and are served family style. A lobster bake on a Maine island is featured on every six-day cruise and on most three-day trips. Cabins are simple but comfortable and all the boats have running water and hot showers. The actual itinerary is determined by the winds, but cruises begin and end at the boat's home port of either Camden or Rockland/Rockport. Crew tends to be young, energetic, friendly, and extremely competent. For an information packet on member boat cruises, call the **Maine Windjammer Association** at 800-807-9463 or check their website: www.sailmainecoast.com.

◆ **CAMDEN**

Angelique. *Captains Mike and Lynne McHenry, Box 736, Camden ME 04843; 800-282-9989.* Built 1980, 95 feet, 29 passengers.

Grace Bailey. *Captains Ray and Ann Williamson, Box 617, Camden 04843; 800-736-7981.* Built 1882, 80 feet, 29 passengers.

Lewis R. French. *Captain Garth Wells, Box 992, Camden 04843; 800-469-4635.* Built 1871, 64 feet, 22 passengers.

Mary Day. *Captains Barry King and Jen Martin, Box 798, Camden 04843; 800-992-2218.* Built 1962, 90 feet, 29 passengers.

Mercantile. *Captains Ray and Ann Williamson, Box 617, Camden 04843; 800-736-7981.* Built 1916, 78 feet, 29 passengers.

Mistress. *Captains Ray and Ann Williamson, Box 617, Camden 04843; 800-736-7981.* Built 1960, 46 feet, 6 passengers.

◆ **ROCKPORT**

Timberwind. *Captains Robert and Dawn Tass, Box 247, Rockport 04856; 800-759-9250.* Built 1931, 70 feet, 20 passengers.

◆ **ROCKLAND**

American Eagle. *Captain John Foss, Box 482, Rockland; 207-594-8007 or 800-648-4544.* Built 1930, 92 feet, 26 passengers.

Heritage. *Captains Doug and Linda Lee, Box 482, Rockland 04841; 207-594-8007 or 800-648-4544.* Built 1983, 95 feet, 30 passengers.

J. & E. Riggin. *Captains Jon Finger and Anne Mahle, 136 Holmes Street, Rockland 04841; 800-869-0604.* Built 1927, 89 feet, 24 passengers.

Isaac H. Evans. *Captain Brenda Walker, Box 791, Rockland 04841; 877-238-1325.* Built 1886, 65 feet, 22 passengers.

Nathaniel Bowditch. *Captains Owen and Cathie Dorr, 4 Gay Street Place, Rockland 04841; 800-288-4098.* Built 1922, 82 feet, 24 passengers.

Stephen Taber. *Captain Noah Barnes, Box 1050, Rockland 04841; 800-999-7352.* Built 1871, 68 feet, 22 passengers.

Victory Chimes. *Captains Kip Files and Paul DeGaeta, Box 1401, Rockland 04841; 800-745-5651.* Built 1900, 132 feet, 40 passengers.

■ Canoeing & Kayaking

One of the best ways to discover both inland and coastal Maine is with a paddle in your hand. The following list includes places to rent canoes and kayaks as well as canoe and kayak tour operators. Many outfitters, especially those on salt water, offer guided half- and full-day trips. A directory of registered Maine guides is available by calling 207-442-9006. *Outfitters are listed by region, then alphabetically by town.*

> (CR) = Canoe Rentals | (CT) = Canoe Trips | (KT) = Kayak Trips | (KR) = Kayak Rentals

◆ Portland & Environs
Peaks Island: Maine Island Kayak. (KT); 207-766-2373, 800-796-2373.

◆ Androscoggin River
East Winthrop: Lakeside Motel, Cabins & Marina. (CR); 800-532-6892.
Orr's Island: H2 Outfitters. (KT); 207-833-5257, 800-205-2925.

◆ Kennebec Valley & Midcoast
Belgrade Lakes: Great Pond Marina. (CR) (KR); 207-495-2213, 800-696-6329.
Boothbay Harbor: Tidal Transit. (KR) (KT); 207-633-7140.
Damariscotta: Lake Pemaquid Camping. (CR) (KR); 207-563-5202.
Stetson: Stetson Shores Campground. (CR) (KR); 207-296-2041.

◆ Penobscot Bay & River
Castine: Dennett's Wharf Kayak Tours. (KT); 207-326-9045.
Lincolnville Beach: Ducktrap Sea Kayaking. (KT) (KR); 207-236-8608.
Rockport: Maine Sport Outfitters. (CT) (CR) (KT) (KR); 207-236-8797.

◆ Mount Desert Island
Bar Harbor: National Park Sea Kayak Tours. (KT); 39 Cottage Street; 207-288-0342, 800-347-0940.
Town Hill: National Park Canoe Rental. (CR) (KR); 207-244-5854.

◆ Down East
Eastport: Tidal Trails Eco-Tours. (KR) (KT); 207-726-4799.
Springfield: Maine Wilderness Camps. (CR) (CT) (KR) (KT); 207-738-5052.

◆ Western Lakes & Mountains

Bethel: Outdoor Adventures/Riverside. (CR) (CT) (KR); 207-824-4224, 800-533-3607.

Brownfield: River Run Canoe Rentals and Camping. (CR); 207-452-2500.

Fryeburg: Saco River Canoe & Kayak. (CR) (CT) (KR) (KT); 207-935-2369.

North Windham: Sebago Lake Lodge & Cottages. (CR) (KR); 207-892-2698.

Oquossoc: Cupsuptic Campground. (CR); 207-864-5249.

Raymond: Kokatosi Campground. (CR); 207-627-4642.

◆ Great North Woods

Allagash: Allagash Sporting Camps. (CR) (CT); 207-398-3555.

Ashland: Bradford Camps. (CR) (CT); 207-746-7777.

Ashland: Libby Sporting Camps. (CR) (CT); 207-435-8274.

Greenville: Allagash Canoe Trips. (CT); 207-237-3077.

Greenville: Beaver Cove Camps. (CR); 207-695-3717.

Greenville: Chesuncook Lake House. (CR) (CT); 207-745-5330.

Island Falls: Birch Point Campground. (CR); 207-463-2515.

Jackman: Sally Mountain Cabins. (CR) (CT); 207-668-5621.

Medway: North Country Rivers. (KT); 207-672-4814, 800-348-8871.

Millinocket: New England Outdoor Center. (CR) (CT) (KR) (KT); 800-766-7238.

Rockwood: The Birches. (CR) (KR) (KT); 207-534-7305.

Rockwood: Old Mill Campground & Cabins. (CR) (CT); 207-534-7333.

■ Alpine Skiing

Big Squaw Mountain. *Mountain Rd. off Rte. 15, Greenville; 207-695-1000; www.bigsquawmountain.com.* 1,750' vertical, 33 trails, 3 lifts, 70% snowmaking.

Black Mountain of Maine. *39 Glover Rd., Rumford; 207-364-8977; www. skiblackmtnofme.org.* 1,150' vertical, 20 trails, 5 lifts, night skiing, 90% snowmaking.

Camden Snowbowl. *20 Barnstown Rd., Camden; 207-236-3438; www.camdensnowbowl.com.* 950' vertical, 11 trails, 3 lifts, night skiing, 55% snowmaking.

Eaton Mountain. *89 Lambert Rd., Skowhegan; 207-474-2666; www.eatonmountain.com.* 622' vertical, 18 trails, 1 lift, night skiing, 100% snowmaking.

Hermon Mountain Ski Area. *Hermon; 207-848-5192.* 350' vertical, 20 trails, 2 lifts, night skiing, 100% snowmaking.

Lost Valley. *200 Lost Valley Rd., Auburn; 207-784-1561; www.lostvalleyski.com.* 240' vertical, 15 trails, 3 lifts, night skiing, 100% snowmaking.

Mt. Abram. *308 Howe Hill Rd., Locke Mills; 207-875-5000; www.skimtabram.com.* 1,150' vertical, 41 trails, 5 lifts, 75% snowmaking.

Mt. Jefferson. *Lee; 207-738-2377.* 432' vertical, 12 trails, 2 lifts, night skiing.

Saddleback Inc. *Dallas Hill Rd., Rangeley; 207-864-5671; www.saddlebackmaine. com.* 2,000' vertical, 50 trails, 5 lifts, 80% snowmaking.

Shawnee Peak. *Rte. 302, Bridgton; 207-647-8444; www.shawneepeak.com.* 1,300' vertical, 43 trails, 5 lifts, night skiing, 99% snowmaking.

Sugarloaf/USA. *5091 Access Rd., Carrabassett Valley; 207-237-2000 or 800-843-5623; www.sugarloaf.com.* 2,820' vertical, 130 trails, 15 lifts, 92% snowmaking.

Sunday River Ski Resort. *Skiway Rd., Newry; 207-824-3000 or 800-543-2754 (lodging reservations); www.sundayriver.com.* 2,340' vertical, 128 trails, 18 lifts, 92% snowmaking.

Titcomb Mountain. *180 Ski Slope Rd., West Farmington; 207-778-9031; www.titcombmountain.com.* 340' vertical, 15 trails, 3 lifts, 75% snowmaking.

■ NORDIC SKIING

Most of the ski resorts listed under "Alpine Skiing" also offer cross-country skiing trails, as do the following commercial cross-country ski centers:

Bethel Inn Ski Touring Center. *Bethel; 207-824-6276;* 36 trails.

Birches Ski Touring Center. *On Moosehead Lake, Rockwood; 207-534-7305;* 25 trails.

Carter's X-C Ski Center. *Rte. 26, 420 Main St., Oxford; 207-539-4848;* 35 trails.

Harris Farm XC Ski Center. *Dayton; 207-499-2678;* 40 trails.

L. L. Bean XC Ski Center. *Freeport; 207-865-4761;* 15 trails.

Rangeley Lakes Cross Country Ski Club. *Rangeley; 207-864-4309;* 75 km of loop trails.

Ski-A-Bit. *Rte. 112, West Buxton; 207-929-4824;* 40 trails.

Smiling Hill Farm. *Westbrook; 207-775-4818 or 800-743-7463;* 35 trails.

THOMASTON POND

Every winter when I was growing up in Thomaston, Maine, a shallow pond just behind the stores on Main Street (Route 1) would become a communal gathering place. Everyone in town seemed to know how to skate and would come down to the pond in the evenings and on weekends. Fire barrels were placed on either side of the pond, and some kind citizens (invisible to us kids) would provide a constant supply of firewood. Neighborly conversation flowed around those glowing barrels. When it snowed, volunteers would show up with shovels and form teams to push the heavy stuff off the ice. When the ice got rough, the fire department would flood the pond, leaving a mirror of fresh ice.

Among us were several skaters who could cut an elegant figure on the ice, and who left the rest of us in awe of their grace and skill. The pond was a courting place, and the figures were cut as part of a kind of winter mating dance. There were pick-up hockey games in the afternoon after school, and we would organize contests to see who could jump over the most orange crates. After gathering crates from behind the grocery store, we'd begin by setting out one, then take turns flying down the ice and leaping over it. After everyone had cleared the first crate we would add another, then another, until some jumper stuck both skates through the flimsy wood and skidded down the ice wearing the crate up around his knees.

In the fall we'd have a hard time waiting for the ice to get thick enough, so eager were we for the skating season to begin. One year three of us went to the pond and stared at the still thin, transparent pane of ice. We could see the weeds on the bottom of the pond, which was only about four feet deep. Without saying much, we laced on our skates and ventured out on ice we knew we should not be on. White lines streaked off across the ice from beneath our skates with that hollow, almost electric sound ice makes when it cracks.

We skated back and forth until the ice was almost entirely white with the web of fractures. At one point near the middle of the pond, the ice actually began to undulate as we skated across it. The three of us joined arms, laughing, fully expecting, even wanting in the perverse way of small boys, the plunge we knew was coming. A few more runs across the wavy ice, and we were suddenly up to our chests in the breathtaking ice water. Somehow we clambered out after breaking a lot more ice in the process. We weren't laughing anymore. Our skate laces froze immediately when we got out, and our hands were so cold we probably wouldn't have been able to untie them anyway. We got on our bikes with our skates on, no mean feat that, to ride a bike with ice skates on. By the time I got home, my gloves and jeans were frozen stiff as well. The story I told my mother was quite different from the truth. How could I explain something that even today I don't fully understand?

What I do understand is that the bustling life on that Thomaston ice pond is as fresh in my memory as if I had just been there. For me, it has become a metaphor, utopian perhaps, for the kind of convivial community that has largely disappeared from American life—at least the kind I am familiar with in our cities. I hope people still skate there in Thomaston, behind the stores on Highway 1.

–John McChesney, correspondent for National Public Radio, 1994

■ STATE PARK TRAILS

Many of the state parks and public reserved lands also offer cross-country trails. For a listing of those open to the general public, write the Bureau of Parks and Lands, State House Station #22, Augusta, ME 04333; 207-287-3821; www.maine.gov/doc/parks. Here are a few especially popular sites:

Acadia National Park. 207-288-3340.

Aroostook State Park. 207-768-8341.

Baxter State Park. 207-723-5140.

Bradbury Mountain State Park. 207-688-4712.

Cobscook Bay State Park. 207-726-4412.

Lake St. George State Park. 207-589-4255.

Mt. Blue State Park. 207-585-2261.

Pine Tree State Arboretum. Augusta (on east side of Hospital St.); 207-621-0031.

Sebago Lake State Park. 207-693-6231.

White Mountain National Forest. 207-824-2134.

Wolfe's Neck Woods State Park. 207-624-6080.

■ TOURIST INFORMATION

A wealth of information is available on the internet at: www.mainetourism.com. In addition, the Maine Tourism Association maintains visitor information centers at the following locations: **Calais** (15 Union St.), **Fryeburg** (10 Main St.),

Hampden (I–95 North and I–95 South), **Houlton** (28 Ludlow Road), **Kittery** (I–95 and Route 1), and **Yarmouth** (Exit 17, I–295).

■ **STATEWIDE**

Department of Inland Fisheries and Wildlife. State House Station #41, Augusta 04333; request fishing and hunting regulations booklets in writing only.

Maine Campground Owners Association. 655Y Main St., Lewiston 04240; 207-782-5874; www.campmaine.com.

Maine Innkeepers Association. 305 Commercial St., Portland; 207-865-6100; www.maineinns.com.

■ **CHAMBERS OF COMMERCE**

Androscoggin County. 207-783-2249.

Bar Harbor. 207-288-5103 or 800-288-5103.

Boothbay Harbor. 207-633-2353.

Freeport. 800-865-1212 or 800-865-1994.

Katahdin Area. 207-723-4443.

Kennebunks. 207-967-0857.

Machias Bay Area. 207-255-4402.

Moosehead Lake Region. 207-695-2702.

Mount Desert Island. 207-244-7312.

Ogunquit. 207-646-1279.

Old Orchard Beach. 207-934-2500 or 800-365-9386.

Greater Portland Convention and Visitors Bureau. 207-772-4994.

Rangeley Lakes Region. 207-864-5364.

Rockland-Thomaston. 207-596-0376 or 800-562-2529.

Rockport-Camden-Lincolnville. 207-236-4404 or 800-223-5459.

St. Croix Area. 888-422-3112.

Southwest Harbor. 207-244-9264 or 800-423-9264.

Sugarloaf Area. 207-235-2100.

York Area. 207-363-4422 or 800-639-2442.

RECOMMENDED READING

■ The Natural World

AMC Guide to Mount Desert and Acadia National Park. 5th ed. Boston: Appalachian Mountain Club Books, 1993. Essential for anyone hiking or canoeing on Mount Desert Island. Detailed trail descriptions, much nature lore, excellent map.

AMC River Guide: Maine. 2nd ed. Boston: Appalachian Mountain Club Books, 1991. Essential for anyone canoeing or kayaking on the state's rivers and lakes.

Clark, Stephen. *Katahdin: A Guide to Baxter State Park & Katahdin.* Unity, ME: North Country Press, 1985. Definitive guide to the wild Katahdin region.

Kendall, David L. *Glaciers & Granite: A Guide to Maine's Landscape and Geology.* Unity, ME: North Country Press, 1987. Detailed explanation for the non-specialist of why Maine looks the way it does.

Pierson, Elizabeth Cary and Jan Erik Pierson. *A Birder's Guide to the Coast of Maine.* Camden, ME: Down East Books, 1981. Definitive work on enjoying the state's coastal birdlife.

■ History

Brault, Gerard J. *The French-Canadian Heritage in New England.* Hanover, NH: University Press of New England, 1986. First comprehensive account of New England's third largest ancestry group.

Calhoun, Charles C. *A Small College in Maine: Two Hundred Years of Bowdoin.* Brunswick, ME: Bowdoin College Press, 1993. Almost as much about Maine as about its oldest college.

Calloway, Colin G. *Dawnland Encounters: Indians and Europeans in Northern New England.* Hanover, NH: University Press of New England, 1991. New scholarship presents the Native Americans, including the Abnaki, not as victims of colonization but as resourceful peoples quickly adapting to change.

Clark, Charles E. et al. (eds.). *Maine in the Early Republic: From Revolution to Statehood.* Hanover, NH: University Press of New England, 1988. Important collection of essays on Maine from the Revolution to 1820.

Beach weather on Mount Desert Island

Duncan, Roger F. *Coastal Maine: A Maritime History.* New York: Norton, 1992. A popular history of how and why Mainers went to sea.

Giffen, Sarah L. and Kevin D. Murphy. (eds.), *"A Noble and Dignified Stream": The Piscataqua Region in the Colonial Revival, 1860–1930.* York, ME: Old York Historical Society, 1992. Essays on the "invention" of traditional New England in the York and Portsmouth region.

Goldstein, Judith S. *Crossing Lines: Histories of Jews and Gentiles in Three Communities.* New York: William Morrow and Company, Inc., 1992. Comparative account of Jewish communities in Bangor, Calais, and Mount Desert Island.

Leamon, James S. *Revolution Down East: The War for American Independence in Maine.* Amherst, MA: University of Massachusetts Press, 1993. British raids, economic disruption, and near-civil war between loyalists and rebels in the District of Maine.

Morison, Samuel Eliot. *The Story of Mount Desert Island.* Boston: Little, Brown, 1960. Brief, charmingly written history by a longtime summer resident of Northeast Harbor.

Mundy, James H. *Hard Times, Hard Men: Maine and the Irish, 1830–1860.* Scarborough, ME: Harp Publications, 1990. Fleeing famine, Maine's Irish immigrants found jobs but had to fight religious and nativist prejudice.

Rolde, Neil. *Maine: A Narrative History.* Gardiner, ME: Tilbury House, 1990. Best popular history of the state in print.

Taylor, Alan. *Liberty Men and Great Proprietors.* Chapel Hill, NC: University of North Carolina Press, 1990. Backcountry civil war simmered from the 1780s until statehood in 1820 between absentee landowners and farmers squatting on what both claimed as their property.

Trulock, Alice Rains. *In the Hands of Providence: Joshua Lawrence Chamberlain and the American Civil War.* Chapel Hill, NC: University of North Carolina Press, 1991. Definitive biography of Maine's greatest Civil War hero and four-time governor.

Ulrich, Laurel Thatcher. *A Midwife's Tale: The Life of Martha Ballard, Based on Her Diary, 1785-1812.* New York: Alfred A. Knopf, Inc., 1990. Brilliant re-creation of the world of a small Maine community (Hallowell-Augusta), based on a diary kept by its highly skilled midwife.

■ CLASSICS

Beston, Henry. *Northern Farm, A Chronicle of Maine.* Camden, ME: Down East Books, 1948. Lyrical record of a year on the farm near Nobleboro where the author and his wife Elizabeth Cotesworth lived.

Jewett, Sarah Orne. *The Country of the Pointed Firs and Other Stories.* New York: W. W. Norton, 1981. Available in many editions since its appearance in 1896. Quietly lyrical account of the "lost" world of pre-modern Maine, set on the coast near Tenants Harbor and Martinsville.

McCloskey, Robert. *Blueberries for Sal.* New York: Viking Children's Books, 1948. *One Morning in Maine.* New York: Viking Children's Books, 1952. Two classics for young readers, and their parents.

Moore, Ruth. *The Weir.* New York: William Morrow and Co., 1943. The story of a fishing family on Gott's Island, by the novelist (now unjustly neglected) who came the closest to capturing the reality of coastal life in the twentieth century.

Rich, Louise Dickinson. *We Took to the Woods* and *My Neck of the Woods.* New York: J. B. Lippincott Co., 1950. A generation ahead of the counter-culture, the author went to live in Maine's northwestern forest. In *The Peninsula* (The Chatham Press, Riverside, CT, 1958, 1971), Rich tells of life on the Gouldsboro Peninsula during the late 1950s.

Stowe, Harriet Beecher. *The Pearl of Orr's Island.* Hartford, CT: Stowe-Day Foundation 1979. An early attempt (1862) to convey Maine folkways (and Maine accents) in fiction.

Thoreau, Henry David. *The Maine Woods.* New York: Penguin Books, 1988. Many editions since its first, posthumous publication in 1864. This one from the Penguin Nature Library has a notable introduction by Edward Hoagland.

White, E. B. *Stuart Little.* New York: Harper & Brothers, 1945. *Charlotte's Web.* New York: Harper, 1952. *The Trumpet of the Swan.* New York: Harper & Row, 1970. Probably the most famous stories to have been written in Maine.

■ RECENT MAINE WRITING

A number of well-known writers today live or at least summer in Maine—Stephen King, Christopher Buckley, Annie Dillard, Richard Russo, Philip Booth, Frances Fitzgerald—but the authors who follow are known for their insights on Maine life. For an extended list of Maine fiction (also for sale at the Writers Center), contact the **Maine Writers & Publishers Alliance,** 12 Pleasant St., Brunswick 04011; 207-729-6333.

Chute, Carolyn. *The Beans of Egypt, Maine.* New York: Ticknor & Fields, 1985. Chute is to Maine's rural poor what Erskine Caldwell was to the South's earlier in the century. Incidentally, there is an Egypt, Maine—near Hancock—but Chute's is invented. More recent novels are *Letourneau's Used Auto Parts* (1988) and the well-regarded *Merry Men* (1994).

Grumbach, Doris. *Coming into the End Zone.* New York: W. W. Norton, 1991. An urbanite reflects on rural living in Maine's East Penobscot Bay region.

Johnston, Willis. *The Girl Who Would Be Russian and Other Stories.* San Diego: Harcourt Brace Jovanovich, 1986. Short stories about life in the Russian Orthodox community in and around Richmond, Maine.

McPhee, John. *The Survival of the Bark Canoe.* New York: Farrar, Straus, 1975. A twentieth-century writer takes to Maine's North Woods, traveling along its rivers and lakes with a canoe.

Melnicove, Mark. *Inside Vacationland: New Fiction from the Real Maine.* South Harpswell, ME: Dog Ear Press, 1985. A collection of stories designed to show how far the "real" Maine is from the "ideal" one of Robert P. T. Coffin and E. B. White.

Pelletier, Cathie. *The Bubble Reputation.* New York: Crown Publishers, 1993. The Carolyn Chute of far northern Maine, but with a much more manic sense of humor. Also, *The Funeral Makers* (1987) and *The Weight of Winter* (1991).

Phippen, Sanford. *The Police Know Everything: Downeast Stories.* Orono, ME: Puckerbrush Press, 1982. Wry, amusing, affectionate sketches of life in and around Hancock, Maine.

Snow, Wilbert. *Codline's Child: The Autobiography of Wilbert Snow.* Middletown, CT: Wesleyan Univ. Press, 1968. An honest and humorous portrait of a childhood in Maine.

■ The Visual Arts

Beem, Edgar Allen. *Maine Art Now.* Gardiner, ME: Dog Ear Press, 1990. Short essays on contemporary art in Maine by one of the state's leading cultural commentators. A worthy successor to Gertrude Mellon (ed.), *Maine and Its Role in American Art, 1740-1963.* New York: Viking Press, 1963.

Docherty, Linda J., et al. *The Legacy of James Bowdoin III.* Bowdoin College Museum of Art, 1994. Essays on Maine's early cultural history based on the collections of one of America's first great art patrons.

Skolnick, Arnold (ed.). *Paintings of Maine.* New York: Clarkson Potter, 1991. Best recent anthology of Maine landscape painting. Introduction by Carl Little.

■ OTHER USEFUL GUIDES

Acheson, James M. *The Lobster Gangs of Maine.* Hanover, NH: University Press of New England, 1988. An anthropologist's close study of the complex social and economic world of a very territorial trade.

Anderson, Will. *Was Baseball Really Invented in Maine?* Portland, ME: Will Anderson, Publisher, 1992. No, but there were an awful lot of Mainers who played in the majors.

Cross, Amy Willard. *The Summer House: A Tradition of Leisure.* New York: Harper Collins, 1992. Why do people go to such trouble and expense to summer in places like Maine? It all goes back to the Romans.

Duncan, Roger F. and John P. Ware. *A Cruising Guide to the New England Coast.* New York: G. P. Putnam's Sons, 1987. A classic. Intensely practical, but with lots of local lore. Wonderful bedtime reading in winter.

Gould, John. *There Goes Maine!* New York: Norton, 1990.

Henderson, James S. (ed.). *The Maine Almanac.* Maine Times, 1994. Much data on the state, some useful, some quirky.

Isaacson, Dorris A. (ed.). *Maine: A Guide 'Down East'.* Courier-Gazette, Inc., Rockland, ME., 2nd ed., 1970. Updating of the 1937 edition published by the WPA's Federal Writers Project. Still the most comprehensive book on the state, though some of it is based more on local tradition than research.

The Maine Atlas and Gazetteer. Freeport, ME: DeLorme Publishing Co., 1993. Don't go anywhere without it.

Shain, Charles and Samuella Shain. *The Maine Reader.* Boston: Houghton Mifflin Co., 1991. An anthology of writing about the state.

Steadman, Mimi, and Christina Tree. *Maine: An Explorer's Guide.* Woodstock, VT: Countrymen Press, 1993. There is simply no more useful and encyclopedic travel guide to the state than this one. A personal favorite.

Uhl, Michael. *Exploring Maine on Country Roads and Byways.* New York: Clarkson Potter, 1991. A personal account of touring Maine. Good for armchair traveling.

I N D E X

ACKNOWLEDGMENTS

All photographs in this book are by Kindra Clineff unless noted below.

LEARNING MAINE: Page 15, Abbie Sewall ▪ Page 19, Camp Runoia ▪ Page 22, Farnsworth Art Museum, Museum Purchase, 1960

SOUTHERN COAST & YORK COUNTY: Page 26, Historical Society of Wells & Ogunquit ▪ Page 31, Historic New England/SPNEA (photo by Elise Tyson Vaughan) ▪ Page 32, Thomas Mark Szelog ▪ Page 35, Thomas Mark Szelog ▪ Page 39, Colby College Museum of Art, Waterville ▪ Page 40, Thomas Mark Szelog

PORTLAND & ENVIRONS: Page 50, Erich Lessing/Art Resource, NY (ART48889) ▪ Page 53, Maine Historical Society ▪ Page 58, Maine Historical Society ▪ Page 68, Thomas Mark Szelog

ANDROSCOGGIN RIVER: Page 75, Library of Congress Prints and Photographs Division ▪ Page 76, Thomas Mark Szelog ▪ Page 82, Maine Historical Society ▪ Page 83, Dennis Griggs/Tannery Hill Studios ▪ Page 86, Library of Congress Prints and Photographs Division ▪ Page 88, Thomas Mark Szelog

KENNEBEC VALLEY & MIDCOAST: Page 100, Farnsworth Art Museum, Museum Purchase (Elmer C. and Alice L. Davis Fund), 1972 ▪ Page 103, Library of Congress Geography and Map Division ▪ Page 108, Colby College Museum of Art, Waterville ▪ Page 112, Colby College Special Collections ▪ Page 122, Abbie Sewall

PENOBSCOT BAY & RIVER: Page 126, Maine Historical Society ▪ Pages 128-29, Farnsworth Art Museum, Museum Purchase, 1963 ▪ Page 136, Thomas Mark Szelog

MOUNT DESERT ISLAND: Page 151, Thomas Mark Szelog ▪ Page 154, Thomas Mark Szelog ▪ Page 161, Abbe Museum, Bar Harbor ▪ Page 162, Abbe Museum, Bar Harbor ▪ Page 168, The Claremont Hotel

DOWN EAST: Page 178, Colby College Museum of Art, Waterville ▪ Page 184, Maine State Museum

WESTERN LAKES & MOUNTAINS: Page 192, Thomas Mark Szelog ▪ Page 195, Thomas Mark Szelog ▪ Page 198, Stanley Museum, Kingfield ▪ Page 200, Nordica Homestead Museum Association ▪ Page 201, Thomas Mark Szelog ▪ Page 203, Thomas Mark Szelog

GREAT NORTH WOODS: Page 207, © Wolfgang Kaehler Page 210, © Wolfgang Kaehler ▪ Page 213, Thomas Mark Szelog ▪ Page 215, Concord Free Public Library ▪ Pages 218-19, Thomas Mark Szelog ▪ Page 221, Thomas Mark Szelog

■ About the Author

Charles Calhoun grew up in Monroe, Louisiana, studied history at the University of Virginia, and went on to study law as a Rhodes Scholar at Christ Church, Oxford. After a newspaper career in southern Florida, he moved in 1981 to Maine, where he has written and lectured on Civil War history and other topics. He edited *Bowdoin* magazine for seven years, and also published *A Small College in Maine: Two Hundred Years of Bowdoin.* He is on staff at the Maine Humanities Council in Portland.

■ About the Photographers

Kindra Clineff travels throughout the United States and abroad, specializing in editorial, lifestyle, and travel photography. She is the principle photographer for the Massachusetts Office of Travel and Tourism and has shot advertising campaigns for the tourism offices of Connecticut and Rhode Island. She regularly produces feature assignments for *This Old House, Country Home, Coastal Living, Cooking Light, and Yankee Magazine,* and images from her extensive library of New England have been published in numerous books and calendars.

Thomas Mark Szelog, a native of Manchester, New Hampshire, specializes in photographing wildlife, nature, and environmental subjects for clients that include the National Geographic Society, the National Wildlife Federation, the National Audubon Society, the Concord Group Insurance Company, and Patagonia Clothing. He is also a contributing photographer to Maine-based *Down East* magazine. Isolation, weather, and wildlife are Tom's companions when he photographs the natural world; ocean, forests, rivers, and mountains are his studio. Tom has earned national recognition for preserving wildlife and the environment through the art of photography. Tom, whose photography is also featured in the *Maine* Compass guide, presently lives with his wife, Lee Ann, in Marshall Point Lighthouse in Port Clyde, Maine.